# A Learning-Centered Framework for Education Reform

## WHAT DOES IT MEAN FOR NATIONAL POLICY?

# A Learning-Centered Framework for Education Reform

## WHAT DOES IT MEAN
## FOR NATIONAL POLICY?

Elizabeth J. Demarest

Teachers College, Columbia University
New York and London

Published by Teachers College Press, 1234 Amsterdam Avenue, New York, NY
10027

*Library of Congress Cataloging-in-Publication Data*

Demarest, Elizabeth J.
   A learning-centered framework for education reform : what does it mean for
   national policy? / Elizabeth J. Demarest.
      p. cm.
   Includes bibliographical references and index.
   ISBN 978-0-8077-5156-5 (pbk. : alk. paper)
   ISBN 978-0-8077-5157-2 (hardcover : alk. paper)
      1. Educational change–United States. 2. Education and state–United States.
   I. Title.
   LA217.2.D425 2010
   379.73dc22                                                     2010026440

ISBN 978-0-8077-5156-5 (paper)
ISBN 978-0-8077-5157-2 (hardcover)

Printed on acid-free paper
Manufactured in the United States of America

17   16   15   14   13   12   11   10          8   7   6   5   4   3   2   1

This book is dedicated to my daughters,
**Kelly Mayer and Helen Mayer,**
especially to Kelly who teaches 6th-grade social studies in Alexandria, Virginia, with hope that positive changes in policy may soon provide her and other teachers with the infrastructure of support they need and deserve.

# Contents

### PART III: IMPLICATIONS FOR FUTURE NATIONAL POLICY

# Preface

It's time to take stock of education reform. The public school system is under tremendous pressure to produce higher levels of student achievement and attainment and to reduce gaps in learning between more and less advantaged students but, despite decades of reform, the desired results have so far proven elusive. Standards-based reform was promising, but incomplete, and before it could be fully implemented, this approach was overtaken by high-stakes testing policies.

The current round of reform, emphasizing accountability, testing, and market competition, has dominated the scene since the Bush administration's No Child Left Behind Act (NCLB) became law in 2002. Now these ideas are also being pushed by corporate foundations and the advocacy groups they fund. Among policymakers, supporters can be found in both political parties. Even a new president who ran on a platform promising "change" has quickly fallen in line with the status quo upon taking office. These policies may have the force of law and big money behind them, but studies show that they have failed to close achievement gaps as promised and evidence of their harmful effects is growing.

A comprehensive, alternative vision of education reform is urgently needed. Where will it come from? The central argument of this book is that educational research has developed to the point where it should be used as a basis for conceptualizing education reform. Some readers may scoff at this idea, but skeptics should ask themselves this question: What enterprise has ever achieved the kind of breakthrough results now expected in education without the application of new knowledge, new technology, or both? If a body of knowledge were not emerging, policymakers' hopes for significantly better results would be just empty rhetoric, not a rational possibility.

Recent advances in research on knowledge, intelligence, learning, teaching, and the kinds of environments in which people learn provide the theoretical groundwork for real advances in educational policy and practice (Bransford, Brown, & Cocking, 2000; Koppich & Knapp, 1998; Sternberg, 1990). Until recently, the field of education lacked a scientific knowledge base that could inform policy as it does in other fields such as medicine or agriculture. But now new knowledge from educational research and emerging examples of better practice offer potentially more effective ways to frame and conceptualize education reform.

In this book I propose a new framework for education reform that I call "learning-centered" because it focuses on improving the core educational practices of learning and teaching and is derived primarily from research on learning and related fields. This framework can be used as a template for reform at any level of the system. However, I focus on its implications for national policy because in recent years national policy has come to dominate the reform movement. It needs to change first before other levels of the system will have the autonomy to change.

The book has three parts. Part I provides a rationale for *why fundamental change is needed.* National policy is driving education reform, but it is disconnected from the substance of education. In Chapter 1, I trace the evolution of national policy, showing that it has become more focused on improving education outcomes but, ironically, less grounded in sound knowledge about education that might actually produce the desired results. In Chapter 2, I briefly outline a body of educational research that can serve as a foundation for educational reform. These new research advances challenge policymakers and practitioners alike to rethink many of their fundamental assumptions about education as well as their strategies for reform.

Part II focuses on *what to do*–the substance of education reform. I consider two overarching questions: What would education reform look like if it were framed and conceptualized in a way that is consistent with the best available education research? How does the research-based framework compare with past reform frameworks? To address these questions, I construct a research-based framework that offers a substantive vision of education reform by synthesizing research from the lines of inquiry mentioned earlier. Then I use the research-based framework as a benchmark and compare it to the frameworks and concepts underlying recent reform efforts, both standards-based reform and NCLB high-stakes testing policies. Finally, I discuss the implications of the research-based framework for the future of education reform.

Part III considers *how to do it.* Here I shift from the substance of education reform to a more instrumental analysis of future national policy. I discuss the question: What does the research-based, learning-centered reform framework mean for the future federal role and strategies in education? The federal government has used a variety of policy instruments over the years to influence education. My analysis in this part suggests that implementing the proposed framework for reform requires fundamental change in the federal role and strategies in education. The learning-centered framework has short-term implications for the reauthorization of NCLB as well as long-term policy implications that go beyond any one round of legislation.

The book as a whole should be of interest to those who make national policy decisions, those who seek to influence policy, those affected by it, and those who study it. The heart of the book is the learning-centered framework for education reform that is presented in Part II. While I apply the framework to the analysis of federal policy in Part III, readers interested in education reform at other levels of the system, including states, districts, schools, and even readers outside the formal education system should be able to adapt it for use in their contexts. The learning-centered framework is a tool that can be used to analyze and improve policy or practice at any level of the education system.

Finally, because my approach to policy analysis is innovative, the book may be of interest to those who do policy analysis or teach policy analysis methods, especially if they are interested in linking policy analysis with basic research and influencing policy at the formulation stage. Policy analysis most often focuses on either promoting informed decisionmaking by analyzing options or evaluating the implementation of existing policies or programs. However, when fundamental change is called for, then a mode of policy analysis directed toward basic understanding and policy reformulation is needed.

# Acknowledgments

This book has been a long time in the making and, consequently, there are many people who contributed directly or indirectly whom I would like to thank. I first became interested in a framework for education reform when, in the mid-1990s, as Director of the U.S. Department of Education's Blue Ribbon Schools Program, I was asked to revise the program criteria (which provided schools with a comprehensive framework for improvement) by updating the research-base and making them more consistent with the standards movement. As a foundation for change, I commissioned a set of research synthesis papers and organized a series of meetings to provide an opportunity for a dialog of research and practice. In retrospect, I look back on those revised criteria as a first draft of the learning-centered framework presented in this book. I would like to thank all the paper authors and reviewers, as well as over 100 program participants, including application peer reviewers, site visitors, and principals from winning schools, who participated in that effort (and to let them know that their work is still bearing fruit).

The broad background knowledge of educational research I drew upon for this book is the result of over a decade of experience in monitoring national research centers and field-initiated studies at the U.S. Department of Education, Office of Educational Research and Improvement (OERI). I created plans for and monitored the Center for Research on the Context of Secondary School Teaching (CRC) at Stanford University, a pioneer in linking new knowledge about learning and teaching with research about the broader contexts of education. I am indebted to Milbrey McLaughlin, Joan Talbert, and many other CRC researchers in numerous ways for the knowledge and insights I gained by working with them. Later I monitored the Consortium for Policy Research in Education (CPRE), a center that studies the progress of education reform and developed many of the concepts we use to think about it, such as content alignment and capacity-building. I want to thank Susan Fuhrman, Dick Elmore, and all the other CPRE researchers who influenced my thinking about education reform.

Thanks are due to Judy Segal, my colleague at OERI, who collaborated with me for several years in co-leading a discussion group we called the "Learning Group." Judy is a cognitive psychologist who monitored the Learning Research and Development Center (LRDC) at the University of

Pittsburgh. Our group, which eventually expanded to include colleagues throughout the Department, systematically read and discussed research on learning, teaching, and educational contexts and the implications of this research for policy and practice. These discussions provided me with many ideas about how these diverse lines of inquiry might coherently connect.

One project at the National Education Association (NEA) is also part of the intellectual history of this book. In 2003, I led a project to develop a concept of educational achievement. After reviewing the literature, I concluded that educational achievement was multifaceted and intimately connected to educational goals. I believed the best approach was to bring together experts in cognitive psychology, sociocultural theory, child development, and educational philosophy to consider the problem from multiple perspectives. I organized a full-day brainstorming session that included Wade Boykin, Gary Fenstermacher, Robert Rueda, Robert Sternberg, and Deborah Stipek (they also contributed short papers). Due to changes in management at NEA, the work was never published as intended. I have drawn upon this project in Chapters 3 and 4 and, although these experts are cited in those chapters, citations cannot fully capture their contributions. I am very grateful to this group, and to Tiffany Cain for her expert assistance on the figures and tables.

I originally intended to develop the learning-centered framework as a tool for school level improvement (and readers can still adapt it for that purpose). However, after No Child Left Behind became law, was implemented amid growing evidence of its harmful side effects and failure to close achievement gaps, and reauthorization efforts began, I was increasingly frustrated by narrow policy debates that, in my opinion, focused on details and missed fundamental flaws in assumptions and strategies. I gradually came to realize that the research-based, learning-centered framework evolving in my mind could, if articulated and published, be used as the basis for fundamental critique of past policy and, more importantly, as the foundation for a comprehensive alternative. Therefore, I shifted my focus from practice to national policy. My longtime friend and colleague, Harold Wechsler, encouraged me to publish a book and advised me on the details.

Thanks are due to Mary Metz and Jack Jennings who read earlier versions of this work and provided helpful suggestions. I am also grateful to Emerson Elliott and to two anonymous peer reviewers recruited by Teachers College Press whose thorough reviews and extensive comments resulted in rewrites that greatly improved the manuscript.

It has been a pleasure to work with an excellent team of professionals at Teachers College Press. Brian Ellerbeck, Meg Hartmann, Karl Nyberg, Pam LaBarbiera, Nancy Power, and Beverly Rivero have each contributed in many ways to making this book possible.

# Part I

# INTRODUCTION

This part consists of two introductory chapters. Chapter 1 is a brief overview of the evolution of national education policy since the 1960s, when a significant federal role began. In the past, national policymakers focused on noneducational goals, such as allocating money or desegregating schools. Substantive knowledge about education had little impact on national policy. However, now national policymakers have decided that the educational goals of substantially improving student achievement and attainment are their primary concerns. If policymakers are to succeed in these ambitious goals, national policy must make educational sense. Effective future policy should be based on the best available knowledge about education.

A sound body of educational research has emerged that can serve as a foundation for education reform and national policy. New theories of knowledge, learning and teaching, and the kinds of contexts in which people learn have the potential to transform policy and practice. Chapter 2 outlines that body of knowledge and related research, its significance for reform, and how it was used in this book. The nature of scientific research has recently become controversial. The lines of research I have used as the foundation for a framework for reform are consistent with the definition of scientific research developed by the National Academies (Shavelson & Towne, 2002). Research on learning and related fields has been accumulating for decades. While many issues remain contested, as is typically the case in science, this research has built a coherent theoretical understanding of the core processes of education through multiple methods of empirical research.

The Bush administration, and some federal statutes, defined scientific research more narrowly, by emphasizing research that tests hypotheses using experimental and quasi-experimental designs. This is only one type of scientific research. My primary interest is in frameworks and concepts that lie outside the purview of experimental research. I am also interested in understanding the complexities of the education system and how to change it. Experimental research is not well suited to understanding complex environments, such as classrooms or educational systems, where all the ingredients are interactive and mutually defining. It isolates variables and, therefore, produces piecemeal findings (Salomon, 1991).

Although national policymakers have been pushing for the use of "scientific research," "evidence," and "data" to inform policy and practice, federal policy itself shows little influence of research. Despite the rhetoric, national policies that are inconsistent with research may actually constrain the use of research at other levels. It is not enough to simply advocate in general terms for the use of research; it is important to follow through and actually use it. In applying research to policy and practice today, the important questions are: What research? For what purpose?

# CHAPTER 1

# Evolution of National Policy

In this brief overview of the evolution of federal education policy, I focus selectively on areas that provide background for the themes of this book. The history I present emphasizes changes in how policy has been framed at different times since the 1960s, when significant federal involvement in education began. I outline evolving conceptions of the federal role, goals, and strategies; the political forces that shaped policy; and the role of research. Also, I describe trends over time in student achievement, although these trends cannot be linked causally to specific policies.

## EQUITY AND EXCELLENCE

Since the 1960s, the federal government has sought to promote both equity and excellence in education, but initially played a different role in pursuing each of these goals. Within the context of a broader civil rights movement and President Johnson's "War on Poverty," early federal initiatives to promote educational equity included a combination of categorical program grants and civil rights mandates. At the same time, many states acted to reduce funding disparities between rich and poor school districts through school finance reform and various court decisions that mandated school desegregation.

Title I of the Elementary and Secondary Education Act (ESEA), was created in 1965 to provide extra supplementary services to educationally disadvantaged students in poor school districts. Issues of religion and local control were impediments to federal aid at this time. The program was designed to get around them. Federal aid was targeted to children so that it could "follow the child" and serve children in both public and parochial schools. Local control of education was preserved because the law contained few substantive education requirements. Instead, it provided a funding stream with requirements for how funds must be allocated to ensure that the targeted children were served and that federal funds did not replace local funds. Although local districts had a great deal of program discretion, Title I typically provided remedial programs to elementary students emphasizing basic skills (Manna, 2008; McGuinn, 2006).

*3*

Similar categorical programs were soon added for other special-needs groups, including migrant, neglected and delinquent, limited English proficient, and Native American students. The program for students with disabilities, currently called the Individuals with Disabilities Education Act (IDEA), has since the 1970s included both mandated service standards and funds allocation requirements (Manna, 2008). While antidiscrimination and school finance policies affected whole schools and districts, categorical programs for special needs students generally operated on the periphery of the education system. These programs did not change the core practices of teaching and learning for all students.

Head Start, an early childhood program that was also part of the War on Poverty, may be one of the best examples of a federal education initiative whose design was informed by basic research. The program was created in the Office of Economic Opportunity by a committee of experts, including research psychologists, physicians, and early childhood educators. With few models of practice, they drew upon emerging child development theory. Thus, Head Start was designed as a comprehensive child development program for poor children that included attention to health; social, emotional, and cognitive development; and motivation. The program sought to motivate children by maximizing "opportunities for the child to *succeed* in what he is doing" (Zigler & Muenchow, 1992, p. 19).

In its efforts to promote excellence at this time, the federal government deferred to state and local governments. The federal role was limited to funding small discretionary grant programs and supporting research and development. Two strategies were employed to improve practice. The first, exemplified by ESEA, Title III, provided seed money for local innovation. It was based on the assumption that the ideas needed for improvement were somewhere "out there" at the grassroots and that local experimentation would produce new knowledge. In fact, this approach tended to support local priorities and functioned simply as grants-in-aid to the local recipients (Turnbull, 1982). The other approach assumed that innovative model programs could be developed by experts, then disseminated and replicated at the local level. Evaluation of these change efforts found that implementation of effective projects was characterized by a process of "mutual adaptation" rather than uniform implementation (McLaughlin, 1990).

This early era of reform was distinguished by a general satisfaction with the education available to advantaged students and a desire to make that same education available to disadvantaged students. There was great optimism about the potential for broad social change, a belief in education as the engine of change, a commitment to equity, and a disposition to use knowledge to inform policy. The primary problems facing schools were thought to be a lack of integration and inadequate resources. Policymakers assumed that if these problems could be solved, student achievement would increase

(McGuinn, 2006). Therefore, education reform focused on equalizing resources, eliminating racial and other forms of discrimination, and providing
supplementary services to special needs groups. On a more limited scale,
educational innovation was encouraged and support for research and development was increased.

The results of the War on Poverty did not live up to the great expectations
it created, and its results are usually characterized as disappointing. However,
in retrospect, education outcomes are more accurately described as mixed.
The period between 1965 and 1980 shows substantial increases in graduation rates for African American students and more dramatic achievement
gains in reading and math on the National Assessment of Educational Progress (NAEP) for the 1960–1980 birth cohort of African American students
than we have ever seen since (Consortium for Policy Research in Education,
1991). NAEP provides evidence about trends in educational outcomes, but it
does not explain the causes of these trends. So we can only speculate about
whether these rising achievement and attainment trends resulted from ame-
lioration of poverty, reduced racial isolation, greater educational access and
opportunity, a combination of these, or some other factor.

Initial national evaluations of Head Start were disappointing, but a more
recent one found small to moderate positive effects on prereading, writing,
and vocabulary (Dotterer et al., 2009). These measures of cognitive development are insufficient to evaluate preschool programs that seek to develop the
whole child. In a synthesis of the evaluations of early childhood education,
including intense, high quality programs like the Perry Preschool Project,
Barnett (1995) found that programs can produce sizeable and persistent positive effects on achievement, grade retention, special education placement,
high school graduation, and socialization. In high-quality programs participating children do better over the long term than similar nonparticipants, but
the performance gap is not closed between the poor and middle class.

Title I has been evaluated both in terms of its success in allocating funds
to needy students and its effects on student achievement. Although the intent
of the law is to serve the most disadvantaged students in poor districts, as a
result of the national formula and local choices, funds are dispersed fairly
widely. Some very educationally disadvantaged students in poor districts are
not served and less disadvantaged students in better off districts are. National
evaluations of the impact of Title I on student achievement indicate that
some participants have made academic gains, but that these students still
perform at low levels and that gaps remain between Title I students and their
more advantaged peers (Manna, 2008).

During this time, groups representing educators, along with civil rights
groups, had the most influence on education policy. A bipartisan consensus developed around the circumscribed federal categorical role. What political scientists call an "iron triangle," a coalition of program participants,

members of congressional committees, and interest groups, developed to protect and expand federal equity programs and mandates. Eventually opposition to proliferating regulations and court-mandated busing arose. The election of Ronald Reagan brought on another period of controversy over the federal role.

During this early era of federal policy, emerging knowledge about child development informed the design of Head Start, but lack of knowledge about cognition and learning hampered efforts to develop more effective approaches to elementary and secondary education. By 1968 an influential study of ESEA concluded that "we do not know how to teach the poor" (Bailey & Mosher, p. 222) and advocated that far greater resources be plowed into basic research. A few years later the National Institute of Education was created with just that mission. However, basic research on learning subsequently revealed that assumptions about educating all children were faulty.

## HIGH STANDARDS FOR ALL STUDENTS

In 1983 a publication entitled *A Nation at Risk*, from a commission established by the U.S. Secretary of Education, decried "mediocre educational performance" and argued that higher education standards were essential to maintain U.S. economic competitiveness in an era of globalization (National Commission on Excellence in Education [NCEE], 1983, p. 5). The report got a tremendous amount of attention from the press and was followed by a number of similar reports that kept up the momentum for change. The slogan "high standards for all students" became the rallying cry of a standards movement that initially elicited broad consensus and public support. During the 1980s there was a remarkable level of state reform activity. Most states increased education spending, raised high school graduation requirements, instituted new student testing programs, and tightened teacher certification requirements (Fuhrman, 2001).

The political reform initiative coincided with important research advances that suggested that the whole education system, not just education for the disadvantaged, was less than optimal and needed to be transformed. Two findings are illustrative. One key finding of cognitive science is that basic and higher-order thinking skills do not develop in a fixed, hierarchical sequence, but are intertwined. This means that the teaching of thinking should begin in the early grades. Another insight is that almost all students can be taught to think if they have access to rich learning environments and are willing to put in the effort. Thus, there is no justification for reserving a challenging curriculum only for the most promising students. A "thinking curriculum" should be available to all (Resnick, 1987). This kind of basic research provided a strong intellectual foundation for the standards movement.

The standards movement shifted the federal focus from the periphery to the core in matters of educational excellence as well as equity. In addition, it started to move national education policy from an input to an output orientation. Both the conception of the federal role and the instruments used to implement policy changed.

In the 1980s the National Council of Teachers of Mathematics (NCTM), in collaboration with researchers and other stakeholders, began developing content standards for school mathematics that drew not only upon teacher expertise, but on the learning research, international curriculum benchmarks, and new developments in the field of mathematics. When these standards were published in 1989, they became a model for voluntary national standards in other subject areas. Because they wanted standards that were national, but not produced directly by the government, the first Bush administration funded other subject-matter professional associations to develop standards. Some organizations produced standards without government funding. National standards were completed and published throughout the 1990s, but they varied greatly in format, level of specificity, and quality (Wixson, Dutro, & Athan, 2003). Most states developed their own content standards and assessments; some drew on the national standards as models, others did not.

As the standards movement progressed, policy implementation researchers played a role not only in studying but in shaping how it was framed. They pointed to problems of incoherence as more challenging standards were added on top of old curriculum and assessment systems and called for better "alignment." The need to build system "capacity" to meet new learning goals was emphasized as well as the need for "accountability" for results (Fuhrman, 1993). Standards-based reform gradually evolved into "systemic" reform. O'Day and Smith (1993) published the classic definition of systemic reform: A common, high-quality curricular vision serves as a foundation for aligning all parts of a state instructional system, including core content, materials, teacher training, professional development, and assessment to support the goal of higher student achievement. The key components of a research-based systemic reform framework might be summarized as standards, capacity, and accountability.

The national policy emphasis shifted to excellence, but the standards movement had significant equity implications as well. The more challenging standards that reformers envisioned applied to all students, not just the elite (Resnick, 1987). Advocates for disadvantaged students in low income districts pushed the idea of opportunity to learn standards as a means of forcing more equal funding to build capacity to meet standards (Wixson, Dutro, & Athan, 2003). In a new round of school finance equalization cases, plaintiffs argued that funding provided by the states in many poor districts was inadequate to enable students to meet educational standards. Finally, because disadvantaged students were disproportionately assigned to low curriculum tracks that did not provide exposure to the thinking curriculum, efforts to detrack often became part of the reform agenda (Resnick, Stein, & Coon, 2008).

The Clinton administration in the 1994 reauthorization of ESEA, which was called the Improving America's Schools Act (IASA), required states to develop content and performance standards for all children as well as aligned assessments as a condition of receiving Title I funds. Instead of being voluntary, state standards and assessments became virtually mandatory. To gain necessary moderate Republican support, the Act also authorized the use of Title I money for public school choice programs and for charter schools. Capacity-building was deemphasized. The opportunity to learn standards that liberal Democrats wanted was bitterly opposed by conservatives and became optional. During the 1990s, various proposals to further nationalize reform by creating mandatory national content standards, a national body to certify the quality of state standards and assessments, or a national accountability test ran into anti–federal control opposition and were defeated (McGuinn, 2006; Resnick, Stein, & Coon, 2008).

Thus, during the Clinton administration a version of standards based reform was codified in federal law, but its components and the emphasis among them differed from the research-based formulation of systemic reform in significant ways. The key components of the Clinton version of reform have been described as standards, accountability, and choice. As a result of conservative Congressional pressure, choice replaced capacity-building as a major component of the national policy framework. In addition, over the years Clinton increasingly emphasized accountability, as evidenced by his unsuccessful attempt to enact a national test toward the end of his term. The practice of disaggregating and publishing assessment results to highlight achievement gaps is sometimes cited as a positive change introduced by NCLB; however, data disaggregation and action to correct gaps was first required in Title I by IASA (McGuinn, 2006).

When the initial call to action came, business interests and the governors were leading advocates of standards-based reform. Subject-oriented education groups and researchers were involved in the development and implementation of voluntary national standards. Moderate Democrats and Republicans were the main supporters of standards based reform. Some liberal Democrats had reservations about standards and accountability without sufficient resources for poor schools. As the movement developed, there was a resurgence of anti–federal control sentiment among conservatives (McGuinn, 2006). At the state and local levels, antireform parent groups initiated "math wars" (Wilson, 2003) and "reading wars" (Pearson, 2000) that opposed changes in curriculum, pedagogy, and tracking.

There was some progress toward the goal of higher achievement for all students during the standards era. NAEP long-term trend data show significant gains in mathematics for 9- and 13-year-olds between 1986 and 2004, with gains accelerating after 1999. There were also gains in reading for 9-year-olds and significant achievement gap reductions for younger Black and Hispanic students in both subjects between 1999 and 2004. However, 17-year-olds showed little progress (National Center for Education Statistics, 2009). NAEP describes trends, but does not explain what causes them. Nevertheless, it is interesting to note that mathematics, the subject in which achievement gains are most evident, came closest to the reform ideal of a content system aligned around new learning goals.

The standards movement envisioned very difficult and complex changes in educational policy and practice. There was tremendous variation in the interpretation and implementation of standards-based reform both over time and in different places around the nation. Reformers can point to islands of success in some states, districts, and schools where most of the components of systemic reform could be seen and student achievement increased substantially. But success was very hard to scale up. By 2000, there was still an absence of standards-based curricula, materials, and assessments in most places (Fuhrman, 2001). It seems reasonable to conclude that standards-based reform was an idea that was never fully implemented. Before its goals could be realized, the national policy framework changed again.

## FOCUS ON ACHIEVEMENT GAPS

The No Child Left Behind Act (NCLB) became law in 2002, and it represented a fundamental change in national education policy. NCLB moved national policy to the center of the educational stage, where it now has a significant impact on core educational decisions formerly left to state and local discretion. It shifted the policy framework from standards-based reform for all students to test-driven accountability that focuses on closing achievement gaps between more and less advantaged students. The focus is clearly on outputs, with little concern about inputs. NCLB relies upon several strategies to accomplish its achievement goals: performance mandates, high-stakes testing, sanctions, market competition, and teacher credentialing (McGuinn, 2006).

The law mandates that each state must attain academic proficiency in reading and mathematics for 100% of its students by 2014, set annual performance targets to gradually reach that goal, and then demonstrate "adequate yearly progress" (AYP). The focus of the AYP requirement is on closing achievement gaps between more and less advantaged students. States must define academic proficiency and develop annual assessment systems in reading and mathematics that provide individual student scores. They must report both overall progress and disaggregated results by race, income, English language ability, and disability status. "Report cards" containing these data must be published at the state, district, and school levels (McGuinn, 2006).

NCLB makes individual schools the legally accountable entity responsible for student performance. Schools face stiff sanctions for failure. If a school does not make AYP for each subgroup for 2 consecutive years, the district must provide technical assistance to that school and public school choice. After 3 years, the school is required to offer parents the option of outside supplementary educational services. After 4 years, the district must take corrective action such as replacing staff or adopting a new curriculum. Finally, after 5 years, a failing school must be reconstituted or taken over by the state. NCLB requires state education agencies to assist failing schools, but ignores the fact that the expertise of these agencies is in channeling funds and enforcing regulations, not in substantive school improvement (McGuinn, 2006; Sunderman & Orfield, 2006).

NCLB employs market mechanisms, emphasizing competition and choice, as strategies for school improvement to a greater extent than any previous federal legislation. A proposal to pursue private school choice by giving vouchers to parents of children in failing schools that they could use in private schools was defeated. In the final legislation, children can transfer out, but only to other public schools. Private firms may provide the supplementary services that failing schools must offer, and they may manage state takeovers. The law also promotes public charter schools by authorizing a small grant program to assist states and localities with design, facilities costs, and evaluation. In combination with the labeling of schools, these market provisions encourage families to exit troubled schools, rather than to exercise voice in improving them (Kantor & Lowe, 2006).

The law also requires schools to staff all core academic subjects with what it calls a "highly qualified teacher." NCLB defines highly qualified teachers as those who have a bachelor's degree and full state certification, and have demonstrated knowledge of their subject matter (Manna, 2008). These requirements, emphasizing as they do preservice education and initial licensing, are more descriptive of a minimally rather than a highly qualified teacher. The law assumes that professional development can facilitate effective teaching. Substantial federal support for teacher professional development is now available through both the Higher Education Act (HEA) for preservice and NCLB, Title II, for inservice.

NCLB and several other recent federal statues mandate the use of "scientifically based research" and various kinds of "data" as evidence to justify decisions about the use of federal funds. The National Research Council, speaking for the research community, argued in congressional testimony that definitions of research have no place in federal law because standards for research are generated by the community of researchers. Definitions of research in federal statutes are inconsistent with one another and incongruent with principles of scientific quality generated by researchers (Eisenhart &

Towne, 2003; Shavelson & Towne, 2002). In addition, statutory definitions of evidence and its uses do not fully encompass the actual scope of evidence use by practitioners (Coburn & Talbert, 2006; Honig & Coburn, 2008).

Ironically, although NCLB requires federal grantees to use scientific research, such research was apparently not used in developing the law itself. A recent study of how research was used in formulating NCLB found that members of Congress and their staffs gravitated toward research that supported their own preexisting ideologies and that the think tanks they relied upon most facilitated and mediated this behavior. A list of the most frequently appearing witnesses included people who were all policy researchers, most of them associated with a conservative perspective, but no nationally recognized experts in basic educational research (Manna & Petrilli, 2008).

The NCLB Act was a compromise among insiders. It was negotiated by a small group of key senators and congressmen working in conjunction with the Bush White House. Groups representing educators focused on increasing education funding and opposing privatization, but these groups have been losing influence (DeBray, 2005). NCLB shifted national education policy to the right by locating the responsibility for educational inequality in the school without reference to the larger society and emphasizing a combination of test-based accountability and market strategies for school improvement. It scrambled traditional political alliances, splitting both the right and the left. Many conservatives, who might be expected to support a Republican president's law, strongly oppose it because it intrudes on local control. Some liberal civil rights groups and advocates for poor children support it because of its emphasis on achievement gaps (Kantor & Lowe, 2006).

During the NCLB era a new political coalition gained ascendancy in national education policy, according to Ravitch (2010). Aptly dubbed "the Billionaire Boys Club," it is an alliance of billionaire entrepreneurs operating through their foundations, advocacy groups funded by these foundations, and politicians from both parties. Unlike traditional foundations that give grants in response to proposals, these new "venture philanthropies" aggressively pursue their own agendas. The biggest and most influential ones in education, the Gates, Walton, and Broad foundations, have coalesced around an education agenda that mirrors corporate values, including competition, choice (especially charters), incentives (such as performance pay for educators), data systems, and other market-based strategies.

NAEP long-term trend data provide some insight into achievement trends during the NCLB era. Overall reading and mathematics scores for 9- and 13-year-olds continued their generally increasing trends between 2004 and 2008, but the pace of improvement slowed from the immediately preceding testing period (1999–2004). There were small gains in reading for 17-year-olds. However, between 2004 and 2008 there has been no significant change in either White–Black or White–Hispanic score gaps in either subject (NCES, 2009). This plateau in reducing achievement gaps since 2004 contrasts unfavorably with both long-term gains since the early 1970s and gains during the preceding testing period (Fuller et al., 2007). In addition, NCLB has had numerous negative side effects on educational practice such as narrowing the curriculum, adoption of easier tests, and teaching to the test, that will be discussed more fully in later chapters.

## A PROMISE OF CHANGE

President Barack Obama premised his campaign on the promise of fundamental change. Almost 2 years into his first term, his education policy is still a work in progress. As in earlier administrations, education policy has served as a means to other ends—this time, economic recovery. The American Recovery and Reinvestment Act (ARRA), popularly known as the Stimulus Act, is the biggest federal investment ever in education, with about $100 billion earmarked. Of this, $95 billion is intended to prevent recession related cuts in education spending and expand existing programs such as Title I, IDEA, and Head Start. The remaining $5 billion is for education reform. Of this, $4.35 billion is being allocated to the states through "Race to the Top" discretionary grants.

Early in 2010 the Obama administration released its proposal for reauthorizing ESEA in a document called the *Blueprint for Reform.* Both the ESEA proposal and the Race to the Top initiative reaffirm raising student achievement and closing gaps as national goals. These policy initiatives add the goals of raising graduation rates and reducing attainment gaps.

Obama's promise of change extends to process as well as substance. In many speeches, including one to the National Academies on April 27, 2009, Obama said that "the days of science taking a backseat to ideology are over" and stated his commitment to "a new effort to ensure federal policies are based on the best and most unbiased scientific information." He pledged more involvement of both researchers and the public in the policy process. Specifically, he said "we also need to engage the scientific community directly in the work of public policy" (Obama, 2009). These changes in process are critical if education policy is going to make sense educationally and have a chance to succeed in meeting national goals for achievement and attainment in the future. Chapter 14 assesses the extent to which the President has fulfilled the promise of change.

## CONCLUSION

This brief historical background has identified three different frameworks that have dominated policy at different times. Each framework arose from the politics of the times. With rare exceptions, such as the design of Head

Start, scientific research about education has not significantly influenced national education policy.

Educational equity was part of a larger movement to reduce poverty and promote racial integration between the mid-1960s and 1980. Some progress was made with a combination of civil rights mandates and categorical programs, but these strategies were inadequate to the high aspirations of the era. National policy operated at the margins of the education system to achieve specific purposes related to equity and innovation. Fundamental issues about education, such as what students should learn, how to teach it, and the intricacies of assessment, were left to the state and local levels. National policy focused on inputs. There was a disposition to use research, but not much useful educational research was available.

In the mid-1980s, a new framework emphasized the need for higher standards for all students to improve U.S. global competitiveness. Standards were potentially a vehicle for applying research advances in the concepts of learning and achievement to policy and practice, but this opportunity was only partially realized. Research suggested that the greatest challenge was to build system capacity to meet higher expectations, but national policy invested little in capacity. Clinton-era legislation framed the components of standards-based reform as standards, choice, and accountability. The vision of systemic reform driven by high standards, with a balance of capacity and accountability, was never fully implemented.

The third transformation of national policy frameworks came about in 2002 with the Bush administration's NCLB. With little public deliberation, NCLB moved the federal government to the forefront of core educational matters. This legislation mandated performance targets for the elimination of achievement gaps between subgroups of students. Its high-stakes testing policies and stiff sanctions are narrowing the curriculum and driving instruction. Its market-based strategies are privatizing public education. There is no evidence that the strategies emphasized in NCLB have improved achievement. Much of the debate about NCLB policy has centered on the specifics of the legislation (such as the AYP requirement); the underlying assumptions about the federal role and strategies have not been adequately addressed.

Today we have layer upon layer of policy embedded in federal legislation. Over time, the combination of layers has become increasingly incoherent. The link between many national education policy initiatives and research knowledge about what might actually improve educational practice is dubious at best. Federal policy has not been designed to make educational sense. Nevertheless, better education outcomes, first implicitly and now explicitly, are expected. It is logical to assume that if policymakers expect significantly better educational results, they must use knowledge about education to frame reform. NCLB policy falls far short of meeting that test.

President Obama has indicated that the goals of raising overall student achievement and attainment and closing gaps among subgroups will continue to provide a sense of direction for national policy in the future. He has made a twofold promise of change. The first part of his promise involves substantive change. The second part of his promise involves change in the way policy is made, both grounding policy in research evidence and opening up the process to broader participation.

It would be naive to think that research will replace politics as a foundation for education policy. Politics and research knowledge interact in complex and varied ways in the policymaking process. However, there is a middle ground. The National Institutes of Health (NIH) seeks to operate at the intersection of national needs and scientific opportunities (NIH, 1992). Their work strategically emphasizes areas of public need where knowledge is accumulating and important advances are thought to be possible. It is hard to find similar examples in education. The time may be right to start looking for areas in education where science and public needs converge. The next chapter considers the scientific opportunities.

# CHAPTER 2

# Research and Education Reform

Education reform currently lacks a commonly accepted framework or theory of action that makes educational sense. Without one, it is not possible to substantially improve student achievement or attainment. Educational research is the best source of a coherent and effective framework for education reform. Following a line of reasoning developed by Shavelson (1988), I argue that the utility of today's educational research lies in its potential to challenge existing assumptions about education, to generate new ways of conceptualizing the central components of education, and to fundamentally reframe how we think about policy and practice. In this chapter, I identify lines of inquiry that offer scientific opportunities for education reform. I describe the significance of this research for framing and conceptualizing reform as well as how I used it in this book. I also describe my research synthesis approach and methods.

## THE LEARNING RESEARCH

Research on learning and its contexts are the most important lines of inquiry for education reform. According to a report by the National Research Council (Bransford, Brown, & Cocking, 2000), research on learning and its contexts has developed to the point where it "is beginning to provide knowledge to improve significantly people's abilities to become active learners" (p. 13). Moreover, "the emerging science of learning underscores the importance of rethinking what is taught, how it is taught, and how learning is assessed" (p. 14).

In the first half of the 20th century, educational research was dominated by behaviorism. This view of learning emphasized the passive accumulation of facts and skills in a linear and sequential manner through practice and repetition (Koppich & Knapp, 1998; Marshall, 1994). Individual behavior, including learning, was seen as a reaction to external stimuli. Theories of reinforcement assumed that behaviors such as learning could be manipulated by the application of rewards and punishments (Stipek, 2002). Ability, including intelligence, was thought to be inherited and static (Martinez, 2000). However, as early as the 1920s and 1930s, researchers demonstrated that the environment had positive and negative impacts on human development.

They concluded that ability was a product of both nature and nurture and was, therefore, malleable to some extent (Lagemann, 2000).

Today's education practice and policy still reflect the strong practical influence of the behaviorist perspective. For example, facts and skills dominate most curriculum frameworks and mandated accountability tests. Teachers teach accordingly. Many teachers doubt the ability of students from disadvantaged backgrounds to achieve. Students are often tracked based on their preexisting abilities. Rewards and punishments are the mainstay not only of school motivation and discipline, but of education policy.

Beginning around 1960, two waves of change took place in research on learning that today are sometimes referred to as the "cognitive" and "sociocultural" revolutions (Cobb & Bowers, 1999; Koppich & Knapp, 1998). These new paradigms share the assumption that learning involves the active construction of knowledge. Currently, educational research and many significant reform initiatives are influenced by constructivist theories of learning. There are two main branches of learning theory–the cognitive and the sociocultural.

Cognitive theorists focus on the workings of the individual mind. They have studied the complex conceptual processes involved in higher-order thinking, sense-making, and understanding. By comparing the performance of novices and experts, these researchers found that expert knowledge is organized around important concepts. Also, experts know when and how to apply their knowledge. Learners always bring some background knowledge to a learning situation, and teachers must build upon these initial understandings as they assist students in acquiring new knowledge. Learning is viewed as a process of active cognitive reorganization that includes, but extends far beyond, fact accumulation. Cognitive research has redefined the nature of knowledge and changed our understanding of how people learn (Bransford, Brown, & Cocking, 2000; Resnick, 1987).

Sociocultural theorists take the individual-in-social-action as their unit of analysis. These theorists assume that "(h)umans develop through their changing participation in the socio-cultural activities of their communities, which also change" (Rogoff, 2003, p. 110). A child (or any newcomer) learns the ways of a community by participating with guidance from more experienced members. Engagement in community activities develops not only competence, but also a sense of identity and membership in the community, through which participants experience meaning. In modern society people engage in multiple communities that may be culturally congruent or incongruent, and they need to learn to negotiate the boundaries of these communities (Wenger, 1998).

Sociocultural theory offers an expanded view of learning that foregrounds its social and cultural dimensions. This research suggests that identity development, community membership, and meaning are important aspects of education that should receive more attention in the future. Very important new insights about how to improve outcomes for students outside the mainstream and potentially reduce gaps in achievement and attainment can be found in this research.

## TEACHING AND EDUCATIONAL CONTEXTS

Early research on teaching, like the learning research, reflected the behaviorist perspective. The focus was on teacher characteristics and behaviors. Studies of "effective teaching" tried to link isolated teacher behaviors with student outcomes. Pedagogy was believed to be a set of simple generic skills that could be applied across subject areas and with all students. The belief was that teaching could be improved if researchers could just identify the right set of teaching behaviors and skills, codify them, and disseminate them to teachers. At the same time developers tried to produce pre-packaged "teacher proof" materials that specified what teachers should do in great detail (Koppich & Knapp, 1998; Richardson, 2001).

Research on teaching changed dramatically after 1975 when the National Institute of Education hosted a conference to create a research agenda on teaching. Influenced by emerging learning theories, participants made the case for what Koppich and Knapp described as "a more cognitive, complex, and contextual view of teaching" (1998, p. 11). The research focus shifted to teachers' thought processes and eventually to teaching in particular subject areas and different classroom contexts. The new teaching research found that teaching was a complex process that required considerable expertise in both pedagogy and subject matter and that effective teaching approaches were not generic, but varied with different subjects and students (Richardson, 2001).

The more sophisticated view of teaching that has emerged from more recent research has profound implications for teacher preparation, inservice learning, the kind of supports practicing teachers need, and our understanding of productive school and policy environments (Koppich & Knapp, 1998). The upshot of this research is that teaching is not a simple task whose elements can be prescribed from above or improved significantly by external rewards and sanctions. Instead, teaching should be viewed as a real profession because it is grounded in a growing body of knowledge. Effective teaching requires considerable expertise and the kind of infrastructure of supports for learning and peer accountability that other professions enjoy. The best way to scale-up good teaching is to strengthen the teaching profession (National Commission on Teaching and America's Future, 1996).

More recently attention has expanded to teaching and learning environments. An emergent line of inquiry hypothesizes that the core educational processes of teaching and learning involve dynamic interactions among the "triangle" of teachers, students, and content and with various environments. For researchers, this framework defines what is important to study—what makes their research "educational" (Ball & Forzani, 2007). For reformers, this triangular schema has the potential to focus education reform efforts on the stuff of education that matters most (McLaughlin & Talbert, 1993). It is the heart of the learning-centered framework because it provides a strategic focus for reform.

Years ago, Bronfenbrenner (1981) provided a theoretical framework for linking teaching and learning with educational environments when he proposed a comprehensive "ecological" framework for understanding the interaction between individual development and the environment. His ecological framework is composed of multiple contexts. He envisioned a series of concentric circles, with the developing child and the environments h/she directly experiences at the center (i.e., home, school, neighborhood). The outer circles include more indirect social and cultural influences on development. Bronfenbrenner saw development as multidimensional (i.e., encompassing intellectual, social, emotional, and physical aspects) and focused on studying the environmental conditions that constrain or enable it. Bronfenbrenner had a direct impact on policy because he was a member of the expert committee that designed Head Start. His theoretical orientation influenced the comprehensive nature of that program (Zigler & Muenchow, 1992) and is still influential today.

Research on schools and the education system used to be disconnected from learning and compartmentalized in separate fields (e.g., curriculum, finance, leadership). By the mid-1980s, researchers in various fields that study larger education environments became interested in the connections between learning theory and their work. Some researchers adapted the ecological model and began using it to analyze how factors in the multiple contexts of education enable or constrain learning and teaching (e.g., McLaughlin & Talbert, 1993, 2001; Newmann & Wehlage, 1995). Other researchers examined the larger education system through a sociocultural lens (e.g., Tharp & Gallimore, 1988). The idea of learning communities as productive educational contexts emerged from sociocultural research conducted both inside and outside of schools (Rogoff, 2003).

Research on learning, teaching, and education contexts became more integrated. Very significantly, the notion arose from this research that reform needed to be comprehensive and systemic because without an infrastructure of content, teacher learning opportunities, student supports, and so on that are consistent with new research-based goals for learning and achievement, the kind of classroom, school, and other environments necessary to produce better outcomes would not materialize. Thus, the need to build capacity is a central focus of learning-centered reform.

Over the course of more than 50 years, scientific knowledge has accumulated in a number of lines of inquiry, including cognitive science, sociocultural learning theory, human development, teaching, and educational contexts, that today provide an intellectual foundation for education reform. The research on knowledge and learning is more advanced than the research on teaching and educational contexts. Further research and development are needed to fill remaining gaps in knowledge and to apply these theoretical advances, but research frameworks and concepts available today already offer more productive ways to envision education reform.

There are many barriers to using these new ideas, but one of the most difficult to overcome is that incorporating them successfully into practice or policy involves significant conceptual change. Therefore, reform involves rethinking the nature of knowledge, learning, teaching, motivation, and other key aspects of education (Bransford, Brown, & Cocking, 2000; Marshall, 1994). This rethinking, as Wilson and Peterson (2006) point out, does not mean "throwing the baby out with the bathwater" and completely abandoning behaviorist theories and ways of doing things, but it does imply deep conceptual reorganization, as well as practical change to develop new system capacity.

## OTHER RELEVANT RESEARCH

Research on learning and its contexts offers a basis for conceptualizing several key components of a framework for education reform: achievement, learning and teaching, educational environments, and system capacity. However, these lines of inquiry do not fully address some other possible components. Logic suggests that a framework for reform should also include both educational goals and an assessment system to measure progress. The research already described has implications for goals and assessments, but there are additional relevant lines of inquiry in each of these areas.

Student achievement is the focus of current policy, but student achievement must be defined with reference to the broader goals of education (Cole, 1990). Only within the context of educational goals can we answer the obvious question: Achievement for what? Educational goals are inherently normative, and empirical research is of limited use in conceptualizing them. Cognitive research suggests that more emphasis should be placed on thinking, and sociocultural research suggests more emphasis on goals such as identity development, but the empirical research does not offer adequate resources for a complete analysis of educational goals.

However, research in the history and philosophy of education does offer a rich source of insight for reflecting on educational goals and how they have evolved. Recent public opinion data and other research on local perspectives offer a more current view of the goals that matter to people today. In combination, these lines of inquiry provide a basis for a critique of recent national policy rhetoric on educational goals and contribute to a more comprehensive concept that can inform future discourse.

Assessment research was until recently separate from learning research. However, any assessment is grounded in theories of knowledge, learning, and measurement. Existing assessments are products of prior theories, but now assessment is being reconceptualized in light of cognitive (Pelligrino, Baxter, & Glaser, 1999) and sociocultural (Gipps, 1999) learning theories. Both the purposes and methods of assessment are changing (Pelligrino, Chudowsky, & Glaser, 2001).

Most commonly used assessments do a reasonable job of measuring knowledge of basic facts, skills, and procedures. However, cognitive research points to important aspects of knowledge not adequately addressed by current assessments, such as students' concepts, problem representations, use of strategies, and self-monitoring skills (Pelligrino, Chudowsky, & Glaser, 2001). Sociocultural theory suggests that assessment should be broadened to include not just what individual students know, but what they can do in social settings. For example, a more complete assessment system might evaluate students' contributions to group problem solving or the level of performance they can attain working dynamically with a teacher (Gipps, 1999). Because new knowledge builds upon prior knowledge, both theoretical perspectives assume that greater emphasis on formative assessment that takes place during the learning process and provides feedback to both students and teachers is essential to facilitate improved learning.

The research evidence supports the idea that assessment should be a key component of reform. However, assessment theory and practice lag behind learning theory. Progress was made during the standards era in developing assessments more aligned with new conceptions of learning and competence, but high stakes testing policies, especially NCLB, have diverted attention and resources to accountability initiatives that use obsolete assessment approaches. With sufficient investment and a different policy environment, today's research provides the foundation for designing new, cutting-edge assessment systems.

Does the research evidence support accountability and choice as components of a framework for education reform? Accountability is an underdeveloped concept (Adams & Kirst, 1999). Some research indicates that change is a product of both pressure and support (Fullan, 1993). However, the notion that higher performance can be mandated and induced by sanctions is not consistent with learning theory. As noted earlier, learning theory suggests that improving performance involves engaging students in challenging intellectual work and creating more educative learning environments, preferably both in and out of school.

Despite decades of implementation in some states, empirical evidence of the effects of high-stakes accountability on student achievement is at best ambiguous. According to several recent research syntheses, studies using state test data may show improvements in some grade levels and subjects, but most researchers consider state tests to be unreliable. Studies using NAEP data do not show positive effects on student achievement (Mintrop & Sunderman, 2009). Since NCLB, one meta-analysis showed modest positive effects on average test scores, but not on achievement gaps (Lee, 2008); another analysis of long-term NAEP data showed slower overall gains (Fuller et al., 2007). A comparison of student reading and mathematics achievement gains prior to NCLB in states that emphasized supports with those that emphasized accountability found that accountability alone had no significant effect, but that a combination of supports and accountability had positive effects in mathematics (Lee, 2006).

The emphasis on accountability has spurred research on alternative conceptions of accountability that may help advance student learning and improve teaching. This new research points to several areas that deserve attention in reframing accountability: how shared accountability among stakeholders might work (Heubert & Hauser, 1999); the reciprocal relationship between accountability and capacity (Elmore, 2003a); the relationship among individual, within-school, and external accountability (Abelmann & Elmore, 1999); and the efficacy of different forms of it, such as professional accountability and public accountability (Adams & Kirst, 1999). Although there is little or no research support for the kind of accountability regime required by NCLB, alternative approaches to accountability are promising. Therefore, accountability is included as a component of the research-based framework for education reform, but the research behind the accountability concepts discussed is more tentative than the research behind other components of the framework.

The notion that choice should be a component of education reform is not based on educational theory or research; it is an application of economic theory to education. The underlying assumption is that market competition will result in school improvement (Friedman, 2002). Over the years a variety of strategies to facilitate choice have been tried, including vouchers, charter schools, and magnet schools, but the results have been mixed. Syntheses of research on market strategies have found that some studies show a modest positive effect on student achievement, but that none of the market-based strategies have significantly and consistently improved student achievement (Belfield & Levin, 2009; Hannaway & Woodroffe, 2003).

Charter schools have now become the leading edge of the choice movement. A recent synthesis of research on charter schools found that some are better and others are worse than regular public schools. Thus, charter schools increase inequality of opportunity without raising student achievement

(Carnoy, Jacobsen, Mishel, & Rothstein, 2005). More recent studies of charters continue to show mixed results on achievement, some positive (Hoxby, Muraka, & Kang, 2009) and others negative (Center for Research on Education Outcomes, 2009). Since the rationale for choice is not based on educational theory and there is little evidence of the significant success its proponents envisioned, inclusion of choice as a component of a framework for reform derived from educational research is unwarranted.

## EXEMPLARS OF BEST PRACTICE

What evidence is there, the reader might well ask, that new research theories will actually lead to improved learning outcomes, especially for all students? For a variety of reasons, there is not as much evidence as we would like. First of all, in the United States there are few examples of learning, teaching, and school contexts consistent with new theories to study, so large-scale evaluations are not feasible. Also, the learning sought by research-oriented reformers is not just better performance of the conventional type; it is qualitatively different. Until very recently, there have been few available assessments appropriate to measure it.

Yet where conditions have made observation and assessment of learning outcomes based on these new theories possible, there are examples of success. There is positive student outcome evidence from evaluations of a variety of teaching experiments based on these theories (see Atkinson & Jackson, 1992; Bransford, Brown, & Cocking, 2000; and Resnick, 1987, for syntheses of findings and results). In more natural settings, there are case studies of individual schools and school districts with outstanding performance results for diverse students who had been low achieving prior to reform (Ancess, 1995; Bensman, 2000; Resnick & Harwell, 1998). On a larger scale, Bryk and his colleagues (2010) compared the top quartile (117 schools) in Chicago that had substantially improved with the bottom quartile (118 schools) that had not. Using the learning triangle as a theoretical guide, they identified a comprehensive set of practices and conditions that interact to improve student outcomes.

International comparative studies in education represent an additional line of inquiry that is useful in constructing a framework for educational reform. A report by the National Research Council (NRC) recently discussed the purposes and potential of international comparisons (Chabott & Elliott, 2003). Policymakers are well aware of the comparisons of student outcomes in such studies as the Program for International Student Assessment (PISA) and the Trends in International Mathematics and Science Study (TIMSS). According to the NRC, the information that these studies provide about policy and practice can help us to see new possibilities, to define what is achievable, and to question existing beliefs and assumptions. None of the international studies are designed to establish causality between inputs and outcomes. However, the NRC maintained that these studies can strengthen the grounds for speculating on causes, especially when promising policies and practices are also consistent with other research knowledge.

The research on learning consists of multiple lines of inquiry, ranging from experimental studies that support causal inferences to case studies that illustrate theory in practice. Although new research on learning, teaching, and educational contexts is extraordinarily promising as a foundation for reform, its implications for practice and policy have not been made sufficiently clear. Therefore, throughout the book I use examples drawn from case studies and international comparisons to illustrate how concepts derived from basic research might be applied in practice. The examples are intended only as illustrations; they do not prove the theory.

Four case study examples are used extensively to provide continuity. Reform in three of these sites (called "high-performance" case studies) was congruent with learning theory, and their students became high-performing. The locale for one case study is Community School District #2 in New York City (Elmore & Burney, 1997, 1998; Stein & D'Amico, 1999; Stein, Harwell, & D'Amico, 1999). Two others are mini–case studies of reform in selected districts and schools in the states of Wisconsin (Odden et al., 2007) and Washington (Fermanich et al., 2006) that have made outstanding student achievement gains, sometimes doubling or tripling student achievement scores. The fourth case study explicitly ties together research on learning and school organization. It analyzed both improving and stagnant schools in Chicago (referred to as the highest- and lowest-performing schools in Chicago)(Bryk et al., 2010). Other case studies are used selectively as exemplars of particular state policies or local practices.

## SYNTHESIS APPROACH AND METHODS

When the consensus behind policy has eroded, policy is not producing the desired effects, or policy has become incoherent, then policy research directed toward basic understanding, policy reformulation, and fundamental change is called for, according to Rein and Schön (1977). Because I believe that these conditions characterize education policy today, I have developed a mode of policy analysis designed to promote fundamental understanding and serve as a rationale for change. This kind of policy research focuses on building a new framework within which action can be organized. It also involves discovering the tacit frames behind existing policies and challenging them (Rein & Schön, 1977). These authors contend, and I agree, that better policies can be formulated through the critical comparison of policy frames because this kind of analysis encourages reflective awareness of our existing assumptions and the stance we wish to take in the future.

Policy analysis concerned with developing understanding of social problems and creating new options is one of three types of policy research that have been identified in the literature. A second type promotes informed decisionmaking by analyzing a variety of alternative courses of action. The third evaluates the implementation of existing policies or programs (Wiley, 1992). In education over the years the greatest emphasis has been placed on implementation studies. These studies are typically used not just to understand the effects of past programs and policies, but to guide the next round of policy formulation to the extent that they identify program weaknesses or gaps. However, because these studies generally deal with individual programs and accept program goals as givens, the evidence they produce can only justify incremental change.

In developing a framework for education reform and comparing it to past alternatives, I used qualitative, interpretive research synthesis methods (Eisenhart, 1998; Suri & Clarke, 2009). My literature search was purposeful rather than exhaustive. The scope of this book makes an exhaustive search impossible. Generally, my focus is on what we can learn from major lines of inquiry, rather than individual studies. I relied heavily upon authoritative research syntheses from the National Academies and various American Educational Research Association (AERA) handbooks and journals, as well as seminal books and articles (e.g., Wenger, 1998). I was already familiar with the research from the most relevant government-sponsored Research and Development Centers, including the Learning Research and Development Center (LRDC), the Center for Research on the Context of Teaching (CRC), the Consortium for Policy Research in Education (CPRE), the Center for the Study of Teaching and Policy (CTP), and the Center for Research on Education, Diversity, and Excellence (CREDE), and I searched their publications further. I conducted targeted literature searches in specific areas as needed to fill gaps. As noted earlier, to make ideas more accessible, I used case study material to illustrate concepts. The introduction to Part II describes more fully my rationale and methodology for developing the specific components included in the learning-centered framework.

In Parts II and III, I drew upon descriptive policy research as well as studies of the implementation of programs and policies to describe standards-based reform and NCLB policy. My purpose was to compare these policies to the learning-centered framework. In Part III, where I discussed the implications of the learning-centered framework for federal policy, I used a line of inquiry in the field of policy analysis that identified a range of policy instruments (e.g., capacity-building, program grants) and studied the conditions under which they are likely to achieve their intended purposes (Hannaway & Woodroffe, 2003; Honig, 2006a; McDonnell & Elmore, 1987). I also relied on my own practical experience in developing government policies and programs at the national level.

## CONCLUSION

Research on learning, teaching, and classroom contexts has a strong scientific foundation. This research supports higher expectations for student learning and achievement and potentially offers a comprehensive and coherent framework for education reform. In order to realize the promise of better outcomes for students, the research suggests that reformers should reconceptualize the goals of education and the nature of school knowledge; transform curriculum content and teaching practices; and ensure that all students have access to rich, challenging, and nurturing learning environments. Today's educational research offers exciting scientific opportunities in each of these areas that are ripe for development and application.

Many researchers who study schools and broader education system contexts have linked their work to research on the core processes of learning and teaching. Taken together, these fields now make it possible to operationally define systemic capacity and to focus change efforts on components of capacity most likely to improve learning and teaching. Research on learning has also transformed ideas about the purpose and methods of educational assessment. With significant long-term investment, it is feasible to create a new generation of assessments that will facilitate learning and achievement.

The strategies for education reform embedded in NCLB have little or no basis in research. Performance can be improved if students have access to better learning environments, but high performance cannot be mandated. Top-down accountability that relies on high-stakes testing does not improve student achievement or reduce gaps, but it does have undesirable side effects. Accountability may be a useful component of reform, but it needs a thorough conceptual overhaul. The idea that market competition and choice can improve educational outcomes comes from economic, not educational, theory. Its efficacy is unproven.

To summarize, education reform is currently driven by national education policy. That policy focuses on areas where research is nonexistent or weak; it ignores areas where significant research advances offer the potential to make a real difference in improving outcomes. Key questions for the future are: What would education reform look like if it took advantage of scientific opportunities and were based on the best available knowledge about education? How does that vision compare with present and past efforts? These questions are addressed in Part II.

# Part II

# A LEARNING-CENTERED FRAMEWORK FOR REFORM

In this section I use the research described earlier to construct a framework for education reform. I call it a "learning-centered" framework because I rely primarily upon advances in research about learning, teaching, and the educational contexts that support learning as a foundation for the framework. The term "learning-centered" also emphasizes the fact that the focus of the framework is the improvement of learning and teaching and, therefore, it encourages reformers to think of the classroom as the core of the educational system. What is the value of a framework for education reform and policy? Before considering its potential in these spheres, it may be useful to consider how frameworks are used in scientific research and in the improvement of practice.

Scientific paradigms have been variously defined as worldviews; conceptual frameworks; constellations of beliefs, sets of values, and techniques; and exemplars or models. However described, according to Kuhn (1970), paradigms provide a focus for the work of particular scientific communities. When a new scientific paradigm gains acceptance, it serves to identify important puzzles to be solved and provides exemplars of how to solve them. In the preparadigm period, there are as many opinions about the nature of the work and how to do it as there are scientists. Once agreement on a paradigm is achieved in a scientific community, researchers share a sense of direction and a set of tools for achieving their goals. If the paradigm proves fruitful, the work proceeds efficiently and rapid progress is possible.

Turning to educational practice, over the years a number of frameworks have been used by schools, and sometimes school districts, for various improvement purposes. There are frameworks for school accreditation (e.g., AdvancED, 2009; National Study of School Evaluation, 2005). Some award programs use self-assessment frameworks as an application form (e.g., Baldrige National Quality Program [2002] and the early Blue Ribbon Schools Program [U.S. Department of Education, 1996]). Education associations sometimes have frameworks their members can use as school improvement tools (e.g., the National Education Association has KEYS). The components of these frameworks differ because they draw upon different research bases and philosophies of change. Nevertheless, all of them seek to promote school improvement by encouraging goal definition, identifying key areas for capacity-building, and in some cases providing ways to assess results. None of the major school improvement frameworks currently in use is systematically derived from research on learning and its contexts.

As in scientific research and the improvement of practice, a coherent framework for education reform and policy could provide a common focus and a strategic direction for future work. A better framework is needed because the NCLB framework that is driving reform has lost its credibility. Current policy rhetoric calls for change and for the use of research. But key questions go unanswered: What kind of change? What research? Part II addresses those questions. Research on learning, teaching, and related fields offers the most promising scientific opportunities for reform. A learning-centered approach to reform would use new knowledge to transform the core practices of education in order to improve the achievement of all students.

The learning-centered framework offers both a sense of direction for the future and a template that can be used to evaluate past and present reform initiatives. There is no way of proving in advance, not even in the hard sciences, that the work suggested by a framework will produce the desired results. Frameworks are accepted because they seem better than the alternatives (Kuhn, 1970). In this part, I synthesize important lines of research inquiry in the form of a framework for reform and then compare it to recently implemented policy frameworks, standards-based reform, and high-stakes testing. I argue that the research-based framework is better than the alternatives.

Like the scientific paradigms and the school improvement frameworks, the learning-centered framework developed here has three essential components: a concept of educational goals, a theory of how to attain the goals, and a way of assessing progress. In all of these areas, current research challenges and has the potential to change current assumptions about education reform.

Within the area of educational goals, national policy emphasizes improving student achievement and attainment. Current research challenges the tendency to equate student achievement with standardized test scores and raises concerns about how attainment is defined and measured. Lines of research dealing with learning, intelligence, and child development offer better ways to conceptualize educational outcomes in the future. New research perspectives expand and deepen our concept of achievement, but they are not well integrated. Merging new perspectives on achievement in practice is both an opportunity and a challenge for future reform.

Student achievement and attainment must be viewed within the context of the broader goals of education (Cole, 1990). Research in the history and philosophy of education as well as current public opinion data give reason to question the narrow emphasis of national policymakers on education as preparation for work and international competitiveness. The empirical research suggests the need for both a broadening and a deepening of educational goals. Research on goals at the local level indicates that educators are cognizant of a range of goals and need to be adept at balancing them.

Educational goals, student achievement, and attainment are closely connected. However, there is a logical distinction in that educational goals are normative, whereas achievement and attainment are empirical. The lines of inquiry synthesized to conceptualize educational goals are different from and would be difficult to combine with those synthesized to conceptualize achievement and attainment. Therefore, educational goals are treated as one component of the learning-centered framework in Chapter 3, and student achievement and attainment are presented as another component in Chapter 4.

Capacity-building and accountability are two possible strategies to reach higher educational goals for which there is some research support. Capacity is not well understood and is insufficiently emphasized. However, the strong research base on learning, teaching, and educational contexts can contribute to an operational definition of capacity. Accountability is overemphasized, and not defined in a way that promotes educational improvement. Some research is emerging that can help to tentatively reconceptualize accountability. The learning-centered framework includes both capacity and accountability as components of reform, reconceptualizes them, and reverses the relative emphasis.

The next two chapters present a framework for building capacity to meet more challenging educational goals in classrooms and throughout the educational system. In Chapter 5, I define classroom capacity around a triangular schema, emphasizing interactions among teachers, students, and content within environments, that, as indicated earlier, has become prominent in the research to represent core educational processes. Because the theory implies that all aspects of this core interconnect, a comprehensive approach to reform is necessary. In Chapter 6, I extend the logic of the learning triangle to the education system as a starting point for comprehensive and systemic reform.

Capacity-building might have been one component of a learning-centered framework, but I have broken it into two, one focusing on the classroom and the other on the rest of the education system, for several reasons. The kind of change that needs to take place at these levels is functionally different. Capacity at the classroom level involves the transformation of practice. In the rest of the system, it involves building a systemic infrastructure of support related to all aspects of the learning triangle. There is a great deal of research on learning, teaching, and educational contexts. Splitting capacity into two pieces makes it easier to synthesize the many relevant lines of research inquiry and, hopefully, easier for readers to use the ideas.

The research suggests that change requires a balance of support (capacity) and pressure (accountability). However, research does not support an approach to change that treats accountability as a panacea or defines it in almost entirely negative terms. The research base for conceptualizing accountability in a way that would provide the right type and degree of pressure is not as strong as it is for capacity, but research on new approaches to accountability is beginning to emerge. In Chapter 7, I use this new research on accountability to understand how it actually works in practice and to suggest a set of alternative accountability principles for future policy.

There is strong research support for assessment as a critical component of a framework for reform. Certain types of ongoing, formative, classroom-level assessment can significantly improve learning and achievement. This implies that there needs to be a better balance of formative and summative assessment. Consistent with the learning-centered approach, in Chapter 8 I reframe assessment by starting in the classroom with a balance of formative and summative assessment, then considering better approaches to assessment at the school and policy levels. A research-based assessment system would combine multiple measures to meet the needs of a variety of stakeholders at various levels of the system. There are substantial scientific opportunities in the area of assessment, but taking advantage of the opportunities requires a long-term investment.

To summarize, in Part II I focus on six central components of education that, in combination, constitute a comprehensive framework for thinking about education reform:

- Educational Goals
- Student Achievement and Attainment
- Classroom Capacity for Learning
- Systemic Capacity and Infrastructure
- Accountability
- Assessment Systems

In Chapters 3 through 8, I develop a new way of conceptualizing each of these components of education that is derived from basic educational research and I discuss its implications for the reform of educational practice. Case studies and international comparisons are used to illustrate key research concepts. For explanatory purposes these components are in separate chapters, but in practice they interact and are highly interdependent. A coherent approach to reform requires attention to all these components and to their interrelationships.

In the concluding section of each chapter, I use the learning-centered framework as a lens to examine and critique past national policy—both standards-based reform and high-stakes testing policy. Are these approaches to reform consistent or inconsistent with the concepts suggested by the learning-centered framework? Finally, I suggest how future national policy can be framed in a way that is congruent with the research-based concepts and, therefore, more supportive of best practice. Chapter 9 summarizes the learning-centered framework and compares it with standards-based reform and high-stakes testing policy.

# CHAPTER 3

# A Balanced Set
# of Educational Goals

This chapter discusses the educational goals emphasized in recent national policy statements within the context of a framework that draws upon the history and philosophy of education, new insights from educational research, and public opinion data. The question of what educational goals should be in the future is a normative one that, in a democracy, is best addressed through public deliberation. Including the public opinion data in this analysis is a step in that direction.

## ECONOMIC

In a world increasingly characterized by globalization, today's national policy rhetoric focuses on the economic goals of education—sustaining economic competitiveness and preparing students for higher education and work. For over 2 decades, beginning with the publication of *A Nation at Risk* (National Commission on Excellence in Education, 1983), policymakers have linked the public benefits of a competent workforce and a strong economy with educational excellence and equity. Many parents are also preoccupied with the economic aspects of education, but tend to view education as a way to achieve economic and social mobility for their particular children (Labaree, 1997).

Decrying a "curricular smorgasbord" and "extensive student choice" as hallmarks of mediocracy, *A Nation at Risk* called for high standards, specifically a more focused and rigorous academic curriculum for all students (p. 18). But, driven by economic goals, the "Five New Basics" of the academic core it recommended—English, mathematics, science, social studies, and computer science—were relatively narrow. Subjects traditionally included in the core of a liberal arts education, such as the arts and foreign languages, were deemphasized. The focus of today's NCLB is even narrower—schools are held accountable for student performance in reading and mathematics. Because performance is judged by standardized tests that usually only measure proficiency in basic skills, the goal of high standards has been effectively abandoned.

Overwhelming percentages of voters (81% in one poll) agree that a strong economy requires good public schools (Learning First Alliance, 2005). The public recently ranked helping people to become "economically self-sufficient" second on a list of reasons why America needs public schools. Clearly, the economic aspects of education represent one important goal dimension. There is an important difference, however, in how policymakers and the public think this goal should be addressed: the public prefers a wide variety of courses to a narrow focus on the basics (Rose & Gallup, 2006).

## CIVIC AND MORAL

Although almost absent from recent national policy discourse, the original purpose of public education in America was to promote civic goals. The statement of purpose for the Northwest Ordinance, our earliest federal education legislation, stressed good government, morality, and happiness as aims of public education that made it worthy of support (Fenstermacher, 1995). Ideas about the nature of civic education have evolved over the years, but there is a fairly consistent set of core objectives that can be traced from the founders to the present. It includes understanding of democratic ideals and principles, awareness of civic rights and responsibilities, knowledge of government institutions and processes, capacity to deliberate, public spiritedness and civic commitment, and participatory and leadership skills (Kaestle, 2000; Pangle & Pangle, 2000; Parker, 2003; Ravitch, 2001).

Today citizenship education is in decline in the United States. Schools require less relevant coursework than they did in the past. Key participatory skills such as deliberation, practical reasoning, and public speaking are generally not emphasized. Opportunities to experience at least some aspects of the democratic process directly are rare. Democratic values are less likely to be emphasized than the mechanics of government (Center for Information and Research on Civic Learning and Engagement & Carnegie Corporation, 2003).

Although an argument can easily be made by citing pervasive scandals in corporations, Wall Street, and government that our nation is at risk morally as well as economically, recent national policy has paid little attention to students' moral development. Our constitutional separation of church and state makes it difficult but not impossible to achieve consensus on what the nature of moral education might be in the public schools (Strike, 1991). In the late 1980s and 1990s, a consensus was created around the need for character education, and a variety of programs that built upon commonly shared values and the practice of the virtues were developed and widely adopted (McQuaide, 1996). Most of the packaged character education programs provide students with basic knowledge and skills. There is limited federal support for character education, although about 28 states mandate or encourage it (Cohen, 2006).

Despite the silence of most policymakers and declining emphasis in practice, the public still ranks preparing students to "become responsible citizens" as an important, and in some polls the most important, purpose of public education (Rose & Gallup, 2000). Voters stress citizen activism, or "preparing students to be citizens who can actively participate in improving their communities" (Learning First Alliance, 2005, pp. 12–13). Likewise, a majority of public school parents favor character education (defined as courses on values and ethical behavior). But when asked whether the schools should teach specific moral values, such as respect for others, fairness, and compassion, agreement rises to over 90% (Elam, Rose, & Gallup, 1994). When it comes to civic and moral education there are values and objectives that Americans share and want public education to emphasize (Learning First Alliance, 2005).

## SOCIAL AND CULTURAL

The workplace and the state constitute only part of the social and cultural environment that people must be educated to live in. Modern civil society encompasses a rich array of groups, organizations, and subcultures. These include families, diverse ethnic groups, community improvement groups, cultural and artistic organizations, churches, and sports teams. Participation in these many social groups "enables people to be themselves in all their dimensions" (Elshtian, 2001) and contributes to the vibrancy of our culture.

Like adults, students participate in many social settings in their everyday lives, including families, peer groups, schools, and communities. They must be able to function effectively in each of these social settings, experience a sense of membership, understand and coordinate multiple perspectives, transition between contexts, and integrate their varied experiences of self into one identity (Wenger, 1998). In homogeneous societies when the values, beliefs, and experiences in these different contexts are compatible, students are likely to find these developmental goals to be manageable. However, in heterogeneous societies, these contexts are often incongruent. Some students may find the challenges of negotiating cultural and social class boundaries difficult or even insurmountable, resulting in negative educational consequences (Phelan, Davidson, & Yu, 1998).

Today all students need competence in ways of acting and participating in multiple social groups as well as a heterogeneous set of cultural knowledge and skills (Lam, 2006). Students from groups that have been marginalized may need extra assistance in negotiating cultural and social class boundaries and learning the ways of the mainstream (Delpit, 2006). Research on learning suggests that in the future, developing the social and cultural competencies necessary to function in a diverse school setting and a diverse world should be recognized as an educational goal. The public values both the common cultural tradition we share as Americans and diverse cultural traditions. Polls indicate that the majority believes that schools should emphasize both (Elam, Rose, & Gallup, 1994).

## EDUCATIONAL

In his book *What Are Schools For?*, Goodlad emphasized that the purpose of education is not just to serve the instrumental goals discussed so far, but "to make human beings who will live life to the fullest" (1994, p. 36). Citing Dewey, he argued that education is a process of "individual becoming" and that the value of schooling should be judged by the extent to which it makes lifelong growth and learning possible. An emphasis on self-realization is the essence of what distinguishes education from training. Despite its philosophical and practical importance, this central educational purpose has been neglected by policymakers and apparently by schools as well. When a recent poll asked the public whether students achieve their full academic potential in school, it found that an overwhelming 80% of respondents said students achieved only a small part of their potential in school (Rose & Gallup, 2001).

Recent research on intelligence and identity development has deepened our understanding of aspects of self-realization. The intelligence research offers new insights into students' innate talents as well as what it takes to succeed in life. Gardner (1985, 1999) proposed a classification of valued intellectual competencies or talents. He identified eight, including linguistic, logical-mathematical, intrapersonal, interpersonal, bodily-kinesthetic, musical, spatial, and naturalist. If schools sought to develop each child's full potential, they would offer opportunities to develop a wide spectrum of talents. Sternberg (2003) found that in order to succeed in life people need not just the analytical abilities that schools have traditionally emphasized, but practical abilities, creativity, and wisdom. This broader set of abilities, he says, can and should be taught in school.

Researchers who study the social and cultural aspects of learning have stressed the importance of student identity development as an educational goal. In forming their identities, students seek answers to questions like: Who am I? Where am I going in life? According to Wenger (1998), "Students must be able to explore who they are, who they are not, who they could be. They must be able to understand where they came from and where they can go" (p. 272). He goes on to say that education is fundamentally about the opening of identities. This is especially true for students from groups that have been marginalized. If schools do not enable these students to experience new possibilities and imagine new trajectories, then their educational and life outcomes will most likely reproduce existing inequalities. Because identity development is an interactive process where the self is formed within a social context, schools can hardly avoid contributing to their students' sense of identity. Unfortunately, some school practices–like putting deficit labels on students–close off rather than open up possible life trajectories.

## COMPARISON AND CONCLUSION

This brief survey of the literature yields a broad set of economic, moral and civic, and social and cultural goals that education serves, as illustrated in Figure 3.1. The intrinsic educational goals of self-realization and identity formation surround the more specific instrumental goals in the figure because unless educators recognize and develop all students' potential to the fullest, none of the other goals will be optimized. Educational goals are not separate and compartmentalized, but overlapping and interconnected in many ways.

Set within the context of Figure 3.1, the incomplete nature of the educational goal concepts expressed in recent years by national policymakers is quite striking. Policymakers have emphasized the economic goals

**Figure 3.1. A Balance of Educational Goals**

Economic Goals

Civic and Moral Goals

Social and Cultural Goals

**Educational Goals
Self-Realization/Identity**

☐ Current Policy Emphasis
☐ Little/No Policy Emphasis

of education–preparing students for work in a competitive economy–to the near-exclusion of other goals. Even within the economic sphere, the idea of a challenging core curriculum for all students that characterized the standards movement has now been reduced to proficiency in reading and mathematics. There has been some attention to the basic but not the more advanced aspects of character development. Civic goals, social and cultural goals, and educational goals are entirely missing from the national policy schema. The challenges that students face growing up and forming their identities in the midst of a complex, diverse, and fast-paced social context also go unrecognized.

What goals do schools actually pursue? Goodlad (1994) analyzed the goals for schooling articulated by state and local school boards and various special commissions in the 1970s. He classified these goal statements into 12 broad categories that span the gamut of the goal categories discussed here. More recently, Rothstein and Jacobsen (2006) analyzed goal statements over 250 years of history, then asked a sample of adults, school board members, and local legislators to rank their importance today. They found that eight goal categories were highly ranked. A nationally representative survey of goals actually pursued by educators in high schools (before NCLB) indicated that they emphasized a broad combination of goals, but gave them different weights depending on the nature of their student body and their school mission (Talbert et al., 1990). The authors of all these analyses stressed the legitimacy of a broad and balanced set of educational goals and expressed concern that overemphasis by policymakers on economic goals threatened to displace other goals valued by significant segments of the public.

In summary, educational philosophy and history, actual school practice, and public opinion are all reasonably congruent in envisioning the need for a broad, balanced, and interconnected framework of educational goals. National education policymakers have a much narrower perspective that is confined to economic goals, interpreted in NCLB as proficiency in the basic skills of reading and mathematics. The national policy orientation is displacing other educational goals and increasingly narrowing the scope of American education.

A recent survey of voters found that there is "a disconnect" between what voters want in education and the goals that they are hearing and getting from national policymakers (Learning First Alliance, 2005, p. 21). This disconnect is a serious problem in a representative democracy. It is also a problem for education reform because it is important for any reform movement to have clear goals that energize support. The time has come to expand and rebalance educational goals through open and inclusive public deliberation.

# CHAPTER 4

# A Multifaceted View of Educational Outcomes

Student achievement is currently the focus of education policy and practice. Raise student achievement! Close the achievement gap! Amid all the rhetoric and performance pressure on schools, few people stop to ask the question that this chapter attempts to address: What is student achievement? What is an educated person? Ever since the advent of standardized tests, there has been a tendency to equate achievement with test scores. Ideally, tests should be based on some prior concept of intelligence and achievement. But history has worked the other way around—our concept of achievement has been driven by assessment practices, according to Sternberg (1990). Here I draw upon several lines of inquiry to define important dimensions of achievement.

The Obama administration has expanded educational outcome expectations by adding the goal of increasing high school graduation rates and reducing gaps among subgroups in attainment. Like achievement, the concept of attainment is problematic. Should graduation rates include only students who earn regular diplomas or also those who earn GEDs? Should only students who complete high schools in 4 years count, or also students who take longer? What should high school graduates know and be able to do? How can more students be motivated to graduate? Of the many thorny issues related to attainment, this chapter focuses on the content of a high school education and its relationship to student motivation, achievement, and attainment.

## THE CONCEPT OF ACHIEVEMENT

There is very little research literature that deals directly with the concept of educational achievement (Cole, 1990). However, recent research advances in the fields of cognitive science, social learning theory, and child development have important implications for how we conceptualize achievement. In combination, these lines of inquiry suggest that educational achievement is a complex and multifaceted concept.

## Basic Knowledge and Skills

Schools have always been expected to produce students who are competent in the basic skills of reading, writing, and arithmetic. Students have also been expected to master the basics of the academic disciplines, traditionally defined as knowing the facts and procedures. Routine comprehension and analysis skills, such as classifying, comparing and contrasting, and summarizing round out the concept of achievement defined at a basic level. Behaviorist learning theory assumed that knowledge and skills were hierarchical and should be learned sequentially, starting with the most simple. Thus, educational objectives at the elementary and secondary levels focused on basic knowledge and skills. This view of achievement was codified in a taxonomy developed by Bloom and his associates in the 1950s. It had a tremendous influence on curriculum, assessment, and popular conceptions of achievement from the time it was published until the present day (Anderson et al., 2001; Anderson & Sosniak, 1994).

## Advanced Knowledge and Skills

Since the "cognitive revolution" over 4 decades ago, research in cognitive science has greatly enhanced our concept of achievement. By comparing the performance of novices and experts, cognitive researchers have made great progress in understanding and describing achievement at advanced levels. High performers in any field have well-organized conceptual schemas; they know when and how to apply knowledge; they can (among other things) find meaning, solve problems in a variety of ways, and regulate their own thinking (Bransford, Brown, & Cocking, 2000).

A key message of this research is that, contrary to earlier assumptions, basic and advanced competencies are not hierarchical. Instead, they develop concurrently and interconnect in complex ways. Therefore, conceptual knowledge and thinking skills, as well as the basics, are important dimensions of achievement for all students at all educational levels (Resnick, 1987). Cognitive research has provided a better understanding of what proficiency means and raised expectations for achievement.

## Doing and Finding Meaning

Researchers interested in the social and cultural aspects of learning have studied learning and achievement "in action"–focusing on what people do as they participate in a variety of social contexts both in and out of school. People often do things with others and can achieve more when working with assistance from someone with greater expertise. Because people use tools as they work, the adept use of tools is another dimension of achievement.

Most people would easily recognize the contribution that tangible tools such as books, computers, and science equipment make in accomplishing a task. But sociocultural theory has also shown that people are always using, and sometimes advancing the development of, cognitive tools such as literacy, mathematics, and logic. In fact, the academic disciplines that make up the school curriculum can be viewed as cultural tools that enable people to understand different aspects of themselves and the world around them (Rogoff, 2003; Rueda, 2004).

As people become more accomplished, their participation in school or community activities is transformed. For example, they can take on more responsible roles, assist others, and perhaps even become leaders. Sociocultural research has sensitized us to the fact that achievement is not just a matter of what people know, but of what they can do both alone and with the assistance of other people and tools in a social context (Rogoff, 2003; Rueda, 2004). When people engage in valued enterprises, they experience meaning (Wenger, 1998). The ability to find meaning or purpose in life is associated with happiness and well-being and, some researchers argue, should be taken more seriously as an educational goal and outcome (Cohen, 2006).

## Competence and the Whole Child

Additional dimensions of achievement are suggested by child development research and by research in noncognitive domains. The more we learn about human development the more apparent it becomes that the cognitive, social, emotional, physical, and other aspects of development all intersect, proceed at different rates, and need to be continually integrated by children with adult assistance (Ayoub & Fischer, 2006). Schools have traditionally emphasized primarily the cognitive or intellectual aspects of development, but it is not feasible to ignore "the whole child." Noncognitive skills are more difficult to define and measure, but their intrinsic importance as well as their relationship to academic achievement is increasingly recognized (Heckman & Krueger, 2003). Balanced development in a variety of domains is necessary for well-being and success both in school and in later life.

Research has led to a better understanding of social and emotional competence (Goleman, 1997, 2006) as achievements in their own right and sensitized us to how unaddressed problems in these domains may interfere with academic learning. A few states are beginning to incorporate social and emotional learning into their standards and curricula (Cohen, 2006). National standards for physical education emphasize lifelong health, fitness, and good nutrition (National Association for Sport and Physical Education, 2004), important achievements for all children, but especially for poor children, who experience more challenges in these areas (Rothstein, 2004). Motivation and affect deserve more emphasis as aspects of achievement because they contribute significantly to the development of competence in all areas of endeavor (Alexander, 2003). Expanding the definition of achievement to encompass the whole child has implications not only for the curriculum, but for the classroom and school environment, for student support services, and even for extracurricular activities (Stipek, 2004).

## The Many Facets of Achievement

Figure 4.1 illustrates a concept of achievement that is derived from the various lines of research inquiry just reviewed. It suggests that there are multiple dimensions of achievement and that they connect with one another and with the educational goals discussed in the previous chapter. Attaining each goal involves multiple facets of achievement. For example, the goal of character development involves the head (knowledge and skills), the heart (affective), and the hand (doing), according to Lickona (1997). Perhaps the most striking thing about the figure is all the blank white space indicating dimensions of achievement that research has identified as important, but policy ignores. Science has expanded the definition of achievement; policy has not kept pace. The concluding section of this chapter returns to this figure for a more detailed comparison of the multifaceted concept of achievement with conceptions of achievement in standards-based reform and NCLB policy.

## THE CONCEPT OF ATTAINMENT

There has been considerable controversy over the past decade about the high school graduation rate. Some researchers argue that it is lower than previously believed and that there are huge disparities among different population groups. After comparing competing estimates, one source recently suggested that the overall graduation rate based on National Center for Education Statistics (NCES) data is about 74%. When that number is disaggregated, however, the estimate for Whites is about 80%, Blacks 60%, and Hispanics 64% (Barton, 2009a).

The U.S. ranking in international comparisons is also an issue. In 1985, the United States ranked third in high school graduation and first in college graduation among Organisation for Economic Co-Operation and Development (OECD) countries (Baldi et al., 2000). However, by 2007 the United States had dropped to 20th in high school graduation and 16th in college graduation. Other countries are increasing their graduation rates, but the United States is not (OECD, 2009).

The debate is not just about increasing the number of graduates, it is also about standards for high school graduation. Critics of current practices say students can get a regular diploma without being "college-ready" (i.e., with-

**Figure 4.1. Multifaceted Concept of Achievement**

| | Basic Knowledge/ Skills | Advanced Knowledge/ Skills | Doing/ Meaning | Noncognitive Competence (Whole Child) |
|---|---|---|---|---|
| Prepare for Work/ Economic Mobility | | | | |
| Character/ Citizenship | | | | |
| Function in Diverse World | | | | |
| Self-Realization/ Identity | | | | |

NCLB Emphasis ▢

Standards/Character Emphasis ▢

Little/No Policy Emphasis ▢

out having the academic course sequence and the level of literacy required by minimally selective 4-year colleges) (Greene & Winters, 2005; Mishel & Roy, 2006; Warren & Halpern-Manners, 2007). Thus, the attainment push also includes the idea of a more rigorous high school curriculum.

Is it possible to raise graduation standards and, at the same time, increase the graduation rate and reduce attainment gaps? A good way to start thinking about this question is to consider why students drop out. The research indicates that dropping out is a long-term process of disengagement from school, not a single event. A combination of out-of-school and within-school factors relates to dropping out. Factors outside of school include pregnancy, wanting or needing to go to work, and incarceration. Factors within school include low grades, absenteeism, grade retention, and disciplinary problems (Barton, 2009a).

A recent survey of dropouts found that the number-one reason cited by 47% of these students for leaving school was that "classes were not interesting." Seventy percent of students in this survey were confident that they would have been able to graduate, but said they were not motivated or inspired to work hard (Bridgeland, Dilulio, & Morison, 2006, pp. 3–4). What would better motivate all students? Student engagement is facilitated by more challenging work, topics that are related to students' lives, active participation in learning, collaborative activities that provide meaningful student interaction in pairs or groups, and a sense of belonging (National Research Council, 2004). Thus, a high school curriculum that not only serves the broad goals of education and addresses the multiple facets of achievement, but also motivates and engages more students is one approach to improving achievement and attainment.

In the history of American education, the pendulum has swung a number of times between an emphasis on a common core curriculum for all students and a differentiated curriculum reflecting students' individual talents and interests. Both are needed, according to Goodlad (1999). The balanced set of educational goals discussed earlier reinforces the need for both commonality and differentiation in the school curriculum. Some educational goals, like citizenship, push toward commonality; others, like identity formation, pull toward differentiation and student choice. The educational ideal of a balanced curriculum for all students has not been realized in recent years.

In the 1960s and 1970s the emphasis was on curricular choice and flexibility. Unfortunately, curricular choice was combined with tracking so that students could choose not only between courses, but between different levels of difficulty. Students could earn credit for courses that were nonacademic or consisted of low-level or remedial content. The combination of choice and tracking resulted in considerable segregation and stratification. High-achieving, predominantly White students took demanding courses, and college entrance requirements motivated them to stay within the academic core. Low-SES, minority, and other non-college-bound students often took an undemanding curricular hodgepodge (Lee & Ready, 2009). Thus, the differentiated curriculum became associated with mediocrity and inequality.

The standards movement swung the curriculum back to a constrained common core as advocated by *A Nation at Risk*. Some reformers envisioned a core liberal arts curriculum with no student choice (Adler, 1982). Standards era reforms involved more specification of which courses students had to take in order to graduate. Yet tracking and inequality persist. The latest "College Prep for All" phase of curriculum reform features a college-prep curriculum, expanded AP offerings, extra support in ninth grade for students who need it, and elimination of remedial courses (Lee & Ready, 2009).

The common core approach has broad support today among reformers. However, some reformers argue that the common core in the United States has become too narrow, and overly focused on the basic skills and "STEMs Without Flowers" (Finn & Ravitch, 2007). In order to lead intellectually satisfying lives, they say young people need more exposure to history, literature, music, and art. They recommend a broader and more balanced curriculum consistent with the traditional liberal arts ideal. International comparisons indicate that the U.S. curriculum is less comprehensive than those of other OECD countries, where the common core includes greater emphasis on foreign languages and the arts (Benavot, 2007). A broad and balanced core curriculum is also more likely to provide a match between students' interests and school subjects.

In the United States the high school curriculum options have been perceived as either a differentiated curriculum associated with mediocrity and inequality or a constrained core curriculum associated with greater rigor and equality. Unfortunately, neither of these options makes schooling more interesting and motivating for students, and therefore they are unlikely to increase attainment. A better third option might be to adapt the postsecondary curriculum structure for high school. The typical college curriculum is partly common core and partly differentiated (student-chosen majors). However, the differentiated area is not associated with mediocrity; rather, it is the most advanced part of the curriculum, where students are expected to produce their best work. This arrangement is consistent with research on intelligence that suggests that people are most likely to excel in areas that best match their individual talents (Gardner, 1985; Sternberg, 2003). It is consistent with research on motivation that indicates that people are more engaged in work that they find interesting and relevant (National Research Council, 2004).

An alternative option for the high school curriculum might be summarized as follows. First, to prepare students for work, higher education, and citizenship, there would be a common liberal arts curriculum that is broader and more balanced than what we have seen in recent years. About 80% of the curriculum would be allotted to the common core, and all students would be expected to achieve proficiency. Second, to develop each student's identity and full potential, there would be an individualized curriculum component closely connected to student talents and interests. About 20% of the curriculum would be devoted to the individualized component (one course each year). Students would be expected to reach more advanced levels of proficiency, even to excel, in their differentiated area (or areas). Students would make their curriculum choices with the help of adult guidance and formative assessments designed to assist them in identifying their strengths and interests in relation to academic and vocational subjects.

Researchers have begun to study what it would take to turn college aspirations into college attainment, and their findings have implications for the high school curriculum. Four areas of knowledge and skills development have been identified as essential: disciplinary content knowledge and skills, core academic skills (e.g., high-level reading and writing, thinking, and analytic skills), noncognitive skills and norms of performance, and college knowledge. The importance of the first two is generally recognized, but the last two are typically overlooked. Relevant noncognitive skills include self-awareness, self-monitoring, self-control, study skills, work habits, time management, help-seeking behavior, and social problem-solving skills. College knowledge includes understanding academic prerequisites, college admissions processes, financial aid processes, and available college options (Roderick, Nagaoka, & Coca, 2009). High schools should provide students with opportunities to acquire knowledge and skills in all four of these areas. Thus, closing gaps in attainment and college readiness requires a broadening, not a narrowing, of the definition of educational achievement and the school curriculum.

Curriculum reform is important but by itself is insufficient. Recent research has identified some relatively simple indicators that can predict as early as middle school whether a student will graduate from high school. Middle school "early-warning flags" include attendance, math and English course failure, and behavior grades (Balfantz, Herzog, & MacIver, 2007). High school "on-track" indicators include the number of credits earned and the number of F's in core subjects (Allensworth & Easton, 2005). Development of data systems that would enable schools to use these indicators and respond early with effective interventions is a very promising strategy to increase attainment. The What Works Clearing House currently contains 16 intervention programs found to have positive effects related to staying or progressing in school or preventing dropouts (What Works Clearing House, 2009). Also, Balfantz and colleagues are refining a three-stage intervention model for middle schools that would address about 75% of students with schoolwide reforms, provide more targeted individual assistance for another 15 to 20% of students, and focus intensive clinical interventions on the remaining 5 to 10% of students.

## COMPARISON AND CONCLUSION

High-quality school content standards have the potential to serve as tools to translate new research-based concepts of achievement into practice. The standards movement significantly expanded the concept of achievement beyond the basics that schools traditionally taught to include more advanced levels of proficiency in subject knowledge, thinking skills, and what students should be able to do. A look back at Figure 4.1 illustrates (lightly shaded areas) that during the standards era progress was made in incorporating new knowledge from both cognitive and sociocultural theory into national standards. The standards movement focused on academic content areas. Other dimensions of achievement emphasized in the research that fall outside of the disciplinary boundaries, like social and emotional competence or student identity formation, received little or no attention.

National standards developed during the 1990s differed in quality from subject to subject (Resnick & Zurawsky, 2005; Wixson, Dutro, & Athan,

2003). Subjects associated with economic goals, such as mathematics and science, had stronger research bases and made the most progress in using new knowledge to redefine proficiency; subjects associated with the neglected goals, such as social studies and the humanities, had fewer resources upon which to draw and were less successful. The challenge of developing high-quality standards that encompass all dimensions of the multifaceted concept of achievement remains unfinished.

The concurrent character education movement added a focus on the basics of moral development (also lightly shaded in Figure 4.1), but character education programs typically do not serve more advanced objectives, such as initiating students into our cultural conversation about fundamental values and reflecting on their meaning (Nord, 2001). The study of ethics in middle or high school might be a step to fill the gap in advanced moral development. However, as Dewey pointed out long ago, character and citizenship are learned not only through courses, but through the lived environment. Classroom management practices and the school environment can contribute to or detract from education in these areas.

NCLB policy does not build upon advances in the concept of achievement made during the earlier era. Because achievement is equated with standardized test scores in reading and mathematics that focus on the lower end of the curriculum, current policy serves "to hijack broader educational goals" (Resnick & Zurawsky, 2005, p. 10). Schools are pressured to return to a definition of achievement that is limited to basic knowledge and skills (only the darkly shaded area in Figure 4.1). The curriculum is getting ever narrower as time devoted to subjects such as social studies, science, and foreign languages is reduced. According to one survey, 71% of districts reported spending less time on other subjects in order to increase time for tested topics in reading and mathematics (Center on Education Policy, 2006). When the one aspect of achievement emphasized by NCLB is compared with the multifaceted concept depicted in Figure 4.1, it becomes clear that NCLB trivializes the concept of educational achievement.

NCLB was successful in sensitizing us to the existence of achievement gaps and the importance of addressing them. Now President Obama wants to close gaps in attainment as well as achievement. Mandates and sanctions will not close these gaps. The logic of the argument in this chapter implies that actually closing these gaps involves expanding educational goals and the definition of achievement, motivating and engaging students, rethinking the high school curriculum, and early identification and intervention for potential dropouts. Later chapters discuss other important factors in gap reduction, including intensive support services for the least advantaged students. A focus on achievement and attainment gaps is useful as a tool to advocate for educational equity, but the NCLB version of it is deeply flawed and needs to be substantially reframed.

A more adequate set of goals for achievement in the future would encompass the multiple dimensions suggested in Figure 4.1, provide a balance of commonality and individuality in the curriculum, and sacrifice neither excellence nor equity. A broad and balanced concept of achievement is a prerequisite for improving attainment and college readiness. There is a great deal of unfinished work to be done in conceptualizing and setting goals for educational achievement and attainment. Current policy ignores most of what matters. Because times change and new knowledge is always accumulating, each generation must ask and answer the question: What is an educated person?

# CHAPTER 5

# Comprehensive Classroom Capacity for Learning

The next two chapters deal with building capacity in classrooms, schools, and school systems to attain a set of broader and more challenging educational goals for all students. This chapter focuses on the capacity to transform classroom practice. The definition of capacity is derived from Figure 5.1, "The Learning Triangle," which foregrounds the classroom and provides a strategic map of what matters.

**Figure 5.1. The Learning Triangle: Components of Classroom Capacity**

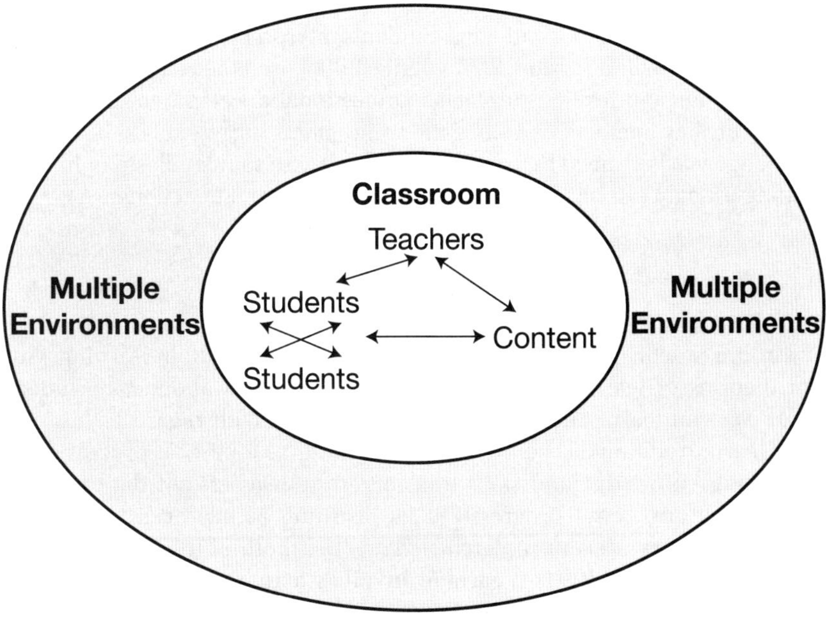

*Sources:* Adapted from Cohen, Raudenbush, & Ball (2000) and McLaughlin & Talbert (1993).

The figure illustrates that the core practices of education–learning and teaching–consist of interactions among teachers, students, and content within the classroom and other environments. If we want to build classroom-level capacity to improve student achievement and attainment, we must focus on these three core components–teachers, students, and content–how they interact, and how they are supported or constrained by the multiple environments in which the classroom is embedded (Ball & Forzani, 2007; Cohen, Raudenbush, & Ball, 2000; McLaughlin & Talbert, 1993). The discussion in this chapter is limited to the classroom environment; the next chapter discusses how broader environments, such as schools, communities, and school systems, also influence teaching and learning.

This chapter begins with the three key components of the classroom core suggested by the triangle and discusses how recent research challenges us to rethink each one of them–learning, teaching, and content–as well as the classroom environment. Rethinking classroom practice is the logical starting point for education reform. The schema used here emphasizes that learning-centered reform is *comprehensive*: it encompasses all aspects of the learning triangle, the dynamic interactions among them, and interactions with various environments (Bryk et al., 2010).

The interactions among the components, represented by the two-way arrows, are also important, but are not covered in this chapter. The processes of teaching and learning involve multiple, complex, and dynamic interactions among teachers, students, and content. For example, teachers interpret and represent subject matter to students. Students interpret their teachers, then respond and act (Ball & Forzani, 2007). Little (2006) used the learning triangle to develop strategic priorities for teacher professional development by focusing on what the key interactions among the components suggest about the kinds of knowledge teachers need to teach well. Both of these sources illustrate how the learning triangle can be used to understand classroom interactions.

## STUDENTS AND LEARNING

Classroom practice is often based upon misconceptions about learning. Current theories of learning challenge older assumptions about *how* students learn, *who* can learn, and *what* they should learn. With regard to how students learn, traditionalists tend to view learning as a passive process of accumulating knowledge and skills transmitted by teachers. At the other end of the spectrum, some progressives see learning as a process of unaided student discovery. Recent research suggests that both of these positions are incomplete (Rogoff, 1994). Learning involves a more complex three-way interaction–learners actively construct knowledge through interactions with others and with the content offered by the environment (Bransford, Brown,

& Cocking, 2000; Marshall, 1994). To improve learning and achievement, effective education reform must "*begin* with rethinking the *nature of learning* and with newer *knowledge about how students learn*" (Marshall, 1994, p. 2).

The high-performance case studies provide examples of what it means to rethink learning. In NYC District #2, school improvement began with a focus on literacy. Study groups were formed to identify the leading edge of literacy research and exemplary practice in order to bring it into the district (Elmore & Burney, 1998). The Wisconsin case studies describe how research served as a foundation for mathematics reform in Monroe. A leadership committee reviewed state and national standards, read books and journal articles, attended national conferences, and visited other districts. They identified best practices, such as a focus on thinking, practical application, and use of multiple strategies to solve problems. Then they searched for and adopted a research-based curriculum that fit the notion of learning they developed from the literature (Odden et al., 2007). If new research about learning is to improve practice, teachers need opportunities to study it, make sense of it, and apply it (Spillane, Reisner, & Reimer, 2002).

Advances in research have changed assumptions not only about *how* students learn, but about *who* can learn. In the past, most people assumed that ability was fixed–a student was either smart or not smart. Now research shows that ability is malleable and can grow with effort. In other words, students can become smart by working hard in an educative environment, according to Resnick (1995). The slogan "All Students Can Learn" is well grounded in research (Martinez, 2000).

However, motivating all students to put forth the considerable level of effort needed to achieve at high levels is a very significant problem. Studies from the student perspective indicate that the majority are chronically disengaged, exert little effort, and claim to be bored (National Research Council [NRC], 2004). Turning this situation around involves revising beliefs about student ability and effort (Resnick, 1995); changing approaches to motivation, discipline, and teaching (NRC, 2004); building a collective commitment to close gaps in achievement and attainment; and providing extensive support systems for the most disadvantaged students (Fermanich et al., 2006; Odden et al., 2007).

Student support systems encompass families and communities as well as students themselves. At the classroom level, in the highest-performing Chicago schools, teachers were knowledgeable about their students' home culture and community and they drew upon this awareness in their teaching. Research on learning suggests that it is critical to build upon students' background knowledge, skills, and interests. Knowledge of students' backgrounds also helped teachers to establish personal connections with them. Teachers and other school personnel sought to involve families directly in student learning by communicating with parents to reinforce study habits and expectations, providing learning activities for students and parents at home, and strengthening parenting skills (Bryk et al., 2010).

## CHALLENGING CONTENT

New theories of knowledge and international comparisons indicate a need to rethink assumptions about what students learn. This involves transforming content standards, the school curriculum, and—most importantly—what is actually taught. Because thinking is not limited to more advanced levels of intellectual development (Resnick, 1987), school content needs to include not only the simple "what" (i.e., facts) of a discipline, but the more advanced frameworks and concepts, the "how" (i.e., procedures and disciplinary habits of mind) and the "why" (i.e., explanations of one's reasoning and conclusions) throughout all the grade levels (Wilson & Peterson, 2006). Students also need to know "when" to use their knowledge. In other words, they must understand the conditions under which particular aspects of knowledge apply to real-life situations (Bransford, Brown, & Cocking, 2000).

International comparisons indicate that in higher-performing countries the content taught is more advanced, it is explained and elaborated more fully, it is more logically and coherently organized, and more explicit connections are made between ideas (Stigler & Hiebert, 1999). Findings like these provide benchmarks that can be used to improve school capacity in the area of content.

The high-performance case studies describe schools and districts that selected one or two subjects as foci for reform and completely transformed the curriculum, either by using research to develop a new curriculum or by adopting an externally developed, research-based curriculum. NYC District #2 developed its own "balanced literacy" curriculum based on the latest research. Later, as their reform emphasis expanded to include mathematics, the district adopted a curriculum called "Investigations in Number, Data, and Space," one of several funded by the National Science Foundation and designed to be consistent with the NCTM mathematics standards (Stein & D'Amico, 1998, 1999). Similarly, the schools and districts in the Wisconsin and Washington case studies all "*threw out* the old curriculum and *replaced* it with a different and more rigorous curriculum" (Odden et al., 2007, p. 45; see also Fermanich et al., 2006).

## TEACHERS AND TEACHING

For at least a century, debates about teaching in the United States have pitted those who favor teacher-directed (traditional) approaches against those who favor student-centered (progressive) approaches. As with learning, the instructional triangle suggests that teaching is considerably more complex—it involves effectively coordinating all aspects of the learning triangle (Cohen, Raudenbush, & Ball, 2000; Little, 2006). Successful teachers have not only a deep understanding of their subject, but also strong pedagogical content knowledge that enables them to make the content accessible to students (Shulman, 1986). They use a variety of teaching techniques appropriate for different learning goals, such as lecture, demonstrations, modeling, experimentation, and group work (Gallimore & Tharp, 1990; Wilson & Peterson, 2006). Effective teachers also know how students connect with subject matter: how they understand (or misunderstand) content, how to diagnose their progress in learning, and how to assess their achievement (Pelligrino, Chudowsky, & Glaser, 2001). Finally, teachers must constantly orchestrate relationships and create a social environment that supports learning (Evertson & Neal, 2006).

In the highest-performing Chicago schools, teaching included but went beyond facts and basic skills. Teaching focused on students' active engagement in tasks that required applications of knowledge. Teachers facilitated classroom discussions. Students were given opportunities to do longer-term projects and their progress was assessed based on their actual work products. Teachers had high expectations for student performance that were reflected in the content and pacing of the curriculum. Students said they felt a combination of academic press and personal support from both teachers and peers for learning. Classroom and school environments were safe and orderly; discipline problems were minimized (Bryk et al., 2010).

Teachers in high-performing schools do not work on instructional improvement in isolation. They work collaboratively in professional learning communities on all aspects of the instructional triangle, such as embracing new norms for student learning and achievement, changing the curriculum and raising the level of content, understanding students and examining student work, sharing pedagogical ideas, and developing shared standards of teaching practice. An emphasis on professional learning communities addresses the problem of uneven teaching quality found in the typical school by building the collective capacity of entire faculties to continuously improve their teaching practice, hold themselves accountable for learning, and raise student achievement (Cohen & Hill, 2001; McLaughlin & Talbert, 2001, 2006; Spillane & Thompson, 1997).

## CLASSROOM LEARNING COMMUNITIES

The learning triangle emphasizes the importance of interpersonal relationships—both how students and teachers interact as well as how students interact with one another. Because learning is a social phenomenon, productive relationships among people are very important. Effective teachers connect with students on a personal level and continually orchestrate interpersonal relationships in ways that support learning. Students say that having a teacher who "cares" is very important. Students prefer an environment where everyone feels they belong and where interaction among diverse peer groups is possible (Phelan, Davidson, & Cao, 1992). To ensure congruence between academic and social goals in their classrooms, teachers often find that they must change their approach to classroom management so that instead of behavior control, it emphasizes student engagement, responsibility, self-regulation, cooperation, and a sense of membership in a learning community (Evertson & Neal, 2006).

The image of a "learning community" is used in the research to describe the ideal classroom environment—one organized around rich, intellectually stimulating activities. Caring and supportive interpersonal relationships as well as high expectations for learning characterize these classrooms. When students' basic psychological needs are met, their motivation and engagement increase. Personalization and classroom communities are related to a large number of positive outcomes for students, especially disadvantaged students, including higher academic performance, commitment to democratic values, social competence, self-esteem, and active participation (Battistich, Solomon, Watson, & Schaps, 1997; Cornelius-White, 2007). A sense of community at the school level is also associated with positive student outcomes (Bryk & Driscoll, 1988).

## COMPARISON AND CONCLUSION

Reforms consistent with research and today's higher expectations require teachers, and everyone else involved, to rethink an entire system of interacting attitudes, beliefs, and practices (Spillane, Reisner, & Reimer, 2002). "Everyone involved has almost everything to learn," according to Cohen (1995, p. 752). Elmore (2005) emphasized that this kind of fundamental change is very difficult—it is completely unattainable given the current capacities of most schools. The small minority of schools and districts he has observed that have displayed remarkable progress built successively higher capacities over extended periods of time. Thus, capacity-building is a critical foundation for education reform. The value of the instructional triangle as an analytical tool is that it focuses attention on the comprehensive and interactive nature of the classroom-level capacities needed for success.

How do recent national policies look when viewed through the lens of the learning triangle? The standards movement initially focused on content reforms, such as raising coursework standards for high school graduation, developing more rigorous national and state content standards, and implementing assessments aligned with the standards. Content standards made visible an expanded concept of educational achievement that was more consistent with learning theory and public expectations for higher performance. Later, a "second wave" of standards-based reform recognized the pivotal role of teachers and emphasized instructional improvement and teacher professional development (Goertz, Floden, & O'Day, 1995). However, policy emphasis on other key elements of the instructional triangle—students, interpersonal relationships, and learning environments—was missing. When compared to either the learning triangle or to the high-performance case studies, the theory of action behind the standards movement was incomplete.

Studies of classroom-level change during the standards era indicated mixed results. Teachers generally supported the idea of high standards, but there was little evidence that teachers fully grasped and internalized the more complex vision of achievement behind the standards. Changes in actual practices tended to be superficial. For example, the more easily imported practices, such as the use of manipulatives in mathematics, were widely adopted, but often used without understanding of the concepts these activities were supposed to teach (Brown & Campione, 1996; Cohen, 1990; Cohen & Ball, 1990; Knapp, 1997; Spillane, 2005). Teaching fully consistent with new research advances, sometimes called "teaching for understanding," and the professional communities that foster this kind of instruction were rarely observed in practice (McLaughlin & Talbert, 2001, 2006; Stigler & Hiebert, 1999). The combined commitment to standards and professional development paid off where it took place, but few states and school districts made adequate investments in professional learning, according to Cohen and Hill (2001).

High-stakes testing policies are having a more striking impact on classroom practice—they are driving instruction in many schools. But because most accountability tests are not consistent with research-based concepts of learning and achievement, or with challenging content standards, they are driving instruction in undesirable ways (Banicky & Noble, 2001; Resnick & Zurawsky, 2005). The evidence suggests that the effects of existing high-stakes testing policies are the opposite of what is intended because school responses vary. High-capacity schools feel less threatened and continue to make real improvements in learning and teaching based on their knowledge of research and best practice. Not knowing what else to do, and feeling most threatened, low-capacity schools are likely to game the system and teach to the test. These variable school responses increase rather than decrease inequality in school capacity and students' opportunity to learn (Diamond & Spillane, 2005; Herman, 2004).

In summary, standards-based reform began to move classroom practice in a direction that was in line with high expectations for student achievement. The reforms were consistent with recent advances in education research, but the scope of the reform agenda was incomplete and the time frame for such fundamental change was far too short. Now, high-stakes testing policies are pushing classroom practice in the opposite direction by "dumbing down" instruction, especially in low-performing schools, and exacerbating disparities in opportunity to learn. It is important to recognize that high-stakes testing constrains rather than enables student learning and achievement and, in the future, to shift emphasis to more effective capacity-building policies.

The key to success in education reform is a comprehensive capacity-building approach that addresses all aspects of the learning triangle. Future capacity-building policies should build upon the progress made during the standards era in improving content and introducing reforms related to teaching and professional communities. However, the agenda for classroom capacity-building should be significantly expanded to fill in the missing pieces related to students, interpersonal relationships, and learning environments.

# CHAPTER 6

# Systemic
# Capacity
# and Infrastructure

Strategic opportunities for building capacity throughout the system are extensions of the classroom learning triangle: the focus at all levels should be on supporting teachers, students, and content, and facilitating productive interactions among them (McLaughlin & Talbert, 1993). The outer ring of Figure 6.1 foregrounds the school and system-level context and moves the inner classroom core discussed earlier to the background.

**Figure 6.1. The Learning-Centered School System**

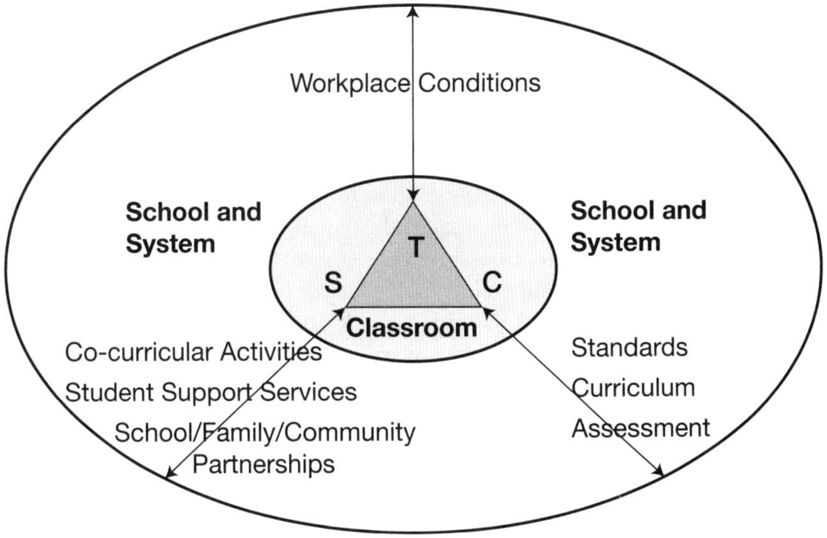

Key for the Learning Triangle: T = teachers, S = students, and C = content.

The figure illustrates the kinds of capacities and support systems needed beyond the classroom to significantly improve teaching and learning. For example, professional development and good workplace conditions support teachers; a variety of school level services and co-curricular activities support students; and standards, curriculum, materials, and assessments aligned around challenging learning goals strengthen content. Leadership is also strategically important at the school and system level because effective leadership recognizes the importance of and coordinates the key components of the learning triangle. Thus, leadership brings coherence to the system and serves as a catalyst for change (Bryk et al., 2010).

Most policymakers do not conceptualize the education system in a learning-centered way; they think instead of a hierarchical bureaucracy. Figure 6.1 radically reframes the education system. In this learning-centered system, classrooms are at the center, surrounded by a multilayered infrastructure of support systems. According to Tharp and Gallimore (1988), in a learning-centered system, teachers assist students to learn, principals assist teachers, district administrators assist teachers and principals, and so on. Building a system that advances learning and provides the necessary infrastructure of support means replacing "chains of command" with "chains of assistance." Learning-centered reform means completely rethinking how the education system works and how the people within it relate to one another.

## SUPPORTS FOR CONTENT

As noted earlier, the standards movement focused primarily on building capacity related to one of the points in this diagram—content. Reformers recognized the *systemic* nature of the problem. The idea was to create an aligned infrastructure in each subject area that would embody a more challenging, rigorous, "thinking" curriculum throughout the grade levels and to raise graduation requirements. The vision called for getting "all parts of a state instructional system—core content, materials, teacher training, continuing professional development, and assessment—to support the goal of delivering a high-quality curriculum to all children" (O'Day & Smith, 1993, p. 267). Moving away from a system that provided weak and inconsistent instructional guidance focused on the basics and toward a new content infrastructure that would provide strong and coherent guidance built around a challenging conception of knowledge is a huge and value-laden task.

During the standards era, national professional organizations and states developed content standards in most academic subjects. In general, the standards were intended to redefine the common core of knowledge in each field—what students should know and be able to do from K through 12—along more ambitious lines (Wixson, Dutro, & Athan, 2003). Performance standards that made it possible to assess whether and to what degree students met the content standards and serve as the basis for a new generation of assessments that could validly measure the kinds of learning and achievement the reformers sought were also developed (Resnick & Zurawsky, 2005). Curriculum and instructional materials–the concrete and everyday stuff that teachers and students use, such as curriculum and pacing guides, textbooks, and materials–were supposed to be aligned with standards and designed to provide opportunities for teacher learning (Ball & Cohen, 1996).

Very few school systems have been successful in achieving the ideal of fully aligning their content infrastructure around challenging learning goals (Resnick & Zurawsky, 2005). The high-performing case studies are exceptions to this generalization–they *did* succeed in content realignment in at least one or two subjects at the elementary or middle school levels. In NYC District #2, for example, reform began in literacy (later in math) with a focus on instructional improvement, challenging curriculum, and extensive professional development. Student performance standards and aligned assessments were added later (Elmore & Burney, 1998; Stein & D'Amico, 1999). The high-performing case studies in Washington and Wisconsin emphasize content alignment as common elements in the successful sites. The Washington study quotes a district administrator who said that the "alignment of the 'written, taught, and tested curriculum' with state standards was central to the work of their schools" (Fermanich et al., 2006, p. 24).

## SUPPORTS FOR TEACHERS AND TEACHING

Substantial improvements in instructional practice require an infrastructure of supports for teachers and teaching. At the school level, two key supports are opportunities for intensive teacher learning and improved workplace conditions. Opportunities for teacher learning are critical because in learning-centered reform teachers must rethink the nature of knowledge, gain a better understanding of student learning, and expand their repertoire of teaching strategies. An early step in building an infrastructure of support for teacher learning is replacing the typical hodgepodge of training events with a more systemic approach that has school-based teacher learning communities as the core and coherently links these communities with external professional development opportunities (Little, 2006). One study found that the effects of professional development by itself on school improvement were weak, but that the effects were maximized in schools where professional development took place in combination with supportive professional communities and an aligned content guidance system (Bryk et al., 2010).

The concept of within-school professional learning communities linked with external professional development is richly illustrated in the high-performance case studies. In NYC District #2, according to Elmore and Burney (1997), "professional development permeates the work of the organization" (p. 15). A combination of strategies was used to develop shared expertise, including peer collaboration, intervisitation of classrooms within a school and in other schools, instructional coaches, and off-site training both during the school year and in the summer. The importance of intensive, multicomponent professional development is a theme running through the Washington and Wisconsin case studies. For example, at one Wisconsin school the process of researching and selecting a new school curriculum facilitated a sense of unity among the staff that developed into a professional community. Later, implementation of the new curriculum involved more formal professional development and instructional coaching (Odden et al., 2007).

Workplace conditions can facilitate instructional improvement either directly or indirectly. The high-performance case studies illustrate how changes in structure, time, and other features of the workplace often directly support new teaching and learning goals. For example, in some schools in Washington, the school day was restructured either to provide double periods for core content or common planning time for teachers (Fermanich et al., 2006). Better workplace conditions can improve teaching indirectly by reducing high teacher turnover rates—or what some researchers have called the "revolving door" (Ingersoll, 2001). Attention to improved workplace conditions is especially important in schools serving poor children, where conditions tend to be substandard and attracting and retaining good teachers is particularly difficult. Workplace reforms, such as multicomponent induction programs for new teachers, safe and well-equipped facilities, and opportunities for career growth, have been found to improve the quality of teaching and teacher retention (Johnson, 2006).

Considering teacher supports beyond the school in the broader education system, successful reform efforts have built comprehensive and balanced teacher support systems that target several key areas: recruitment, initial preparation, induction, evaluation, and professional development. Just as all aspects of the content system must be aligned around new learning goals, all aspects of the systems for teacher support and evaluation must also be realigned.

Connecticut is often cited as a model of best practice in this area. Teaching standards were aligned with student learning standards. To strengthen recruitment, Connecticut substantially increased and equalized teacher salaries across the state, provided bonus grants for teachers in poor areas, offered scholarship and loan-forgiveness incentives, and made out-of-state licenses more transportable. Preparation was strengthened through a tiered certification system that raised initial licensing requirements and required performance-based assessment and continuing professional development to renew certification. An induction system provided careful observation, feedback, and mentoring for new teachers. Since the vast majority of teachers in Connecticut have partici-pated in this system as new teachers, assessment scorers, or mentors, a com-mon understanding of quality teaching has evolved that provides the basis for professional community. Continuous learning is further enhanced by gener-ous support for professional development (Darling-Hammond, 2004; Wilson, Darling-Hammond, & Berry, 2001).

## SUPPORTS FOR STUDENTS AND LEARNING

The third point in the learning triangle framework—support systems for stu-dent learning and development—has received the least attention recently from policymakers. However, research on what the best schools actually do clearly indicates that comprehensive systems of student support are a key aspect of school capacity. Successful schools "capitalize on every opportunity to extend student learning and well-being" (Ogden & Germinario, 1995, p. 89). These schools provide a wide array of extracurricular activities, oppor-tunities for academic tutoring, counseling, and health services. They extend their capacity to support students by developing school, family, and commu-nity partnerships (Epstein et al., 2002), often collaborating with social service agencies, community youth organizations, and businesses (Honig, Kahne, & McLaughlin, 2001).

Common characteristics of effective student support systems have been identified: they address the whole child, developing the students' identity as well as intellect; they emphasize and build on student strengths (rather than deficits); they model and promote positive social norms; they provide a sense of belonging; and they offer students opportunities for leadership. Effective configurations of student supports vary depending on the school; they are specifically tailored to the neighborhood context and the developmental lev-el of the student (Eccles & Templeton, 2002; Honig, Kahne, & McLaughlin, 2001). Studies that have considered differences in learning and development related to students' social class indicate that much more in the way of aca-demic support, supplementary educational services (such as early childhood, afterschool, and summer programs), and other integrated social services are needed to significantly improve outcomes for poor children (Hart & Risley, 1995; Lee & Burkam, 2002; Rothstein, 2004).

The high-performance case studies illustrate the context-specific nature of student supports as well as the need for systemic policies. Components of the student support infrastructure varied, but each site in Wisconsin and Washington had some combination of extended preschool for poor children, afterschool and summer programs, small class sizes in the early grades, tar-geted tutoring based on identified student needs, and/or special programs for homeless students (Fermanich et al., 2006; Odden et al., 2007). They pieced together a variety of school, district, state, and federal student support programs into a system that met the needs of their students.

Reform in NYC District #2 initially did not emphasize student supports. However, as the district became more concerned with student outcomes and began to analyze disaggregated assessment data, it became apparent that there were variations in achievement between schools serving more and less affluent students. In response, the district developed extended day and summer programs for struggling students. Now all schools in the district have an infrastructure of supports consistent with the learning triangle, but in the high-poverty schools the supports are more intensive (Elmore & Burney, 1998; Stein, Harwell, & D'Amico, 1999).

The learning-centered framework suggests and empirical studies support the notion that schools, homes, communities, and other environments interact to enable or constrain student learning and achievement. A study of Chicago school reform found that a significantly greater percentage of schools located in the poorest, most racially isolated, and distressed neighborhoods remained stagnant despite efforts to improve them. Two kinds of constraints held these schools back. First, they had insufficient resources to address tremendous needs. Second, there was a lack of social capital in both the neighborhood and the school. This study suggests that policies to turn around the lowest-performing schools must take school and community interactions into account and address issues in both of these contexts (Bryk et al., 2010).

## COHERENCE AND LEADERSHIP

Some cross-cutting school-level factors characterize the overall environment of the best schools. Their improvement efforts are coherent—the kinds of supports just described are coordinated with one another and linked to student learning. Resources are used strategically to advance the school's common learning and improvement goals; diffuse, scattered programs are avoided. All of this takes leadership, especially a principal who decides to develop or adopt a comprehensive, learning-centered improvement framework; makes it a common priority for the school community; and persists with it over the long haul (Newmann, Smith, Allensworth, & Bryk, 2001). The best schools exhibit a vitality that comes from continuous self-assessment and ongoing, collective efforts to improve their capacity and outcomes (Ogden & Germinario, 1995).

In all of the high-performance case studies, a critical mass of leaders knew how to galvanize the school community around student performance goals and understood the importance of a long-term commitment to improvement encompassing all aspects of the learning triangle. Effective leaders also built trust and nurtured social relationships while advancing instrumental improvement objectives (Bryk et al., 2010). Compared to a typical school or school system, leadership in these sites was more distributed, more focused on teaching and learning, and more aware of new research and how to use it. Administrative roles were kept to a minimum, and roles related to improving teaching and learning were emphasized (Elmore & Burney, 1998; Fermanich et al., 2006; Odden et al., 2007).

Moving from the school to the system level, the image of an effective leadership infrastructure that has emerged from the literature is one of nested learning communities (Resnick & Hall, 1998). Nested learning communities strengthen human and social capital throughout the system to effectively use advances in knowledge as a basis for reform. A critical mass of education leaders with appropriate expertise in research-based school improvement is needed at each level of the education system. Superintendents can form professional learning communities for principals; state leaders can do the same for superintendents. Because the kind of leadership needed for research-based reform is so scarce, NYC District #2 made developing new leaders a priority. Special program arrangements were made with local universities because traditional administrator training was not consistent with the district's vision of leadership (Elmore & Burney, 1998).

## COMPARISON AND CONCLUSION

Successful capacity building initiatives are both *comprehensive* and *systemic.* Capacity-building is comprehensive when it encompasses all aspects of the learning triangle and their interactions. Capacity-building is systemic when it recognizes that classrooms and schools are embedded in multiple contexts that can enable or constrain teaching and learning and builds a coherent infrastructure of support that cuts across these multiple contexts. The schools and districts described in the high-performance case studies successfully built comprehensive infrastructures of support that spanned multiple contexts.

Do recent national policies facilitate the development of comprehensive, systemic infrastructures of support that build capacity for teaching and learning? The standards movement took a systemic approach to building a support structure to improve content. Judged in relation to its original plan of action, investment in an aligned content infrastructure was never sufficient to realize the ideal, and the desired changes in actual classroom practice were not widespread (Cohen & Hill, 2001; Resnick & Zurawsky, 2005; Spillane, 2005). Standards of uneven quality were promulgated in different subjects. There was a great deal of experimentation with new kinds of assessment.

The classroom-level tools that teachers and students use every day received the least emphasis. A recent report found that "curriculum . . . is woefully inadequate" and often not aligned with standards (American Federation of Teachers, 2001, p. 6). Whatever the subject, evaluations of textbooks have found them wanting (American Association for the Advancement of Science [AAAS], 1999; Brophy, Alleman, & O'Mahoney, 2000). Better curriculum and instructional materials still top the list of what teachers say they need to improve instruction (Sunderman, Kim, & Orfield, 2005). Without widespread policy support, instances of successful transformation of content at the grassroots will continue to be rare.

In comparison to the learning triangle, Figure 6.1 illustrates that the scope of the infrastructure that reformers sought to build during the standards era was incomplete. While the standards movement emphasized the need for systemic content alignment, it did not place equal emphasis on developing aligned systemic infrastructures for other aspects of the learning triangle, specifically supports for students, teachers, and leaders.

NCLB places little emphasis on capacity. Policies in the law touch upon all aspects of the learning triangle, but these policies are piecemeal, not comprehensive and systemic. Current high-stakes testing policies do not build upon earlier advances in creating a rigorous and challenging content infrastructure. Instead, high-stakes tests, rather than the standards and the curriculum, are all too often determining school content. State accountability tests are often not aligned with standards (Goertz, 2001) or with current research-based views of knowledge (Pelligrino, Chudowsky, & Glaser, 2001; Schoenfeld, 2006). Moreover, standardized tests only measure a small sample of curriculum content. NCLB has killed off state-of-the-art innovation in the testing industry and encouraged states to invest in tests that primarily measure low-level knowledge and skills. Therefore, content is being trivialized, and the scarce resources devoted to assessment are being used to build an inferior infrastructure rather than one consistent with the state-of-the-art (Toch, 2006).

As a strategy for improving teacher quality and teaching, NCLB emphasizes credentialing. According to the law, to be considered "highly qualified" teachers need a bachelor's degree, full licensure or certification, and subject-matter competence. Although the evidence is mixed, some studies indicate that fully prepared and certified teachers are more successful with students (Darling-Hammond & Ball, 2004). However, the research on teaching offers more important messages. One is that the strategic emphasis should be on *teaching effectiveness* rather than *teacher credentials*. Another message is that the focus should shift from the individual teachers' skills to the problems of building the collective capacity of entire school faculties and of strengthening teaching as a profession. In addition to preservice preparation and licensure, effective teaching is enabled by standards for accomplished teaching, school professional communities, inservice professional development, and workplace conditions that support teaching and learning (Koppich & Knapp, 1998). The NCLB approach to improving teaching is incomplete.

NCLB-type accountability provisions are associated with perverse rather than positive effects on professional development and workplace conditions. Emphasis on high stakes testing appears to move professional development away from the kind of research-based best practice that leads to real gains in student learning and instead focuses it narrowly on test preparation (Banicky & Noble, 2001; Hargreaves, 2003). Also, instead of improving working conditions, designating schools as "low-performing" negatively affects working conditions, increases teacher turnover, and makes it difficult to recruit good teachers to these schools (Clotfelter, Ladd, Vigdor, & Diaz, 2004).

NCLB addresses student supports by requiring that supplemental educational services be made available to students in schools in need of improvement. These services focus on basic skills remediation rather than on support for the development of the whole child. Moreover, the district must arrange for the services to be delivered by providers outside the school because this requirement (along with another option to transfer out of the school) is intended not just to help particular students, but to promote market competition. There is no evidence that such competition results in positive school change, but based on earlier experience with Title I pullout programs, there is cause for concern that the out-of-school arrangements required will lead to curricular and instructional fragmentation (Sunderman, Kim, & Orfield, 2005). For example, the practical difficulties of coordinating separate providers for regular and remedial education make it unlikely that students will get effective help targeted to their specific learning needs as identified by formative assessment.

National policymakers have raised the bar of expectations for what the educational enterprise is supposed to produce, but have failed to retool the infrastructure and build the capacity needed throughout the system to attain results. Current federal policy emphasizes punishment and market incentives; it pays little attention to capacity. The limited supports that NCLB does include are conceived in ways that are inconsistent with research and unlikely to be effective.

Future policy should shift to a focus on capacity-building. Specifically, policy should aim to build a comprehensive, research-based infrastructure of supports throughout the education system. This approach would complete the unfinished business of strengthening the content infrastructure begun during the standards era. In addition, it would expand the notion of systemic reform to encompass other dimensions of the learning triangle and build coordinated infrastructures to support students, teachers, and school leadership.

# CHAPTER 7

# A Stronger
# Accountability Hybrid

Despite all the recent policy emphasis, accountability is a theoretically un-derdeveloped concept. In an accountability system, a principal conditionally delegates the authority to do something to agents who accept the responsibility and may be called upon to render an account of their action to the principal. Responsibility is central to the notion of accountability–the notion of being "called to account" for one's actions. Key questions are: Who is responsible? To whom? For what? How does accountability work? How will it be enforced? (Abelmann & Elmore, 1999; Adams & Kirst, 1999). Answers to those questions are implicit in one's assumptions about the nature of the education system. This chapter addresses these accountability questions and frames the answers so they are consistent with the learning-centered model and new research on accountability.

Figures 7.1 and 7.2 depict alternative assumptions about the education system and their implications for accountability. Most people think of the educational system as hierarchical, as illustrated in Figure 7.1. Authority flows from the top to the bottom. Accountability is viewed in legal and bureau-cratic terms. Legal accountability relies on statutes to set goals and require-ments, to structure accountability relationships, and to enforce compliance through sanctions. Bureaucratic accountability operates within organizations or intergovernmental systems of organizations. It is based on relationships between superiors and subordinates where subordinates are supposed to carry out defined responsibilities according to standard operating procedures. Rewards and punishments are used to enforce compliance. Traditionally in education, the targets of legal and bureaucratic accountability have been re-sources and processes. More recently, legal and bureaucratic mechanisms have been used to target improved performance (Adams & Kirst, 1999) with little understanding of their limitations for this new purpose.

Figure 7.2 frames the education accountability system in accordance with the ecological, learning-centered model. The classroom is the central focus rather than the bottom rung. The two-way arrows suggest that learning and achievement are co-produced with many possible agents directly or indirectly

**Figure 7.1. Top-Down Accountability**

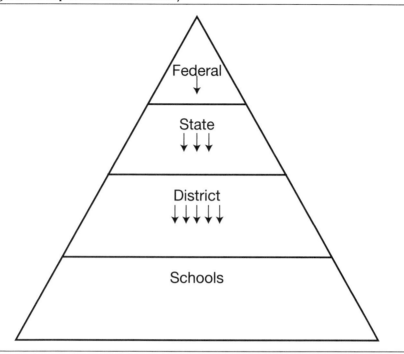

**Figure 7.2. Shared, Reciprocal Accountability**

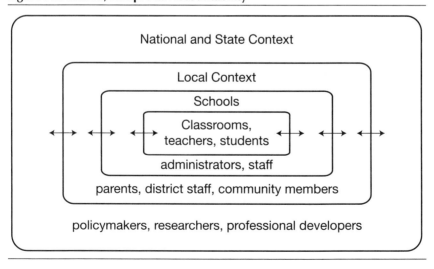

sharing degrees of causal responsibility for student learning and achievement. Within classrooms the teacher, student, and student's peers are directly engaged; outside the classroom, but within the school, administrators, school staff, and coaches have some influence; and outside the school families and community members have an impact. Also depicted are some sources of indirect influence, including policymakers and bureaucrats who supply resources, as well as experts who supply some aspects of knowledge. These examples are only suggestive of the many indirect influences on student learning and achievement. This conceptualization of the relevant environment extends beyond the formal education system and, therefore, beyond the purview of legal and bureaucratic accountability.

## SHARED RESPONSIBILITY

Who is responsible to whom? The answer to this, and the other key questions, varies depending upon whether one has the top-down or the learning-centered framework in mind. One principle of accountability is that the degree of an agent's responsibility should be congruent with the degree of their control over the expected results (Adams & Kirst, 1999).

In accordance with the hierarchical framework, national policy today makes the school the responsible unit. Schools suffer sanctions for not meeting performance goals set by policymakers. Many states have added stakes for students, such as promotion and graduation requirements, to their accountability systems (Fuhrman, Goertz, & Duffy, 2004). School personnel are treated as subordinate agents who are accountable to their superiors at higher levels of the bureaucracy. The responsibility runs in a one-way direction from the top down. The top-down model may work when the objective is to establish accountability for processes and resources that are within the purview of the bureaucratic system, but it is more problematic when applied to the goals of student learning and achievement because control over outcomes extends beyond the bureaucratic system.

As the learning-centered figure illustrates, actual causal responsibility for student learning and achievement is widely dispersed inside and outside the formal education system. Individuals, institutions, communities, and cultures interact in complex ways to affect student achievement. These multiple interacting influences imply the need for multiple accountability relationships. One challenge for the future is to improve the match between causal responsibility and accountability expectations related to performance.

The National Research Council (NRC) has recommended an accountability principle that is more in line with the learning-centered framework and the realities of causal responsibility. According to the NRC, "Accountability for educational outcomes should be a shared responsibility of states, school districts, public officials, educators, parents, and students" (Heubert & Hauser, 1999, p. 5). Shared responsibility goes outside the formal system to include parents and public officials. Instead of having sole responsibility, schools become the linchpins of an interdependent accountability system. Schools cannot do it alone. A better accountability system for the future would build on the principle of shared responsibility.

## RECIPROCAL ACCOUNTABILITY

Accountability for what? Over the past several decades, education policy has moved from a focus on accountability for inputs (e.g., number and type of staff, minimum quality standards, and proper use of resources) to a focus on outputs, specifically student achievement (Goertz, 2001) and attainment. Meanwhile, performance expectations have been significantly raised.

The business literature highlights key conceptual flaws in both past and present theories of accountability in education. At the same time education policy was shifting strongly to a focus on student outcomes, there was a "revolution" in thinking about accountability and performance assessment in the business world, but of a very different kind (Eccles, 1991). Long known for their sole focus on the "bottom line" of profits, today effective businesses are shifting their attention to a combination of input and output measures. The performance inputs businesses track are not the kind of inert inputs educators used to track, but those perceived as enablers of high-performance outcomes (Bogan & English, 1994). The current business approach recognizes the interaction of outcomes and enablers as well as the importance of capacity-building. In fact, there is criticism in the business literature of trends in the public sector toward accountability and control using outcome indicators alone (Smith, 1995).

The view of accountability emerging from educational research is similar to the more enlightened business perspective. It assumes that accountability is inherently reciprocal. Elmore (2004) expressed the idea this way: If I require increased performance of you, I have a reciprocal responsibility to provide adequate resources and assist you in developing the capacity to produce. Performance-based accountability systems generally provide inadequate opportunities for teacher learning and other aspects of capacity-building needed to meet high expectations. This mismatch poses a dilemma. Is it ethical or reasonable to hold teachers responsible for doing things that they don't know how to do and can't do without an increase in knowledge, skill, and resources (Elmore, 2004)?

Empirical studies of school reform illustrate how capacity and results interact in education. For example, an emerging line of research on school responses to external accountability demands indicates that responses vary. In one study schools that responded effectively to external demands for higher performance perceived the policy as aligned with their own mission, had the collective capacity to respond, and had internal structures and processes for translating policy into coherent action. The results in these schools exceeded the expectations of the mandate. In schools that did not respond appropriately, individual school personnel were atomized, there were no shared goals or collective sense of responsibility, and there was a perceived lack of capacity. These schools went through the motions of compliance without results (DeBray, Parson, & Woodworth, 2001; see also Newmann, King, & Rigdon, 1997).

Much remains to be learned about reciprocal accountability, but preliminary studies indicate that a school's response to accountability demands is determined by its prior status on dimensions of capacity. External accountability systems work not through command and control, but by mobilizing and focusing preexisting capacity in particular ways (Elmore, 2003a). If schools are expected to significantly improve performance, especially low-performing schools with the least capacity, then a much greater policy emphasis on capacity-building is a prerequisite. Both practical and ethical considerations point to the need to shift emphasis in the future from a one-sided emphasis on accountability for performance to reciprocal accountability that balances support and pressure.

## INTERNAL AND EXTERNAL INTERACTION

How does accountability work? Most research dealing with accountability in education focuses on the implementation of the predominant top-down, high-stakes model. Existing accountability systems assume uniform responses to standardized requirements. However, once we begin to think about accountability as interactive, questions about the relationship between internal accountability within the school and the external accountability system inevitably arise. A new line of inquiry is addressing issues of internal-external interactions in different kinds of accountability systems. A key question is: How do schools respond to external accountability demands? These studies are finding interesting patterns of variation in school responses.

An emerging theory of accountability posits three interacting tiers in education accountability systems: one is teachers' individual sense of responsibility; the second is the collective expectations of teachers, students, administrators, and parents in a school; and the third is the formal, external accountability system. In one type of school studied, characterized as "atomized," there was no accountability beyond the individual teacher's sense of moral or professional responsibility. Another type of school had developed a culture of expectations that shaped individuals' views around a common purpose. Although these schools did not have visible accountability structures, collective expectations heavily influenced individual perceptions of responsibility. The third type of school had developed their own internal accountability and improvement systems. Sometimes the internal and external systems were aligned; other times they were not. When alignment was absent, the schools followed the norms of the internal system (Abelmann & Elmore, 1999; Carnoy, Elmore, & Siskin, 2003).

These findings about the shared, reciprocal, and interactive nature of accountability have important implications for policy. First, policy can encourage schools to build the internal structures and systems needed to establish collective, professional norms and to take action on school improvement. The findings from accountability research converge with research on professional communities. Both indicate that professional communities within schools can build collective teaching capacity as well as a sense of accountability for student performance. Professional communities serve to mediate external influences (McLaughlin & Talbert, 1993). Second, policy can recognize the limitations of top-down legal and bureaucratic accountability and strengthen other types of accountability that operate within schools (moral and professional accountability) and in the local context (public accountability).

## A HYBRID APPROACH

This section considers how education accountability can be strengthened by creating a hybrid system that combines the legal and bureaucratic approaches that currently predominate with other types. It discusses future possibilities for strengthening professional and public accountability. Each approach has its strengths and limitations. Just as hybrid plants are stronger, a hybrid accountability system may be stronger, too.

Professional accountability is an underutilized resource. It recognizes the importance of expertise in complex work and devolves authority for setting standards to professionals and their organizations. In return, the professionals are expected to develop a sense of ownership and commitment to best practice and to meet the standards they set (Adams & Kirst, 1999; O'Day, 2004). In most professions, the professionals set and enforce their own standards through accreditation of preparation programs, initial licensure, and advanced certification. In education, professional leadership in student content standards presents another opportunity to enhance professional accountability. Widespread teacher involvement in standard settings not only fulfills an accountability function, it serves to build teacher capacity by developing and diffusing the professional knowledge base (Darling-Hammond et al., 2005).

Public accountability received more attention during the standards era than it does today. The publication of school test scores as a means for public oversight is now required by NCLB. However, the concept of public accountability goes considerably further: schools would actively involve their stakeholders in an ongoing improvement process. Data on both capacity and performance data would be published. Events (e.g., town meetings, interpretive panels) would engage stakeholders in the interpretation and application of the data. At the local level, it is possible to use a richer array of standardized and nonstandardized data to paint a more realistic school portrait. Public accountability also involves stakeholders in strategic planning and follow-through (LeMahieu, 1996). In a well-conceived improvement and accountability system, the public would have the data and the capacity to call educators to account for the quality of practice, to call policymakers to account for providing infrastructure and equitable resources, and to hold both responsible for results.

## SANCTIONS AND SUPPORTS

How is accountability enforced? Accountability systems have various ways for agents to periodically provide an "account" to explain and justify their actions and results. Performance has consequences, positive or negative, depending on whether the account is satisfactory. If we reject the one-sided view of accountability, then the high-stakes testing and school-level sanctions system currently in use is clearly inadequate. What alternative accounting mechanism and consequences would be appropriate in the future?

In a shared, reciprocal accountability system, a "balanced scorecard" that can measure both sides of the equation—capacity and outcomes—and also serve the information needs of a variety of audiences at different levels of the system would need to be developed (Kaplan & Norton, 1992). A more balanced reporting system would allow stakeholders to assess gaps in resources as well as in results. Also, it would provide the public with data to hold policymakers accountable for the responsibility they have to build capacity. Chapter 8 discusses a system of multiple measures that meets these criteria and is well suited to serve the assessment functions of a new hybrid system.

When it comes to consequences for inadequate performance, there is considerable research evidence behind the idea of switching emphasis from sanctions to supports. One study compared the predictive effects of state accountability policies that emphasized input guarantees with those that emphasized output guarantees on student performance using National Assessment of Educational Progress [NAEP] data (prior to NCLB). States with more supports and resources for schools had higher achievement; states that emphasized test-driven accountability had lower achievement. In math, when inputs were low, output pressure made little difference. But when supports were high, press for outputs was associated with relatively large gains in achievement (Lee, 2006).

An in-depth research synthesis of different pre-NCLB state accountability systems reported similar results. It found that the more effective states had achievable goals, exerted modest accountability pressures, and provided strong and comprehensive capacity-building assistance to low-performing schools. In these support-oriented state systems, schools were required to develop school improvement plans. Some or all of the schools underwent on-site inspection by a state or district team. Schools judged to be in need of external assistance got on-site personnel to advise and assist them for extended periods of time. Comprehensive capacity-building might include professional development, instructional support, help with assessment, extended school days, or parent services. The authors concluded that "comprehensiveness is a key characteristic that makes interventions sufficiently different from all the other things that schools have tried before and that makes corrective action programs effective" (Mintrop & Trujillo, 2005, p. 17).

## COMPARISON AND CONCLUSION

During the standards era, most states substantially increased demands for student performance and held schools, teachers, and students responsible for meeting these expectations. The states varied considerably in the extent to which they emphasized capacity-building, accountability, or both strategies. Although top-down legal/bureaucratic accountability methods predominated, there were also some efforts to strengthen professional and public accountability. For example, professional organizations were given the responsibility for developing content standards (some also developed teaching standards), and this strategy was somewhat effective in developing professional commitment to improve practice based upon the standards. Teachers involved in the standards-setting process, and in related state-level curriculum and assessment work, often went on to become leaders in the reform movement (Talbert, 2002).

NCLB set achievement targets that manage to be both simplistic and impossible. It is desirable to have performance goals, but they should be grounded in the reality of past experience, according to Linn (2003). NCLB's top-down bureaucratic accountability approach and its neglect of capacity-building is inconsistent with research on how accountability works—by drawing upon preexisting capacity—and helps explain why NCLB's emphasis on sanctions and choice, without capacity-building, has failed to produce results. The punitive approach to accountability has produced numerous negative, unintended side effects. Efforts to build capacity should move to the foreground and drive reform; sanctions should move to the background and be used as a last resort.

The research reviewed here suggests that an alternative accountability system for the future is both possible and desirable. Accountability would be viewed as a shared responsibility of all stakeholders for student learning, achievement, and attainment. A hybrid system combining public, professional, and intergovernmental legal/bureaucratic accountability would open avenues for shared roles and responsibilities. In addition, a future accountability system would be based upon the principle of reciprocity. It would recognize that when performance expectations are substantially raised, there must be a reciprocal commitment to building capacity throughout the system as well as to providing adequate and equitable resources.

# CHAPTER 8

# Systems of Multiple Assessments

Assessment serves a number of purposes, and different purposes require different approaches. One type of assessment cannot fit all purposes. Student assessments should be conceptualized and designed so that they are consistent with theories of learning and achievement (Pelligrino, Baxter, & Glaser, 1999); school assessments should be consistent with theories of organizational change and improvement. Additionally, assessment systems must meet the needs of a variety of stakeholders, including students, teachers, parents, administrators, and policymakers.

This chapter draws upon the literature in assessment and school improvement to consider assessment goals, conceptual and design issues, and audiences. Consistent with the learning-centered framework, I map backward from the classroom to the school level and then to the larger school system in discussing the features of a better assessment system. Finally, I compare the research-based assessment system with assessment policies during the standards and NCLB eras and make recommendations for the future.

## CLASSROOM ASSESSMENT

Research strongly suggests the need for a balance of two types of assessment at the classroom level. The purpose of one approach–formative assessment–is to help students learn and to improve instruction. It takes place at the start of and during a learning sequence. The second and more familiar type of assessment–summative assessment–documents achievement at the end of a learning sequence (Glaser & Silver, 1994).

Formative assessment facilitates learning in a variety of ways. Because we know that new knowledge always builds upon prior knowledge and cultural perspectives, teachers must determine where students start. Techniques such as questioning and conversation can be used at the beginning of a lesson to draw out and informally assess students' initial knowledge. We also know that students learn better when their progress is tracked during the learning process and they receive feedback along the way. Feedback not only helps students learn, it informs teaching because teachers can use it to individualize and adjust instruction (Black et al., 2002; Pelligrino, Baxter, & Glaser, 1999; Shepard, 2001). There is evidence that when it is used systematically throughout the learning process, formative assessment not only facilitates learning and teaching, it produces very significant gains in student achievement (Black & Wiliam, 1998).

Formative assessment is a theme found in the high-performance case studies. At one school in Wisconsin, the principal attributed the schools' success in literacy largely to the use of running records that continuously identify what students know and what they still need to learn. This helped teachers allocate their time to areas where students were weakest and refer students quickly for extra help outside the classroom. Another district-level case in Wisconsin described the benefits of formative assessment in their new literacy curriculum. Here, too, the teachers kept running records and used these data to target instruction to the learning needs of students. The data transformed the kinds of conversations teachers had with one another, with parents, and with administrators about student learning and instruction (Odden et al., 2007). Unfortunately, these cases are the exception rather than the rule. Few teachers know how to make expert use of formative assessment. Building this capacity is a huge challenge that must be addressed with opportunities for teacher learning (Shepard, 2001).

What other elements might a comprehensive classroom-level assessment system include? Because concepts of learning and achievement should guide the design of an assessment system rather than the other way around, Figure 8.1 lists the dimensions of achievement discussed earlier along with some examples of appropriate assessment approaches.

Mastery of basic knowledge and skills represents one dimension of achievement. Most of the standardized tests that dominate assessment today were designed primarily to measure low-level knowledge and basic or routine skills. For example, they contain many more questions that require students to recall and state facts than questions asking students to apply or evaluate information. Standardized tests (e.g., the NAEP) can measure some aspects of thinking and more advanced knowledge, but states have no incentive in a high-stakes testing environment to adopt more demanding assessments.

It is appropriate to evaluate achievement in basic knowledge and skills, and standardized tests can serve as one component of an assessment system, along with school-based assessments, to measure this dimension of achievement. However, standardized tests by themselves are inadequate as overall measures of achievement. Overreliance on these tests gives "a skewed sense of student achievement" (Toch, 2006, p. 15) and fails to represent the full range of valued educational outcomes (Glaser & Silver, 1994).

In the 1990s, there was considerable experimentation with new assessment approaches, such as performance assessments and portfolios, designed to

**Figure 8.1. Classroom Assessment: Toward a System of Multiple Measures**

| Dimension of Achievement | Example of Assessment Approach |
|---|---|
| Basic Knowledge/Skills | Standardized Tests |
| Advanced Knowledge/Skills<br>Competence in Doing | Performance Assessments<br>Portfolios<br>Dynamic/Interactive Assessments |
| Whole Child Development | Noncognitive Assessments |
| Full Potential<br>Identity Development | Project Spectrum (Gardner)<br>Rainbow Project (Sternberg)<br>Progress Files |

NCLB Emphasis [ ]
Standards Movement Emphasis [ ]
Little/No Policy Emphasis [ ]

measure advanced knowledge and skills as well as the ability "to do" a complete and complex task. Consistent with more rigorous achievement goals, instead of multiple-choice questions, performance assessments might ask students to conduct an experiment, explain the thinking behind their response, or provide alternative interpretations of a problem. Portfolios composed of actual student work samples document what students can actually do (Glaser & Silver, 1994). Assessing students' highest ability level requires dynamic assessments that consider what a student can do working with the help of tools or other people, rather than alone, because learning theory suggests that assisted performance represents the upper reaches of one's ability (Gipps, 1999).

If we value the development of the whole child, then assessment related to noncognitive domains might be part of a comprehensive system. In the areas of social and emotional development, two approaches are useful. One is student assessment (both formative and summative). The other approach is assessment of the classroom and school environments to determine whether they facilitate students' social and emotional growth. While some research is under way, and a variety of assessment instruments are in use, we do not yet have evidence-based assessments of either type. Many state education agencies are interested in scientifically sound evaluation of school climate (Cohen, 2006). The Australian Council for Educational Research (ACER) has done research on this type of student and school assessment. ACER has developed surveys that measure students' overall level of social-emotional well-being as well as the quality of school life for use in Australian elementary and secondary schools (Australian Council for Educational Research, 2007).

A variety of assessment tools may facilitate student identity development and assist in identifying student talents. The British have experimented with an innovative assessment approach at the high school and college levels called "progress files" where students systematically document both their academic and nonacademic achievements working with a tutor. This system focuses on student strengths and was found to be somewhat effective in boosting motivation, helping students develop both course-taking and career plans for the future, and fostering student identity development (Office for Standards in Education [OFSTED], 2002). An approach similar to the British progress files could be adapted for use in U.S. schools.

Both Gardner (Gardner, Feldman, & Krechevsky, 1998) and Sternberg (2003) have experimented with assessment approaches designed to identify talents in children consistent with their theories of intelligence. Gardner (1993) has argued that instead of being used to label student deficits, assessments should be used to identify their strengths and show concrete ways to build upon them. These experimental approaches to assessment measure important aspects of achievement, such as creativity, that are currently neglected.

New knowledge makes the creation of better assessment systems possible, but more applied research is still needed. For example, a significant investment is needed to develop empirically validated "learning progressions" that reflect how students actually advance in their learning (Corcoran, Mosher, & Rogat, 2009; Resnick, Stein, & Coon, 2008). New technology also has the potential to enhance both formative and summative assessment. In technology-enhanced environments, assessment is integrated with the learning process. For example, students can work on complex problems with "intelligent" computer-based tutors that guide students along a learning trajectory and provide remediation when students make mistakes (Pelligrino, Chudowsky, & Glaser, 2001). Digital portfolios can be used to organize and display student work within the context of a school's learning goals (Niguidula, 1998). Many advanced applications of technology in the field of assessment are still in the experimental stage, but offer exciting possibilities for the future.

Teachers, students, and parents are the primary audiences for classroom assessment. Research has shown for years that standardized tests are of little use to teachers and students (Glaser & Silver, 1994). For example, a recent survey of school leadership teams found that approximately three-quarters of respondents considered student portfolios, running records, and open-ended assessments "highly useful," but only about one-quarter found standardized tests "highly useful." Standardized test results are not available in a timely manner and lack the detail needed for within-school purposes (Supovitz & Klein, 2003). Insufficient attention has been given to the impact of existing and alternative assessment practices on students. Assessment practices do not just passively measure student achievement; the nature of the practices can affect student learning, motivation, and sense of self (Filer & Pollard, 2000).

Parents want multiple types of assessments. A study asked parents to compare the utility of different types of assessment for understanding their child's progress in school. They gave their highest ratings to talking with the teacher, followed by samples of their child's work, then report cards, and finally standardized tests. When shown actual examples of the kinds of questions used on standardized and performance assessments, they approved of both, but gave stronger approval ratings to performance assessment items. They recognized that scoring the performance assessments would be more subjective, but believed that disadvantage was outweighed by several advantages. For example, they said that performance assessments would make their children think and use imagination (Shepard & Bliem, 1995).

## SCHOOL ASSESSMENT

Assessment can serve both formative and summative purposes at the school level just as it does in the classroom. Formative organizational assessment is a key aspect of continuous school improvement. Research on organizational change suggests that in high performance organizations continuous improvement of practice is a core activity (Senge, 1990; Watson, 1992; Wenger, McDermott, & Snyder, 2002). Effective organizations look outside as well as within for ideas on how to improve. The regional school accreditation process encourages formative assessment and an emphasis on continuous school improvement (National Study of School Evaluation [NSSE], 2005).

The process of continuous improvement in schools is similar to benchmarking in the business world. The benchmarking literature emphasizes the need to consider both performance enablers and outcomes. Benchmarking has been described as "a continuous search for and application of *significantly better practices* that leads to superior competitive performance" (Watson, 1992, p. 2). There is a "planning" stage that involves setting goals and finding new ideas and best practices, a "doing" stage where better practices are adapted and implemented, an "assessing" stage that checks on the results of the change, and a "revising" stage that builds upon what was learned (Tucker, 1996; Watson, 1992).

A strategic framework is needed for systematic school assessment and improvement. One popular framework used in business is called the "balanced scorecard" because it considers four dimensions of improvement, including organizational capacity and results, as well as customer satisfaction and innovation (Kaplan & Norton, 1992). Figure 8.2 sketches a framework for school assessment that combines this approach with the learning-centered approach. It illustrates how the learning-centered framework might be applied to assessment at the school level.

**Figure 8.2. School and System Assessment: Toward a System of Multiple Measures**

| A Balanced Scorecard for Schools | |
| --- | --- |
| **Vision:** <br> Shared and Balanced Educational Goals <br> Multifaceted Concept of Achievement <br> All Students Can Learn | |
| **Enablers** | **Results** |
| Capacity <br>   Students/Learning <br>   Teachers/Teaching <br>   Content <br>   Leadership <br> Resource Adequacy and Use <br> Shared Accountability | Student Learning and Achievement (Multiple Measures) <br> Organizational Performance Indicators <br> Stakeholder Satisfaction |

The school improvement literature emphasizes the need for a shared vision developed through participatory processes, but is often vague about the substance of the vision. However, the learning-centered framework is more specific. It suggests that schools need to consider and balance a variety of economic, civic, cultural, and educational goals; foster multiple dimensions of achievement; and develop a commitment to the idea that all students can learn. The school's vision cuts across and informs its capacity-building, resource allocation, accountability, and assessment efforts depicted in the two columns in Figure 8.2.

The balanced scorecard includes, on one side of the ledger, capacity, resources, and shared accountability as enablers of school performance. Drawing upon the learning-centered framework discussed earlier, Figure 8.2 suggests four strategic focus areas for developing school capacity: students/ learning, teachers/teaching, content, and leadership. Research on school reform indicates that as part of the change process, high-performing schools rethink and strategically redeploy their resources to build capacity in areas related to the learning triangle (Miles & Darling-Hammond, 1997; Odden et al., 2007). Therefore, resource adequacy and use are included. Finally, as Chapter 7 indicated, successful schools have their own internal improvement and accountability processes.

On the other side of the ledger, assessing student and school results, Figure 8.2 encourages the use of multiple measures. In examining their student outcomes, successful schools use various types of standardized and authentic student performance data, aggregating and disaggregating them in different ways to serve a variety of analytical purposes (Smith & Ruff, 1998; Supovitz & Klein, 2003; U.S. Department of Education, 1996). They may also assess indicators of organizational performance such as teacher and student attendance, frequency of serious disciplinary incidents, promotion and graduation rates, and/or percentage of students going on to college (U.S. Department of Education, 1996). Some schools assess the quality of their environment at the classroom or school levels, recognizing that the environment has effects on students' academic, social, and moral development (Cohen, 2006; Goodlad, 1994; Newell & Van Ryzin, 2007). Borrowing from business practice, school assessments may also include surveys of stakeholder satisfaction (Baldrige National Quality Program, 2002; NSSE, 2005).

When school-level assessment data are organized in summative form and publicly reported, they can serve important local accountability purposes. Many schools develop comprehensive school profiles for the benefit of parents and the community (Banicky & Foss, 1999; Supovitz & Klein, 2003). When parents, business leaders, and administrators are asked what kinds of information they need to hold schools accountable, they want far more than standardized test scores. They ask for information about inputs, such as school safety and teacher qualifications, as well as a variety of outputs, including mastery of both basic and advanced competencies along with information about how current performance compares with both standards and previous performance (Banicky & Foss, 1999). Thus, the balanced scorecard not only reflects what current research and exemplary practice suggest schools should assess and act upon to improve, it also provides the kind of data the public wants for accountability purposes.

School-level assessment is a critical aspect of an improvement process that may also include benchmarking, external review, or other means to discover, use, and evaluate best practices. In successful schools, the cycle of assessment, learning, and improvement is continuous and evidence-based (Tucker, 1996). Schools differ in their capacity to assess themselves and use best practices; they need varying levels of external support. A formative self-assessment process builds internal school accountability and public reporting of summative school-level assessment data serves local external accountability purposes.

Despite its importance as the linchpin of a continuous school improvement process, school-level assessment is usually overlooked in the education assessment literature, which focuses on either classroom or large-scale contexts. However, the organizational, school improvement, and accountability research indicates that strengthening school-level capacity for formative and summative organizational assessment and continuous improvement is a promising strategy to consider for the future.

## LARGE-SCALE ASSESSMENT

Beyond the classroom and the school levels, large-scale, standardized assessments are intended to serve the needs of administrators and policymakers at the district, state, and national levels by providing information to monitor achievement and attainment trends over time. During the 1990s considerable investment was made, often by states, in developing large-scale assessments designed to communicate more challenging content goals and standards to teachers as well as to measure progress in attaining them (Shepard, 2005). Also, some large-scale assessments, such as NAEP and TIMSS, began collecting information about the conditions of learning and achievement as well as student outcomes. The intent was to go beyond a myopic focus on results, make useful information available for educational improvement, and provide a kind of balanced scorecard for policymakers.

In current high-stakes testing systems, however, the illusion of accountability displaces the information and improvement purposes. Due to more frequent testing and high stakes, state assessment systems have retreated to standardized tests that are not aligned with challenging standards. It is impossible to track the effects of learning-centered reform on student achievement because the most commonly used standardized assessments are not sensitive to the aspects of a multifaceted concept of achievement that reforms emphasize (e.g., higher-order thinking or problem-solving). Therefore, evaluations that employ these tests will report no differences in outcomes (Schoenfeld, 2006).

Even within the narrow range of outcomes they measure, the results of high-stakes tests are likely to be distorted. Research in a variety of fields shows that the more any social indicator is used for decisionmaking and control, the more it corrupts the process it is supposed to measure. In high-stakes testing environments, teachers teach to the test. Past exams supplant the curriculum. Apparent gains on tests with stakes are typically not confirmed by tests without stakes (Madaus, 1999). In addition to these problems with student achievement measures, recent debates about high school completion and dropout rates reveal inadequacies of both definition and measurement in tracking educational attainment (Warren & Halpern-Manners, 2007).

Many policymakers have recently become interested in assessing student growth and "value-added." Most existing large-scale assessments are status models. They measure student performance at a given point in time, usually in comparison to an established target. Growth models measure student performance by tracking the test scores of the same students from one year to the next to determine the extent of their progress. According to a survey of the states, as of 2010 there are 30 states that have either implemented or are developing growth models (Blank, 2010). Value-added models are a particular type of growth model that uses complex statistical methods in an attempt to attribute some fraction of student performance growth to particular teachers, schools, or programs (Braun, Chudowsky, & Koenig, 2010).

Value-added models are popular with some policymakers who want to use them in accountability systems to reward or punish specific teachers or schools based on their performance in producing student growth. However, assessment experts have warned that the use of value-added models for high-stakes purposes is premature due to numerous technical problems. At this time the best use of value-added models is in closely studied pilot projects (Board on Testing and Assessment, 2009). Other policymakers are interested in growth models because they want to move toward assessment systems composed of multiple measures. Existing growth and value-added models are based on data from state accountability assessments. Therefore, they offer two ways of looking at the same dimension of achievement (generally basic knowledge and skills). This is a useful addition to an assessment system, but it does not yet serve the broader purposes and measure the multiple dimensions of achievement suggested by Figure 8.1.

Are there examples of better assessment alternatives for the United States? Darling-Hammond and Wentworth (2010) studied student assessment practices in high-performing countries that provide good benchmarks for the United States. They found that these countries place greater emphasis on assessment for information and improvement purposes than for accountability purposes. Their systems facilitate learning through formative assessment and measure a broad range of outcomes, including more advanced knowledge, skills, and applications, through a combination of standardized assessments, open-ended performance tasks, and school-based assessments. In countries with high school exit examinations, students often choose the areas in which they will be assessed. International comparisons also offer benchmarks for school-level assessment because many countries have traditions of school self-assessment and/or external review (Cuttance, 2005; Rothstein, Jacobsen, & Wilder, 2008; Wilson, 1996).

The developmental assessment program in Australia is one good example of a user-friendly system of multiple measures designed to support learning and measure student achievement. It bridges the gap between teachers' classroom assessment and large-scale assessment. Progress maps that report student achievement along a developmental continuum are the backbone of this system; these maps serve both formative and summative purposes. Teachers are provided with the resource materials and training needed to use multiple kinds of developmental assessments in specific subject areas and to report reliable and valid data for system-level use. In addition, teachers have a website and assessment resource kits to build their understanding of and capacity to employ best practices in assessment. At the same time, the system provides summative information about trends in achievement across the whole continuum from basic to advanced that is useful to administrators and policymakers for accountability purposes (Forster & Masters, 2004).

## COMPARISON AND CONCLUSION

When we begin in the classroom and work "from the inside out," draw upon research evidence, and consider what a variety of stakeholders want, an assessment system emerges that is radically different from what we have now. It is a comprehensive system of multiple measures that serves a variety of purposes and audiences throughout the multilevel education system. At the classroom level, there is a balance of formative assessment that facilitates teaching and learning and a coherent set of summative assessments that document the many facets of student achievement. At the school level, formative organizational assessment provides a foundation for continuous improvement. Publicly reported summative school profiles serve local accountability purposes. Beyond the school level, large-scale, low-stakes standardized assessments with a balanced emphasis on enablers and outcomes serve the needs of administrators and policymakers by providing the information needed to allocate resources and track trends in results.

There is a stark contrast between the purposes and scope of a comprehensive, multipurpose assessment system suggested by Figures 8.1 and 8.2 and the assessment system currently required by NCLB. The shaded areas in Figure 8.1 (Classroom Assessment) that highlight areas of policy emphasis show that gains were made during the standards era in expanding the types of assessments available to evaluate more advanced knowledge, thinking skills, and task performance. However, these components of a better assessment system were largely abandoned because NCLB high-stakes testing policies encouraged states to adopt inexpensive tests that measure only basic knowledge and skills (Resnick & Zurawsky, 2005; Toch, 2006).

Now the Obama administration is funding consortia of States to develop assessments in mathematics and in English language arts that measure both status and growth in a wider range of knowledge and skills—annually in grades 3 through 8, and once in high school. Funding is also available for "rigorous" high school course assessments in STEM-related fields. Improvement purposes are mentioned, but the procurement continues to emphasize accountability purposes (Comprehensive Assessment Systems, 2010). These assessment priorities will, no doubt, rekindle interest in performance and other types of innovative assessments, but so far support is available only in a few subjects.

The unshaded areas of Figure 8.1 indicate the many aspects of assessment that have been and still are neglected. There has been no national policy emphasis on assessing the nonacademic aspects of student development and achievement, such as social and emotional growth or student identity development. No part of Figure 8.2 (School and System Assessment) is shaded because, despite its use at the grassroots in many high-performing schools and districts and in school accreditation, school-level organizational assessment was not a national policy emphasis either during the standards era or currently. Clearly, existing assessment practices are far from optimal.

In the area of assessment, the message for future policy from the research is clear. National policymakers need to start with new concepts of learning, achievement, and school improvement, then fundamentally rethink and revise assessment policy. A distinguished committee of experts assembled by the National Academies (Pelligrino, Chudowsky, & Glaser, 2001) said: "Policymakers are urged to recognize the limitations of current assessments and to support the development of new systems of multiple assessments" (p. 14). That same committee also recommended a shift in the balance of emphasis from "external forms of assessment to an increased emphasis on classroom formative assessment designed to assist learning" (p. 14). It will take a substantial investment of time and money to develop the new systems of multiple assessments that the experts envision and that school systems need to facilitate high performance.

# CHAPTER 9

# Overview of the Learning-Centered Framework

Sometimes it is useful to view familiar ideas through new lenses. Part II has looked at six key components of education—goals, concepts of achievement and attainment, classroom capacity for learning, school system capacity and infrastructure, accountability, and assessment—and suggested new research-based ways of conceptualizing each one. The learning-centered framework positioned the classroom, where the core educational processes of teaching and learning take place, at the center of the education system. Then it strategically considered how policies at other levels of the system enable or constrain learning. The challenge for policy is to build the necessary enablers for high performance and to remove any constraints.

From the learning-centered perspective, education serves a variety of overlapping economic, civil, moral, social, and educational goals. Future policy should legitimate the full range of educational goals and encourage schools to balance and prioritize them to meet student needs and public expectations. Student achievement is a multifaceted concept that cannot be adequately measured by standardized test scores. If improving student achievement and attainment are central objectives of national policy, it is essential to promote student engagement and effort. A better school curriculum should balance individuality and commonality. A curriculum designed along these lines would connect with student interests and develop each student's full potential as well as address the public purposes of education by developing student proficiency in a common academic core.

Comprehensive and systemic capacity-building is a necessary prerequisite for meeting more challenging educational goals. At the classroom level, this involves rethinking all aspects of practice. Teachers need to be convinced that disadvantaged students can achieve with effort and the opportunity to learn; they need encouragement to learn new theories of motivation, learning, and teaching; and they need opportunities to collaborate in professional communities and to try out better, research-based teaching practices. Throughout the multiple layers of the education system, capacity-building should be the top priority. The entire education enterprise must be retooled so that it provides an infrastructure of supports for content, students, teachers, and leadership.

Despite all the emphasis on accountability in education today, it is not defined or measured in ways that will improve education. An alternative accountability system based on the principles of shared responsibility and reciprocity is needed in the future. Accountability would be viewed as a shared responsibility of all stakeholders for student learning and achievement. This concept would be operationalized in a hybrid system that combines public, professional, and intergovernmental bureaucratic approaches to accountability. The principle of reciprocity suggests that accountability is not a one way street. When performance expectations for students and teachers are substantially raised, there must be a reciprocal commitment to building capacity throughout the system as well as to providing adequate and equitable resources.

Educational assessment systems of the future should be designed to serve a variety of purposes and audiences. Most urgently, there needs to be a balance of summative and formative assessment. At the classroom level, formative assessment facilitates learning by providing feedback to teachers and students. At the school and system level, formative organizational assessment is part of an improvement process that involves setting goals and then tracking capacity-building, resources, and results. Assuming that the concept of achievement is broadened, multiple measures of its many dimensions must be developed. Measures of educational attainment are also inadequate and need to be improved. Research advances in learning, assessment, and measurement provide the scientific opportunities for real breakthroughs in assessment. The needed ingredients are substantial investment and a long-term perspective.

The standards movement was compatible in some ways with the learning-centered framework, but was incomplete in its conceptualization of education goals, student achievement, and the scope of capacity-building needed to transform the education system. Its ideal of an aligned content system built around challenging learning goals for all students was very important, but it was never fully implemented, and this unfinished work remains as a task for the future. Reformers in the standards era placed insufficient emphasis on building a systemic infrastructure of supports for teachers, students, and leadership.

NCLB's high-stakes testing policy has focused public attention directly on the gap in achievement between more and less advantaged students and the importance of addressing it. However, NCLB policy and the learning-centered perspective are worlds apart in their basic frameworks and assumptions about the nature of student achievement and how to improve it. NCLB trivializes educational goals and the concept of achievement. It does little to build systemic capacity for change, but instead assumes that the threat of sanctions and greater reliance on market competition will suffice to close achievement gaps. It emphasizes accountability testing to the near-exclusion of other, more important aspects of assessment.

In summary, basic research suggests new ways of conceptualizing the central components of education and a new framework for future education reform. In every substantive area of education considered–educational goals; the definition of achievement; classroom, school, and system capacity; accountability; and the approach to assessment–the concepts behind recent national policy are dramatically inconsistent with the research-based framework and concepts. Table 9.1 summarizes differences in assumptions about key components of education behind the standards movement, NCLB high-stakes testing policy, and a learning-centered alternative for the future. As they look to the future, policymakers and practitioners should fundamentally reframe their approach to education reform.

**Table 9.1. Summary and Comparison of Education Frameworks**

| Policy Area | Standards Movement | NCLB Policy | Future Alternative |
|---|---|---|---|
| Goals of Education | Economic goals | Economic goals | Balance of goals–economic, civic, moral, cultural, and educational |
| Student Achievement and Attainment | Advanced knowledge/skills and "doing" or practical application<br><br>All students proficient in challenging core academic curriculum | Basic knowledge and skills<br><br>Close the "achievement gap" in math and reading | Multifaceted concept of achievement<br><br>All students proficient in core curriculum; advanced proficiency for each student in chosen area<br><br>Reduce gaps in achievement and attainment |
| Classroom Capacity | Emphasize challenging content | "Teach to the test" | Comprehensive capacity for whole classroom triangle–teachers, students, content, learning environment |
| School and System Capacity | Aligned guidance systems for content<br><br>Supports for teachers, students, and leaders insufficient | Sanctions and market competition<br><br>Supports very limited and mis-specified | Strong systemic infrastructure of supports for content, students, teachers, and leadership |
| Accountability | Type and emphasis varied by state | Schools responsible<br><br>Results only<br><br>Legal/bureaucratic<br><br>Sanctions–driven | Shared responsibility<br><br>Reciprocal–capacity and results<br><br>Hybrid–professional, legal/bureaucratic, and public<br><br>Assistance-oriented |
| Assessment | Summative–new types (e.g., performance assessments, portfolios) | Summative–standardized tests | Balance of formative and summative<br><br>Systems of multiple measures |

# Part III

# IMPLICATIONS FOR FUTURE NATIONAL POLICY

The learning-centered framework is a theory of education reform that can apply to any level of the system. In Part III, I consider the implications of the learning-centered framework for national policy. What federal role and strategies would be consistent with the learning-centered framework? This part provides readers interested in federal policy with an alternative role conception and a coherent set of strategies that are fundamentally different from past policy. Readers at other levels of the system can use the learning-centered framework presented in Part II as a guide to rethinking policy and practice in their own contexts. Also, the national strategies discussed here may be adapted for other levels of the system.

Before discussing national strategies, it is important to consider the federal role. A review of Figures 5.1 and 6.1 is helpful in thinking about the federal role. The learning triangle depicted in Figure 5.1 reminds us that learning and achievement are co-produced by teachers and students. Thousands of "reformers" in national and state legislatures, bureaucracies, and foundations are impotent unless they can activate teachers and students to identify with and commit themselves to the cause. Is national policy framed in a way that inspires teachers and students to become leaders in education reform?

If we reflect on the interactivity and complexity of the education system as depicted in Figure 6.1, the limits of both top-down and bottom-up control become apparent. The philosophy of a partnership among stakeholders is more consistent with the interactive, horizontal, and complex learning-centered framework. Clearly teachers and students need to be full partners, but the learning-centered framework shows the need to look beyond the formal inter-governmental education system for additional partners, including such entities as professional associations, universities, community groups, foundations, and other stakeholders. Over the years there has been plenty of rhetoric about partnerships in education. However, recent top-down national policy has strayed far afield.

A change in the mindset at the national level is a prerequisite to creating a real partnership for education reform. Partnership is built on trust, but NCLB projects a tone of deep distrust for local educators. More recently, teacher-bashing has become commonplace among some reformers and media spokespersons (let's blame all those bad teachers and their unions). Studies of education reform indicate that mistrust and disrespect undermines progress; indeed, trust and collaboration are critical components of success (Bryk et al., 2010; Spillane & Thompson, 1997). Instead of a "them and us" tone, future federal policy needs to project a "we're all in this together" tone that inspires key stakeholders to collaborate and work together as partners in education reform over the long term.

Two theories of reform found in the literature advocate different strategies (Darling-Hammond, 2004; Elmore, 2003b; Shepard, Hannaway, & Baker, 2009). The first theory assumes that the problem with education is a lack of effort on the part of students and teachers. Schools fail because the people in them don't work hard enough, are lazy, or are unmotivated. From this perspective, the purpose of policy is to motivate people and make them work harder. The assumption is that clear standards and assessments combined with a system of external sanctions and rewards will increase effort and channel it in the direction policymakers desire. Past federal policy is generally consistent with this theory.

The second theory assumes that the demands currently placed on schools to increase performance and close achievement gaps are beyond the capabilities of most schools to attain with existing practices. The best hope for success in reform is to apply new knowledge and to transform practices. Judged against more challenging standards, even practices in the best-performing schools are not optimal, and these schools could improve by using new knowledge. Low-performing schools need to improve even more and at a faster pace to close gaps. The challenge is not working harder at doing more of the same, but learning to do something fundamentally different. Schools need policy support to develop new capacities to address the challenges of reform.

The first of these theories emphasizes top-down goals, extrinsic motivation, and accountability; it ignores issues of capacity and resources. The second emphasizes more challenging goals and capacity-building; it de-emphasizes motivation and accountability. The learning-centered framework is generally consistent with the second theory of reform, but it is incomplete and needs to be extended to include an explicit theory of motivation. Adding this component sharpens the contrast between the two theories, exposes weaknesses in the first, and strengthens the second.

In a recent interview about the implications of his synthesis of the motivation research for education reform, Daniel Pink was asked to sum up his message. He said: "Carrots and sticks are so last century" (Von Zastrow, 2010). Why? He explained that decades of research have shown that extrinsic motivation strategies only work in limited circumstances where compliance with relatively simple and routine tasks is expected. When the work is complex, conceptual, and creative, and high degrees of effort and performance are needed, intrinsic motivation is required. The mistaken application of extrinsic motivation strategies in the wrong circumstances can destroy intrinsic motivation.

Education reform is consistent with the latter kind of goals and work expectations and, therefore, needs to emphasize intrinsic motivation. What fosters intrinsic motivation? Relying primarily on cognitive research, Pink argued that the key elements of intrinsic motivation are a sense of purpose (connecting to a cause larger than oneself), mastery (getting better at doing what matters), and autonomy (directing one's own life). Other researchers have emphasized the importance of relatedness (experiencing a sense of belonging) (Ryan & Deci, 2002).

Sociocultural learning theory suggests how these, and some additional elements, work together in a joint enterprise such as education reform. If active engagement and high performance are desired, then it is necessary to negotiate a common purpose: to coordinate perspectives and actions by convincing, inspiring allegiance, building trust and uniting people; to distribute roles and open avenues for participation; and to create the tools and conditions that provide the capacity to accomplish the work (Wenger, 1998).

This new knowledge about motivation has important implications for education reform. Policy *can* and, if it hopes to succeed, *must* shape the environment in ways that foster intrinsic motivation among all stakeholders, especially teachers and students. Appropriate strategies would include participatory activities to formulate shared goals and a sense of belonging; less top-down control, more distributed responsibility, and autonomy; and capacity-building so everyone involved has the expertise, tools, and resources to do their part. In such a joint enterprise, accountability must be shared and reciprocal.

When partnership becomes an operating principle, rather than just a rhetorical flourish, it implies radical change in future education reform roles and strategies. In Part III, I propose a configuration of national strategies consistent with the learning-centered reform framework and conducive to the development of a real partnership for education reform.

Chapter 10 deals with leadership, goals, and standards. In this chapter I argue that policymakers should begin a new round of reform by negotiating a common purpose with all stakeholders that reaffirms a broad and balanced set of educational goals and a multifaceted concept of outcomes. Because standards can be important tools for operationalizing educational goals and concepts of achievement, I discuss criteria for high-quality standards and the kind of process needed to develop them. Finally, I argue that NCLB performance objectives and AYP requirements are inconsistent with the kind of goals and standards that should serve as a foundation for future reform, and should be abandoned.

The case was made earlier for greater emphasis on capacity-building throughout the education system. In Chapter 11, I suggest an operational definition of educational capacity and argue that the ESEA (and other relevant statutes) should be reframed to focus on building capacity. Research and development is the key driving strategy because capacity grows when new knowledge is created and used to improve performance. Using knowledge requires social capital, including networks and learning communities. The learning triangle suggests four important strategic program focus areas (learning, teaching, content, and leadership) where greater capacity is essential throughout the education system. Because capacity-building requires resources as well as knowledge, more equitable distribution and better use of resources are also important strategies.

An overhaul of accountability policies to make them consistent with the principles of shared and reciprocal responsibility is overdue. In Chapter 12, I sketch the outline of a hybrid accountability system built on these principles that would also facilitate educational improvement. The alternative system would combine professional, bureaucratic, and public accountability approaches. I discuss strategies to turn around struggling schools in Chapter 13. The evidence suggests that stigmatizing them with negative labels and applying harsh sanctions is counterproductive and that future policy should emphasize comprehensive and intensive diagnostic and capacity-building strategies. In the concluding chapter, I summarize how future federal policy should be reframed to reflect the learning-centered vision and offer an interim assessment of the Obama administration's still emerging education policies.

Existing national policies have failed to produce the substantial improvements in student achievement that policymakers want. However, an alternative sense of direction has been missing. The learning-centered framework fills that gap with a theory of action for the future that is comprehensive, coherent, and research-based. This part addresses the future federal role and strategies from a learning-centered perspective.

# CHAPTER 10

# Leadership, Goals, and Standards

Education reform needs national leadership, but it has been lacking from the start. President Reagan left education reform to the states. President George H. W. Bush funded national standards. President Clinton wanted to exert stronger leadership but was constrained by an uncooperative Congress. President George W. Bush moved the federal government to the forefront, but his sanctions-driven strategy for change has undermined progress. Now President Obama has promised change in education policy based on knowledge. One lesson about change that policymakers might take from this checkered history is that stable and effective national leadership for education reform cannot be person-dependent. There is a need for deliberative national institutions and processes with the expertise and legitimacy to carry on over the long term.

An old adage says that leaders know what to do and managers know how to do it. Leaders focus on goals and standards because these define what to do. This chapter considers institutional arrangements, processes, and strategies for how national leaders both in and out of government might reinvent education reform as a more knowledge-based and participatory partnership. In the first section, I consider the need to negotiate common goals that would define the nature of the joint enterprise. Next I discuss criteria for high-quality education standards and the kind of process needed to produce them. Finally, I deal with the issue of what to do about the achievement goals and targets in NCLB.

## EDUCATIONAL GOALS

Each generation must consider what it means to be an educated person, if education is to be a vibrant and relevant enterprise. This means reflecting on the goals of education and the weight that should be assigned to them, the meaning of achievement, and the nature of the school curriculum. Periodically convening deliberative bodies to reflect on these matters is an important aspect of national leadership.

Rothstein and his colleagues (2008) recently reviewed the history of efforts to frame national goals. At the turn of the 20th century, two blue-ribbon committees convened by the National Education Association highlighted the tension between emphasis on academics and life skills. In 1893 the Committee of Ten called for an academic high school curriculum, but significantly expanded the subjects then considered appropriate for a high school diploma and college preparation (National Education Association, 1893; Wechsler, 2001). A quarter-century later, another NEA committee issued the *Cardinal Principles of Secondary Education*, a report that emphasized practical life skills (National Education Association, Commission on the Reorganization of Secondary Education, 1918). Rothstein observed, and comparison with the goals suggested by the learning-centered framework confirms, that both of these reports are unbalanced in opposite ways.

The most recent effort to provide a sense of direction for education was the 1983 report *A Nation at Risk* (National Commission on Excellence in Education, 1983). In its basic assumptions and rhetoric, today's national policy still harks back to that report. Yet much has changed in the intervening years, both in the knowledge base and in the social, economic, and political context of education. Young teachers entering the profession today were not even born when that document was published.

Because educational goals evolve over time, policymaker emphasis on particular goals can be useful in bringing new goals to the attention of educators and the public. Sometimes new goals emerge from events. The connection between education and international economic competitiveness was a new idea a quarter of a century ago when it helped to galvanize reform. Today the rise of terrorism, widespread corporate corruption, and growing economic inequality suggest that greater attention to the social and cultural aspects of globalism, students' moral development, and educational equity may be justified. Sometimes research points toward new education goals. New knowledge about learning implies that an emphasis on the goals of student identity formation and the ability to navigate cultural boundaries might make a difference in closing achievement gaps.

A high profile activity to promote deliberation about the goals of education is an important first step in reframing education reform and providing intellectual leadership for national policy. Instead of a "summit" of high-ranking officials, a more appropriate approach for a partnership in a research-based joint enterprise would be a broad-based dialogue among researchers, policymakers, practitioners, and the grassroots public. Topics addressed might include educational goals, the multiple dimensions of achievement, the balance between commonality and individuality in the school curriculum, and requirements for high school graduation. Consensus on these "big-picture" matters is a prerequisite for coherent subject matter guidance systems in particular subjects.

There are many ways that such a dialogue could be organized. I will suggest one example. At the national level, an authoritative, nonpartisan, scholarly organization(s) could take on the task of commissioning research papers and organizing a participatory national symposium to discuss their implications. All the papers would be available on the Internet as background material for grassroots meetings and the symposium itself might be telecast or webcast to promote public participation. This activity would bring in new research perspectives on these issues.

Similar dialogues could be organized by state, district, and school leaders (through their national associations) all around the United States both to apply research-based ideas and to bring in their own perspectives. Teachers, students, parents, administrators, and other community members would gather in local meeting places to deliberate about their education goals and priorities. A dialogue of this type would not be just an academic exercise. It could inform, improve, and breathe life into school mission statements; feed into district and state strategic improvement plans; and provide a coherent overall context for future content standards and assessments. By highlighting the contributions of education to American society, a well-organized activity of this type might also serve to build support for public education.

Where might the impetus for an initiative like this come from? The best route would be for the national organizations representing educational researchers and practitioners to recognize the intellectual and institutional vacuum at the core of education reform today, organize themselves into a leadership consortium, and step in to provide the missing educational perspective related to goals and the overall content of education. It might be an opportunity for the scholarly education associations (e.g. the National Academy of Education, the National Academies, and/or the American Educational Research Association) to make a contribution to education reform and for the practitioner organizations representing teachers, principals, and administrators to regain some of the influence on national policy they have lost in recent years. Alternatively, the executive branch could use its convening authority to organize such an initiative or Congress could authorize and fund it. Some previous initiatives of this type have been educator-initiated; others have been government-initiated.

## EDUCATIONAL STANDARDS

Educational standards are controversial because they reflect values and beliefs about the goals of education and the nature of knowledge, teaching, and learning. After years of experience with uneven state standards, Barton (2009a) recently indicated that a consensus has formed on the need for change. However, controversy continues over the purpose of standards, criteria for quality, who should participate, and the process for development. The learning-centered framework offers some insights on the purpose of standards and criteria for quality; these ideas have implications for the kind of entity and process needed to develop them.

If a key objective of reform is to use new knowledge to improve education, then content standards can be important tools that embody and communicate new concepts of disciplinary knowledge and of learning and teaching. High-quality content standards have the potential to be the basis for a more rigorous curriculum and a new vision for teaching. Performance standards complement content standards and serve as a basis for assessment; they define various levels of competence that students are expected to reach in the subject matter (e.g., basic, proficient, advanced) (Wixson, Dutro, & Athan, 2003).

Content and performance standards should meet criteria for high quality, but there is not a consensus on what these criteria should be. Several evaluations of standards have used different criteria and reached different conclusions. The National Research Council (NRC) recently synthesized quality criteria used in the past and suggested some additional ones. According to the NRC (2008), standards should reflect the state of knowledge of the larger disciplines and integrate it with current research-based knowledge of learning and teaching. These critical criteria have been missing from past evaluations of standards. The Common Core State Standards Initiative led by the National Governors Association (NGA) and the Council of Chief State School Officers (CCSSO) that is working to develop common state standards emphasizes some additional criteria, including international benchmarking and alignment with college and work expectations.

There are many lessons to be learned from the first round of standards about what it takes to meet the criteria for excellence just discussed. Better quality national standards that reflected disciplinary advances were preceded by syntheses of disciplinary content. For example, in mathematics the NRC produced three authoritative documents that laid a foundation for the original NCTM standards. These publications synthesized knowledge, defined the "big ideas" in mathematics, recommended a philosophy for reshaping the school curriculum, and made a case for reform (NRC, 1989, 1990a, 1990b). In science, the American Association for the Advancement of Science (AAAS) produced a report entitled *Science for All Americans* (Rutherford & Ahlgren, 1989) based on 3 years of collaboration among scientists, philosophers, and educators that synthesized knowledge in the fields of science, mathematics, and technology for school content standards. These examples demonstrate the importance of synthesizing disciplinary knowledge as a foundation for standards and including disciplinary experts in the standards development process in all subject areas.

The learning research suggests many facets of achievement that should be considered in developing standards. It is also necessary to understand students' learning progressions–an ordered set of goals that students would be expected to meet as they progress in a subject. In the past, these progressions have been developed by consensus. Now prominent learning experts recommend that learning progressions be developed through empirical research. Only a few well-researched learning progressions currently exist, so developing them for the entire school curriculum involves a major research investment. Learning progressions are potentially the backbone for both standards and assessments. This is a very ambitious project, but it would allow for significant improvement in standards and assessments (Corcoran, Mosher, & Rogat, 2009; Resnick, Stein, & Coon, 2008). Researchers with expertise in learning, teaching, school subject matter, and assessment have critical expertise to contribute to the development of learning progressions.

Content-area teacher associations have both subject matter expertise and knowledge about how to make standards work in practice. Since teachers are the ultimate implementers of standards, their commitment and buy-in are essential. As already indicated, standard setting is a core function of every profession; it strengthens both professional knowledge and accountability. Earlier experience with the development of standards by teacher professional associations shows that participants often went on to become grassroots leaders in the standards movement (Talbert, 2002). NCTM and AAAS produced tools to facilitate standards implementation, such as Project 2061, a model that other content associations could emulate with adequate funding. A focus on standards at the annual conventions and other meetings of these associations is an important means of professional development. A central role for content-area teacher associations strengthens standards development, implementation, dissemination, and professional accountability.

This analysis of the expertise needed to develop high-quality standards and other analyses (e.g., Barton, 2009a) indicates that no existing entity has the right mix of expertise. Therefore, the best approach for the future might be a collaborative or partnership composed of several kinds of organizations to produce common standards. The National Governors Association (NGA) and the Council of Chief State School Officers (CCSSO) have already formed a partnership that includes Achieve, the American College Testing Program (ACT), and the College Board among the inner circle. Achieve brings expertise in international benchmarking, and the other two organizations have expertise in college readiness.

However, the foregoing discussion suggests that the NGA/CCSSO partnership is too narrow and that core participation should be broadened. If standards development is to be a true joint enterprise with the capability not only to produce high-quality products but to galvanize support for implementation, then disciplinary experts, educational researchers (perhaps through the NRC), and teachers (through the teacher content associations) need to be part of the inner circle, not the periphery. The Obama administration is already encouraging states to adopt the consortium standards; they could also require broader membership and give the group a more permanent status.

A recent study of the standards process compared two contexts in which standards have been developed in the past. One was a deliberative context that, while recognizing the political tensions around standards, seeks consensus. The other is a competitive context that focuses on political victories (Wixson, Dutro, & Athan, 2003). Standards products are likely to be of better quality when the environment is more deliberative/professional and less political/competitive. Political leaders cannot fully control the context, but creating an independent entity that consists of a partnership of respected organizations that collectively have the required expertise would be a step toward the deliberative model.

## GAPS IN ACHIEVEMENT AND ATTAINMENT

Emphasis on closing the "achievement gap," and now also the "attainment gap," has focused national attention on improving outcomes for students who have been left behind in the past. The practice of disaggregating data is an important tool for reducing gaps because it makes visible disparities between more and less advantaged groups of students that were hidden when only school averages were reported. However, the standardized "proficiency for all" as defined in NCLB has been criticized as an oxymoron because, in its expectation that performance gaps can be eliminated in specified subject areas, it fails to recognize that there "is no aspect of human performance or behavior that is not achieved in different degrees by individuals in a large population" (Rothstein, Jacobsen, & Wilder, 2006, p. 17).

While NCLB has directed *more* attention to some inequities in achievement that were not previously visible, the other side of the coin is an important limitation. The focus on a narrowly defined achievement gap makes other kinds of inequities *less* visible. The hidden inequities include gaps in other dimensions of student achievement and attainment, gaps in students' opportunity to learn, gaps in school capacity, and gaps in the resources available to schools. The high-performance case studies and other research indicate that successful schools do not focus myopically on gaps in standardized test scores. They use multiple sources of data, and they aggregate and disaggregate them in sophisticated ways to serve a variety of analytical purposes. For example, they might use data to inform instruction, identify weaknesses in their curriculum, select students for extra help, or identify professional development needs (Supovitz & Klein, 2003).

The targets and timetables for making "adequate yearly progress" (AYP) in raising achievement are too narrow, unrealistic, and not statistically dependable (Linn, 2003). There is no evidence that educational outcomes can be mandated or that threats and punishments will close achievement or attainment gaps. Instead, the evidence from learning theory indicates that outcomes improve when students are placed in a rich learning environment that motivates their best efforts (Bransford, Brown, & Cocking, 2000). Because gaps between more and less advantaged children begin at birth, poor children need intense support for learning at every stage of development, beginning with early childhood education and continuing through graduation (Farkas, 2009). While the idea of closing gaps in achievement and attainment is important, a simplistic statutory mandate is not the right place to require performance targets or specify rates of progress in meeting them.

A future statute should affirm, as the Northwest Ordinance did, the important goals that public education plays in American life that make it worthy of public support. The statute can state aspirations to raise achievement and attainment, and to close gaps between more and less advantaged groups, but leave the specifics to authoritative documents produced through the kind of deliberative processes described in the previous two sections. It can retain requirements to publicly report outcome data, specify the use of multiple measures, and require the disaggregation of standardized test data. However, it should repeal the existing 100% proficiency goal, the narrow focus on reading and mathematics, and the AYP requirement.

## CONCLUSION

Education reform is unlikely to succeed as long as national policymakers define it in terms of top-down control. More effective leadership would seek to unite people in a common enterprise. This involves negotiating a consensus on what to do and then forming a partnership to get it done. Education reform should be defined in a way that will inspire widespread commitment and a desire to participate. Leadership roles and responsibilities should be distributed among key stakeholders. Greater emphasis should be placed on using knowledge of research and best practice because without it, progress will be impossible.

Education goals and standards need to be reframed. A high-profile initiative to encourage national deliberation on the goals of education might be an effective early step in creating a partnership for education reform. High-quality standards can be a tool for disseminating new knowledge about learning, achievement, and the disciplines. The nascent state standards collaborative should be expanded into an entity that includes all of the relevant expertise necessary to develop high-quality content and performance standards, especially disciplinary experts, educational researchers, and teachers.

NCLB proficiency targets, deadlines and AYP requirements, and associated testing mandates should be repealed. Assessment experts have found them to be narrow, unrealistic, and statistically problematic. Evaluations of their implementation have described many undesirable side effects. Most importantly, performance requirements that are simple and standardized enough to fit in a statute will necessarily trivialize the broad and challenging goals and standards that should inspire American education. High-stakes testing should be eliminated.

# CHAPTER 11

# An Emphasis on Capacity-Building

Capacity involves "the wherewithal needed to translate high expectations and standards into effective instruction and strong performance for all students" (Massell, 1998, p. iii). High-capacity organizations produce superior results because they know how to acquire new knowledge and use it to transform their practice (Wenger, McDermott, & Snyder, 2002). Very few education organizations—schools, districts, or state and federal agencies—currently have the capacity for high performance, yet, ironically, current federal policy places very little emphasis on capacity-building. Equally problematic is the fact that conceptions of capacity in federal policy and programs are not consistent with current research-based conceptions.

The argument that capacity-building strategies should move from the background to the foreground of national policy and become a top priority was made in Part II. This chapter has two purposes. The first is to describe the compliance-oriented concept of capacity currently underlying federal policy and then redefine it to be more consistent with research. The second is to draw upon the learning-centered framework as a conceptual resource for analyzing existing federal programs and for making recommendations that would streamline and focus future programs around the key dimensions of educational capacity.

## CAPACITY REDEFINED

In federal categorical programs, capacity-building generally has a compliance orientation. A recent study of state capacity to implement NCLB is representative of the categorical program mind-set. It defined capacity as the ability of state education agencies (SEAs) to implement the mandates of NCLB. Examples of capacities included complying with annual assessment requirements and complying with school choice requirements. The study found that there was "a persistent pattern of tension" between bureaucratic compliance and educational quality (Center on Education Policy, 2007, p.

11). Such tension is not surprising when federal program requirements have become increasingly inconsistent with research and best practice.

There are big conceptual and practical differences between capacity as compliance with legal requirements and capacity as learning to use new knowledge to transform practice. In the standards era, SEAs made some progress in moving from a compliance approach toward one emphasizing improved teaching and learning (Massell, 1998), but the highly prescriptive nature of NCLB and the threat of sanctions has apparently forced states back into a compliance mode.

What does it take to develop the capacity for high performance? According to Spillane and Thompson (1997), capacity can be conceptualized as an interconnected combination of human, social, and physical "capital." Growth in one of these dimensions depends on and may contribute to growth in the other dimensions. The necessary human capital includes the ability to learn the substantive ideas behind knowledge-based reform, the commitment and skill to act on these ideas, and a disposition to learn and help others learn. Social capital consists of relations among individuals. The social capital needed for education reform is built through participation in learning communities or social networks that encourage collaboration on continuous improvement and link reformers throughout the system with one another and with critical sources of knowledge. Finally, physical capital includes the tools and materials, programmatic infrastructure, and financial resources needed to support teaching and learning. Capacity is needed not just in schools but throughout the entire intergovernmental education system.

In considering how national policy can promote capacity throughout the system, capacity-building is best understood as an umbrella strategy under which federal policies and strategies can be more coherently framed. Thus, research and development can promote human capital by developing innovative ideas. New policies to promote reform-oriented social networks can build social capital. Grant program designs aligned with the learning-centered framework can build physical capital related to the key components of education—content, teacher and student supports, and leadership. Adequate and equitable funding is also an essential dimension of physical capacity. Efforts to improve coherence among policy instruments are important because fragmentation and incoherence have become an impediment to reform (Hatch, 2002). Policies and programs should not be viewed separately, but as an interrelated set.

## RESEARCH AND *DEVELOPMENT*

Recognized since the early 1970s as an important aspect of the federal role in education, R&D has never been as critical as it is today. Theories about the nature of learning, teaching, achievement, and appropriate contexts for learning have advanced significantly, largely thanks to decades of federal support, and are now "ripe" for development. The breakthroughs in knowledge offered by this research base potentially provide an intellectual foundation for education reform. Today, using this research, it is possible to piece together a coherent picture of what comprehensive and systemic reform aimed at high achievement for all students might look like, as Part II of this book attempted to do. It is also possible to find schools, districts, and states that have used this research as a foundation for reform and achieved impressive results.

Unfortunately, further development of this forward-looking research and its application to practice was stymied by the Bush administration's national research policies. Today a thorough reorientation of substantive research priorities, the scope of research methods, and the theory of utilization are all necessary.

Different configurations of topics have characterized the missions of R&D center and other grants programs over the years, but generally speaking the priorities have included some combination of research on learning, teaching, school subjects, assessment, and policy. This focus on topics related to the learning triangle is what makes the research educational (Ball & Forzani, 2007) and has contributed knowledge relevant to reform (Koppich & Knapp, 1998). During the Bush Administration many of these core educational topics were deleted from the R&D center program and replaced with ideologically driven topics such as school choice and performance incentives.

Today there is a need to move the research focus back to the educational core. Leaders of the educational research community have recommended a strategic research agenda for the future that would focus on cognition, learning, and human development; student motivation and engagement; continuous school improvement; and local research utilization (National Research Council, 1999). Research in these areas would continue important lines of basic research, but place much more emphasis on development and research utilization.

In the area of research methods, rather than build upon the strong theoretical foundation of basic educational research, which implies that fundamental change is needed, the Bush administration's research priorities emphasized the evaluation of existing programs and practices through randomized experiments. Evaluation of what already exists is a backward-looking research orientation. It assumes that the kind of education we need is already out there; it does not advance theory or practice beyond the status quo. This narrow definition of research is at odds with the much broader definition widely accepted in the research community (Shavelson & Towne, 2002). Evaluation is but one component of a much broader research portfolio that should form the foundation for policy and practice.

Experience has shown that knowledge use is not a hierarchical, linear process where researchers produce knowledge and practitioners consume it. Rather, it is a two-way exchange between those who work in schools and those who work in R&D organizations (Turnbull, 1996; Turnbull & Laguarda, 2006). Basic research, applied research, and development are no longer viewed as separate stages of a linear process that must proceed sequentially. Research projects can often be designed to combine these functions in ways that enable the project to advance both theory and practice. More investment in this kind of research is needed.

Investment in *development* has been woefully inadequate. If research theory is to be translated into practice, embedding new knowledge in practical tools, such as standards, texts, and assessments that are created by researchers and practitioners working together, can be an important strategy for change. For example, Ball and Cohen (1996) described how research-based instructional materials could be developed that would improve teachers' understanding of content and how to build upon students' thinking.

Reflecting on his extensive experience as a researcher and a participant in Chicago school reform efforts, Bryk (2008) recently sketched a development-oriented vision for future educational research. He would like to see research organized around the core problems of practice. Researchers, practitioners, and representatives of commercial organizations that produce many of the textbooks, materials, and technologies used in classrooms would work together to co-construct better ideas, tools, and systems to improve long-term educational performance. These teams would have a practical, engineering orientation. To make scale-up possible, they would consider how innovations work in the hands of different individuals and in varied contexts. Doing this kind of development work would involve rethinking the roles and relationships of universities, schools and school districts, and the commercial sector.

The aspiration to use research as a foundation for policy and practice expressed in NCLB is a very important one. If there is a way to significantly improve education, it is through the use of current and future research advances. However, using scientifically based research involves significant learning and conceptual change (Shavelson, 1988). If policymakers want to turn rhetoric into reality, they must begin by recognizing that it is the prerogative of the research community (not the government) to define research. They must invest their own and their staff's time in learning the big ideas that basic research has to offer and then make sure that the framework and provisions of national policy are consistent. Practice is unlikely to be research-based if policy is not. Finally, they must greatly expand support for research, and especially development, that focuses on the core problems of practice so that knowledge will continue to advance and local educators can access and apply new breakthroughs.

## KNOWLEDGE-BASED NETWORKS FOR REFORM

Although research-based definitions of capacity for high performance include a social dimension, in the past there has been little explicit attention to strategies that address the social aspects of change in national policy. If policymakers want to develop capacity for knowledge-based reform in the future, they cannot afford to overlook policies to facilitate social capacity.

Knowledge use involves learning. Learning communities or social networks can function to span boundaries between research, policy, and practice (Turnbull, 1996; Turnbull & Laguarda, 2006). Using new knowledge about education involves significant conceptual change (Spillane & Thompson, 1997) and cultural change (Stigler & Hiebert, 1999) as well as practical change. Learning communities serve as mediators by negotiating the meaning of external knowledge, coordinating multiple inside and outside perspectives, and working collectively to adapt practice (Coburn & Stein, 2006; McLaughlin & Talbert, 2001; Wenger, 1998).

Two kinds of interconnected social networks are important as components of education reform. One is the intergovernmental network of program administrators and practitioners at the federal, state, and local levels. The other is a growing array of networks and other organizations outside the formal system, such as professional networks and associations, private providers, school–university partnerships, and foundations.

Federal, state, and district bureaucracies are under pressure to improve student achievement and attainment, but their capacity to do so varies considerably (Center on Education Policy, 2007; Marsh, 2000). In response to pressure to raise student achievement, these agencies have been forced to change how they perform traditional roles and take on new roles. This chapter discusses the challenges they face in administering programs and services, as well as the growth of professional learning communities that help many of them improve performance. The next two chapters consider their accountability and compliance functions as well as new demands on them to assist low-performing schools to improve.

The fragmentation of existing federal policy contributes to bureaucratic incoherence throughout the system. State and district education agencies tend to be organized in separate silos reflecting fragmented programs and funding sources. However, some of these bureaucracies have enhanced their capacity in similar ways. They adopted strategic plans with clearly focused goals for student learning and implemented them by transforming program infrastructures to focus on the core of educational practice suggested by the learning-centered framework: challenging content and supports for students, teachers, and principals. They pushed more resources into the poorest, lowest-performing schools. At the same time, they cut extraneous programs and administrative overhead that did not fit into their strategic vision. Some agencies addressed fragmentation by encouraging staff to work in teams across programs and departments (Center on Education Policy, 2007; Darling-Hammond, 2004; Hightower, 2002; Massell, 1998; McLaughlin & Talbert, 2003).

These bureaucratic adaptations do not appear to be widespread, however. A recent survey of state education agency (SEA) staff about their capacity found that generally 20% or less felt they had "a great extent" of capacity. In most areas they rated their capacity as moderate to nonexistent. Areas of concern included: insufficient staff (or staff without the necessary expertise), inadequate funding, inability to assist low-performing districts or schools, and inadequate data systems. SEAs with high numbers of low-performing schools and those in less populated states were particularly challenged. Underscoring the intergovernmental nature of the capacity problem, most SEAs did not find the guidance they got from the U.S. Department of Education to be helpful (Center on Education Policy, 2007).

The minority of state and district agencies that have successfully transformed their practices have also become learning-centric and developed a commitment to continuous improvement (Darling-Hammond, 2004; Hightower, 2002). These organizations recognized that the knowledge needed to improve student outcomes was not in regulations but in research and best practice. Some researchers have called for nested learning communities throughout the educational system where principals assist teachers to learn, superintendents assist principals, and so on (Resnick & Hall, 1998). Another image positions learning communities at the hub of an organization with strategic interconnections to external learning opportunities, such as professional networks (Little, 2006).

The formal education system is increasingly supported by external organizations that supplement its capacity, but these partnerships are underdeveloped. Several functions that social networks can play in developing capacity have been identified in the literature. These networks facilitate learning and change among their own members, create and disseminate research-based products, and provide external assistance and support for improvement (Massell, 1998).

Teacher professional associations and networks are examples of organizations that support the learning of their members. Focused on common aims and interests such as building subject-matter expertise, learning new pedagogies, or examining student work, these organizations have played an important role in school improvement. The National Writing Project is one of the best-known nationally funded teacher professional networks. Some states have funded more extensive content networks, such as the Subject Matter Networks in California (Massell, 1998). Studies have found that networks like these espouse aims that teachers find compelling; build knowledge, expertise, and a sense of identity and community; offer varied learning activities (e.g., summer institutes, conferences, ongoing personal and electronic networks); and develop teacher leadership (Lieberman & Grolnick, 1996; Lieberman & McLaughlin, 1992; Lieberman & Wood, 2003).

Networks for principals and district superintendents have emerged to facilitate leadership, collaborative improvement, and change. One example is the Western States Benchmarking Consortium, where seven large school districts have adopted a common improvement framework and the members regularly share best practices. An example of an external intermediary organization that assists districts is the Institute for Learning (IFL), housed at the University of Pittsburgh. IFL helps districts to connect the learning research with educational practice. Their strategy has been called "adaptive assistance" because they customize their assistance to each district's needs and because there is a two-way reciprocal learning relationship (Honig & Ikemoto, 2008). IFL forms partnerships with districts and works to transform districts into learning organizations. In addition to customized, applied knowledge, IFL offers practical tools; professional development opportunities for central office staff, principals, and teacher leaders; and networking opportunities for participating districts (Honig & Ikemoto, 2008; Marsh et al., 2005; Resnick & Glennan, 2002).

Some researchers have observed, "It takes capacity to build capacity" (Hatch, 2001, p. 44). Policymakers have long been concerned with gaps between rich and poor schools, districts, and states in resources and outcomes. However, the gap between the rich and the poor in the more intangible resources of human and social capital is also widening and poses a major policy challenge for anyone concerned about educational equity. The well positioned tend to be rich not only in material resources, but in human capital (especially leaders' knowledge and skills) and in various forms of social capital (connections to sources of knowledge, norms of collegiality, trust). Without human and social capital, it is unlikely that material resources will be used effectively (Spillane & Thompson, 1997).

An education system high in social capital would have interconnected learning communities at all levels: within schools in departments or other subunits; schoolwide improvement teams; task forces or work groups at the district and state levels; district-supported networks of principals; networks linking policymakers, researchers, and educators; and so on (Resnick & Hall, 1998). Multiple sources of external opportunities to learn and sources of assistance would be available at all levels of the system to match organizational needs at different stages of development. Currently, effective professional learning communities are rarely found in schools or elsewhere in the education system (McLaughlin & Talbert, 2006). Contexts that foster social and human capital will remain rare without policy support to scale up this critical dimension of educational capacity.

Future legislation should recognize the importance of human and social capital, and give it considerably more visibility and support, by creating a new title in ESEA to support Knowledge-Based Reform Networks. Like Title V of the original ESEA (which was designed to build SEA capacity), the new title would build the capacity for learning-centered education reform, not just at the state level, but throughout the intergovernmental system and beyond. This new policy initiative would have two main objectives. First, it would support the development of human and social capacity within state and district agencies. Second, it would support external professional networks that would enable practitioners to learn about best practices from one another and to link them in partnerships with sources of formal research knowledge.

Capacity-building funds for SEAs and local education agencies (LEAs) would not be narrowly program-focused. Each SEA might receive an amount that would include funds for itself and some that could be suballocated to districts. These funds could be used to build nested learning communities; to hire new staff in areas needed to improve learning and teaching; to support strategic planning; to collaborate with other states, districts, or external partners; to expand their capacity to provide assistance to low-performing districts or schools; or to upgrade data systems.

With regard to external networks, the descriptions of initiatives by various states and associations in this chapter have already hinted at some programmatic ideas. The new title should also support networks to enable practitioners to learn about best practices from one another, to partner with organizations that can link them with research, or both. Taking a cue from California, the federal government should scale up the National Writing Project by extending this model to other subjects. Networks for principals, district administrators, and school improvement teams to facilitate benchmarking should be supported. The IFL "adaptive assistance" strategy should be scaled up.

The new title should provide for research and evaluation. Because understanding of the human and social dimensions of capacity is still in an early stage, support for further research on how it develops and what effects it has on performance in different kinds of educational settings would be useful. Quality control is an issue mentioned in the literature on professional networks (Lieberman & McLaughlin, 1992). Therefore, more systematic formative and summative evaluations of these networks would also be useful. Increased support for the development of social capital appears to be a relatively low-cost but potentially high-leverage initiative, especially in schools and districts serving poor students.

## LEARNING-CENTERED GRANT PROGRAMS

Future legislation should address two problems with federal grant programs. The first is a philosophical one. These programs are conditional grants that theoretically involve transfers of money in return for the production of goods or services. It is assumed that grantees already have the capacity to fulfill the requirements of the grant, but the will or the resources needed to mobilize action are lacking (McDonnell & Elmore, 1987). The original intent of the large federal categorical programs was to increase the allocation of funds available to provide compensatory services for students with special needs. After some compliance problems in the early years, states and districts generally developed the capacity to administer categorical grant programs.

However, legislation during the standards era, and now NCLB, has created a new layer of capacity problems by going beyond requirements related to funds allocation and service provision. More recent legislation first encouraged, then mandated, student outcome expectations that are beyond the reach of typical schools. As long as challenging outcome expectations are retained as policy objectives, there is a concomitant task of building comprehensive and systemic capacity. Thus, conditional grants in education need to be reconceptualized so that instead of assuming preexisting capacity, they embody a capacity-building strategy.

The second problem involves incoherence and system overload. Schools and local districts are overwhelmed by numerous and conflicting external demands. Policies and programs emanating from multiple levels of government representing different, and often conflicting, philosophies all converge at the local level. Frequent changes in policy exacerbate the problem (Hatch, 2001). Two strategies to address system overload have been identified (Honig & Hatch, 2004). One is called the "outside-in" or top-down approach that seeks simplification and better alignment of policy strategies. The other approach is "inside-out" or bottom-up coherence. It involves strengthening within-school improvement processes so that school leaders can "craft coherence" by setting goals, choosing appropriate improvement strategies, and managing external demands. Future national policy can simultaneously pursue both of these paths.

In this section, I consider how the learning-centered framework developed in Part II might serve as a template for reframing ESEA programs and designing a new educationally sound and coherent infrastructure that focuses on building capacity. National policymakers should reframe the main titles of ESEA around the elements of capacity identified by the learning-centered framework: supporting student learning and achievement, improving teaching and leadership, and strengthening content. These areas, along with the cross-cutting area of adequate and equitable resources that is discussed in the next section, encompass the physical dimensions of capacity. In addition, a title should be created to build social capacity throughout the system (as discussed in the previous section). Finally, there should be a title for accountability and cross-cutting school improvement programs (as discussed in Chapters 12 and 13).

Each of the proposed ESEA titles would specify a limited number of important capacity and accountability objectives. All the programs relevant to those objectives would be moved to that title. Some program gaps might need to be filled. Programs that do not fit within the scope of any objective would be candidates for elimination. The Appendix summarizes a streamlined and simplified ESEA structured along these lines.

Attaining important capacity and accountability objectives will require an unprecedented level of vertical and horizontal coordination throughout the intergovernmental system. Vertical coordination involves federal, state, and local programs throughout the system. Horizontal coordination refers to collaboration among education programs or among education, health, social service, and other program areas at any particular level of government. The ESEA could employ several possible strategies to promote collaboration and better coordination.

Both vertical and horizontal coordination might be enhanced if, instead of the traditional program-by-program state plan application, each state were required to submit a long-term strategic plan to the U.S. Department of Education (USDE) for each of the main areas of capacity and accountability (i.e., each title). State strategic plans would apply the applicable objectives to their circumstances, describe how they plan to use funds from multiple federal and state programs to attain the objectives, and include timetables. Waivers might be allowed, if necessary, to shape specific programs to larger objectives. To foster quality, and bring in perspectives reflecting research and best practice, the USDE should be given the responsibility to organize peer review panels of outside experts who would review plans and provide feedback. However, the states should have discretion in how they utilize the feedback. Studies of successful state and district agencies indicate that some of them already use strategic planning processes to reduce fragmentation and promote coherence (Hightower, 2002; McLaughlin & Talbert, 2003). Federal legislation could scale-up the practice.

The new ESEA might also authorize a federal interagency task force in each of the main areas of capacity to improve horizontal coordination. These groups would work on streamlining, simplifying, and coordinating related federal programs to serve capacity objectives. Mechanisms for horizontal communication have been found to be important for integrating services at other levels of the system (Honig, 2006b), and it is logical to assume that they could also be useful at the federal level.

In the remainder of this chapter, I suggest some objectives for building capacity in the strategic priority areas suggested by the learning-centered framework. Then I consider which existing programs logically fit into each area and the extent to which they address or fail to address the capacity objective(s). I identify gaps where new initiatives are needed as well as constraints that should be removed. The analysis is intended to be illustrative, not exhaustive. It is beyond the scope of this book to analyze all federal programs. In the next chapter, I analyze accountability in the same way.

Since Title I, ESEA, has always been concerned with student needs and services, I begin with the objective of building a comprehensive and systemic infrastructure of supports for all students that will enable them to reach their full potential and narrow achievement and attainment gaps among groups. Every school needs a seamless continuum of supports matched to the needs of each student. All students need a rich environment of academic and extracurricular opportunities, and sometimes they need extra help or tutoring, in order to reach their full potential. However, the most disadvantaged students, especially those in schools with high concentrations of poverty, need a broader and more intense array of supports. They need these comprehensive and intense supports at all ages and grade levels, including preschool (Farkas, 2009). The problem for the future is to figure out how to integrate the core education program, compensatory education, and noneducational services (e.g., health, social services) into a continuum of appropriate student support.

The research on schools and districts that doubled student achievement in some subject areas found that they used a combination of federal, state, and local funds (and sometimes foundation funds) to develop coherent infrastructures of student supports. These support systems included various combinations of such initiatives as early childhood education, smaller classes in the early grades, one-on-one or small-group tutoring, extended-day academic help programs, summer school, and English development programs for English language learners (Odden et al., 2007). Instead of placing an extraordinary burden on local leaders to transform incoherent policies into a student support system like this, how can the federal program infrastructure be more aligned with the basic capacity objective?

Federal policymakers should consider placing all the programs in ESEA that contribute to the goal of building an infrastructure of student supports under the same legislative umbrella in Title I. There are two types of programs that would fit. The first is the equity programs targeted for specific categories of students: low-achieving students in poverty, migrants, neglected and delinquent, English language learners, immigrants, Native American, Alaska Native, and Native Hawaiian children. Unnecessary constraints within these programs, such as the Title I requirement that supplemental education services be provided by outside vendors, should be repealed.

The second type of relevant program focuses on specific student-related problems or services, such as dropout prevention or safe and drug-free schools. Policymakers should consider whether these specific programs are consistent with current priorities and with research about the kinds of supports students need. Some may be retained or revised, others eliminated. For example, in view of the current emphasis on dropout prevention, the existing program may be too small. Perhaps it is time for a more substantial program that would enable every middle and high school to take advantage of current research on early warning indicators (Allensworth & Easton, 2005; Balfantz, Herzog, & MacIver, 2007) and effective dropout intervention programs (What Works Clearing House, 2009).

In the next priority area, building a comprehensive and systemic infrastructure to improve teaching and leadership, two policy objectives related to capacity should be considered. The first objective is to develop an infrastructure of high-quality professional learning opportunities for teachers and administrators that begins with preservice education, continues throughout their careers with a combination of job-embedded and external opportunities, and enables them to meet high standards (Feiman-Nemser, 2001). The second is an equity objective, already in NCLB, that states show progress toward ensuring that poor and minority students are not taught by inexperienced, out-of-field, or otherwise unqualified teachers at higher rates than are other students. More attention is needed to research-based strategies in both professional development and teacher allocation. Additional objectives to improve teaching and leadership through professional accountability are discussed in Chapter 12.

The federal government is currently making a large investment in teacher and administrator development, including NCLB, Title II (primarily inservice); the Higher Education Act (HEA), Title II (primarily preservice); and numerous smaller professional development programs for teachers of specific student subpopulations and subjects. However, a recent GAO audit focusing on the two largest programs in NCLB and HEA concluded: "It is not clear the extent to which they complement each other" (Birman et al., 2007, p. 12). GAO found that the districts spent over 50% of their NCLB program funds in 2004–05 on class size reduction. An evaluation of the NCLB program found that the professional development experienced by 80% of the teachers served was only of a limited duration (Birman et al., 2007).

These two substantial pots of federal funds each contain a fragmented laundry list of allowable activities, but judging from the program evaluations, the choices that grantees appear to be making about the use of these funds are not resulting in a high-capacity infrastructure for improving teaching or leadership. This is an example of an area where having clearly defined objectives for capacity-building could be beneficial. ESEA and HEA might give states the option of submitting a joint strategic plan, describing how funds from those two federal sources plus state funds would be used to achieve the capacity and accountability objectives listed in the Appendix. It is all right to have menus of allowable activities and state discretion in choosing among them as long as the activities work in a coordinated fashion toward worthwhile reform objectives. The idea of a federal-level committee for horizontal program coordination would respond directly to GAO's concerns in the area of quality teaching and leadership.

Future legislation might make allowable activities more consistent with research about best practices by encouraging learning communities as the hub of a system of supports for professional learning (Little, 2006). Also, we have strong evidence that certain characteristics of professional development programs are positively related to student achievement. The content focus should be on helping teachers improve their knowledge of how students learn specific subjects and expand their repertoire of strategies for teaching the subject. Teachers should be able to directly use the program content to improve curriculum and instruction. Finally, programs should involve extended learning time and actively engage teachers (Blank & de las Atlas, 2009).

Attracting and retaining teachers in schools serving predominantly poor and minority students requires a combination of strategies such as improved working conditions, extra efforts to recruit and retain teachers, and leadership and administrative support. Recruitment strategies might include service scholarships and forgivable loans for teacher candidates (Darling-Hammond, 2006) or pay bonuses for practicing teachers. Recruitment strategies are unlikely to be effective, however, unless they are combined with workplace improvements and retention strategies. Because so many teachers in these schools are new, multicomponent induction programs are probably the most important workplace enhancement needed to improve retention (Smith & Ingersoll, 2004). Other workplace conditions that might be addressed include administrative support and student discipline (Ingersoll, 2004; Johnson, 2006). If ESEA, Title II is to focus on teacher capacity and professional accountability, the class size reduction component might be eliminated, capped, or focused on low-performing schools.

In the third main priority area related to capacity, strengthening educational content, there are at least two key capacity objectives. The first one, already discussed in Chapter 10, is to form a consensus around a broad and balanced set of educational goals for all students, a concept of achievement that emphasizes its multiple facets, and what high school graduates should know and be able to do. The second objective discussed here is to create a complete content infrastructure in each subject area, including challenging standards, curriculum, textbooks, materials, and assessments. These content infrastructure components should be aligned with one another, with challenging learning goals, and with teacher professional development.

Currently, there is no central focus in the ESEA on content. Inattention to a better content infrastructure is the result of long-standing political opposition to federal government control of the school curriculum. In our federal system, education has always been recognized as a state responsibility. Supporters of high-stakes testing may not want to admit it, but this NCLB policy is exerting substantial (and inappropriate) control over the school curriculum through the back door. Eliminating high-stakes testing is a necessary, but not sufficient, step toward improving content. It is also a step toward eliminating the excess federal control that many people believe NCLB represents.

Reverting to the pre-NCLB content vacuum, however, is not a good alternative. There is a consensus on the shortcomings of existing state content systems: a great deal of variability in the content and quality of standards, lack of alignment between standards and assessments, and very different proficiency expectations. Some observers think the time is right for another attempt at creating a better content infrastructure (Barton, 2009b). A politically acceptable entity that includes the necessary expertise, long-term strategic planning, and adequate resources is essential to get the job done. Therefore, a new title should be created—let's call it Title III—that begins with the key content capacity objectives stated previously and authorizes appropriate institutional arrangements and strategies.

Nowhere is the concept of partnership more important than in creating an entity to improve the school content infrastructure. The responsible entity needs three types of expertise: knowledge about the states and the education policy context, knowledge about the academic disciplines and the scientific opportunities afforded by educational research, and knowledge about best practice and what teachers need to implement standards. As indicated in Chapter 10, the NGA and CCSSO are already leading a fast-track project to create common standards. If national policymakers are going to support and subsidize this activity, the ESEA should require that the partnership be expanded. Research organizations should be added, such as the National Academy of Education and/or the National Research Council, and they should be charged with bringing in disciplinary and other experts as needed when the work shifts from subject-to-subject. Teacher content associations should also be added both to bring in the practical knowledge and expertise of their members and to encourage the teacher buy-in and support that is critical at the implementation stage.

The type of state strategic plan recommended in the other priority areas is not relevant in the content area. However, Congress should authorize the expanded content entity to develop two types of strategic plans. One is a short-term plan to ensure coordination and coherence among the standards setting and assessment development activities already underway in language arts and mathematics. The short-term plan should also address a variety of other as yet unanswered questions. What work needs to be done to develop curriculum and the other materials needed for a complete, aligned content infrastructure in the language arts and mathematics? What about content infrastructures for other subjects?

If the ultimate goal in developing content capacity is to take full advantage of the scientific opportunities in all of the core subjects, some experts have estimated that it would take about a decade and require a considerable amount of R&D (Shepard, Hannaway, & Baker, 2009). Examples of some of the kinds of R&D needed include developing learning progressions, researching best practices in teaching and learning (especially in subject areas that have been neglected), and synthesizing the most significant concepts and new developments in the disciplines.

A more optimal, state-of-the-art content infrastructure may never come into being unless today's policymakers are farsighted enough to proceed on two tracks at the same time. The short-term track, already ongoing, would yield products that will result in some improvement now. The long-term track would produce a plan for the next round of content improvement. The planning and R&D for the second round would begin now, but implementation would not take place for another decade. The capacity to develop and carry out a long-term project is, of course, contingent upon having a permanent entity with the expertise and resources to do the work.

Compared to the cost of providing direct services to support teachers and students, developing a better content infrastructure is cheap. However, compared to the miniscule amount that has been spent on this objective in the past, it may seem expensive. There is a need for both federal government funding and safeguards against too much federal government control. Precedents exist for "no strings" federal funding of independent entities. One good example is the role the federal government played in supporting the National Board for Professional Teaching Standards.

Programs related to a wide variety of school subjects are scattered throughout the ESEA, including reading, writing, mathematics, science, civics, economics, history, foreign languages, the arts, physical education, and character education. Except for the larger reading programs, most of these are small discretionary grant programs. Many programs are highly prescriptive, directing funds to a particular grantee or a specific approach to the subject (e.g., "traditional" American history). A few (e.g., the arts) authorize a more systemic range of improvement strategies. There is substantial funding for technology programs that can enhance content.

Programs that support state and local efforts to improve content should be continued. The disparate collection of programs related to content should be brought together under the new Title III and organized under a more coherent framework that reflects major disciplinary divisions, such as English language arts, the STEM subjects, social studies, and the arts and humanities. In order to demonstrate a shift from a narrow curriculum to a broad and balanced curriculum that can produce well-rounded students, these major curricular categories should be more equally funded. In addition, there should be a category that includes nonacademic areas, such as physical education, and social and emotional development. The language in some programs that prescribes what and how to teach is not consistent with the limited constitutional role of the federal government in education, and should be repealed.

## RESOURCE DISTRIBUTION AND USE

More equitable distribution of educational resources has been a policy goal for decades and resources are an important dimension of capacity. Two main strategies have been employed: intrastate school finance equalization through the courts and categorical assistance programs to pay for extra services to students with special needs. Despite numerous school finance court cases, fiscal disparities have improved only slightly over the years. Unless they rest on an equitable foundation, compensatory education programs do not provide extra services to needy students as they are intended to do. In fact, the local-state-federal intergovernmental school finance system is a layer cake of inequities at every level. Some school finance experts have concluded that "school finance systems are aging and in need of repair" and that it is time to invent "new school finance structures appropriate for the education goals of today" (Odden & Clune, 1998, p. 157).

A new school finance structure would combine several approaches. It would emphasize the concept of adequacy as well as that of equity. Adequacy directly ties school finance policy to the objectives of higher student achievement and attainment by requiring that every school have a base level of spending that is adequate to enable the average child to attain high minimum standards. On top of an adequate base, the next task is to identify how much extra each school requires to ensure that special-needs students, including those with disabilities, those from low-income backgrounds, and English language learners, can attain outcome standards (Odden & Clune, 1998). The school would be the base unit in the new finance system and would be given more responsibility and flexibility for its own budget (Goertz & Odden, 1999).

These new ideas about school finance have significant implications for federal policy. First, according to Rothstein (2000) the greatest source of disparity in school finance is *interstate* inequality. These interstate inequities have never been addressed by national policymakers, although it would be impossible to set meaningful school adequacy and equity targets without doing so. Per-pupil expenditures in the lowest-spending states are, on the average, approximately half of per-pupil expenditures in the highest-spending states. This means that the poorest children in the high-spending states have more resources available for their education than the wealthiest children in the low-spending states. Action to address inequities in interstate financing is clearly a federal responsibility. Doing so would require a new school finance initiative that brings the low-spending states up to a more adequate level, taking states' capacity to pay and cost-of-living differentials into account (Rothstein, 2000).

The second and third steps in reframing school finance policy involve addressing inequities between districts within states and between schools within districts (Odden & Clune, 1998; Rothstein, 2000). Some experts have advocated putting more teeth in state level school finance equalization by mandating fiscal equity targets for state-to-district finance reform. Most states now have foundation formulas (or similar policies) to ensure some level of minimum expenditure. However, greater equity would be achieved by setting equity policy targets (such as the median or a specified percentile) that would result in a more adequate level of expenditure in all districts (Odden & Clune, 1998).

A substantial source of inequity between schools within districts is the maldistribution of experienced (and, therefore, more highly paid) teachers who gravitate to schools in wealthier communities. When school districts do their budgeting, however, they assume that all teachers are paid an average salary. This practice and other accounting gimmicks shortchange the poorest schools and make it appear that school budgets are more equal than they really are. The first step to correcting this problem is requiring reality-based budgeting that would make the funding differentials transparent. Then, between-school inequities could be offset by such strategies as paying bonuses to teachers in hard-to-staff schools; improving the often unsatisfactory working conditions in these schools; assigning extra teachers, counselors, or other support staff; or increasing student support services such as tutoring, extended-day, or summer programs (Carey & Roza, 2008; Rothstein, 2000).

Finally, federal compensatory education funding formulas and requirements need to be coordinated with overall adequacy and equity goals. Title I is supposed to provide extra funding for children in high-poverty schools, but several program features undermine this intent. First, although Title I funding is distributed by formula to the states based upon the number of children in poverty, because the funding per student is tied to the average amount of state and local funding per student, wealthy states receive more per student than poor states. Title I contains a "comparability" requirement that says school districts must equalize educational services paid for with state and local funds to ensure that the federal funds are extra. However, the comparability requirement disregards salary differentials for seniority and accepts incomplete accounts of expenditures that allow other inequities to be hidden. A better school finance system would correct the disequalizing aspects of the Title I formula and the comparability requirement (Carey & Roza, 2008; Roza, 2008).

At the same time, future federal and state policy should increase compensatory funding overall. Assumptions common in the early days of these programs that a year of Head Start and a little remedial education in the elementary grades would close achievement gaps have proven wrong. Recent studies of what it would take to improve the educational outcomes of poor children have found that to narrow achievement gaps substantially, more extra supports are needed throughout the grades than are typically provided (Hart & Risley, 1995; Lee & Burkam, 2002; Rothstein, 2004). A recent synthesis of the research on achievement gaps indicated that the most powerful factors influencing educational inequality lie outside school. To counteract these environmental effects, early preschool is important, as well as consistent monitoring of student progress throughout the grades, with immediate supplementary assistance provided any time that a student starts falling behind (Farkas, 2009).

Debates about whether money matters in education have gone on for years, but the current research literature reconceptualizes this issue in very significant ways. First, it expands the conventional concept of resources to include such factors as the knowledge and skills that teachers and students bring to a learning situation. Second, research suggests that resources by themselves will not automatically lead to better outcomes—it is *how resources are used* in practice that matters. Thus, student learning and achievement depend on the mobilization and effective use of a complex collection of knowledge and skills, conventional resources, and collective action. In short, "what students and teachers do with resources is no less consequential than the resources which schools deploy" (Cohen, Raudenbush, & Ball, 2000, p. 5).

Effective use must be added to equity and adequacy as a future policy goal related to resources. Successful schools and school systems deploy resources differently and more coherently than less effective ones (Miles & Darling-Hammond, 1997; Newmann et al., 2001). In setting priorities the high-performance schools and districts strategically focused on the learning triangle, and they used research-based ideas and programs as foundations for reform. The next chapter discusses a system of school improvement and accountability that would encourage effective use of resources.

The research on education finance suggests the need for change in federal policy. It is unrealistic to expect that high performance can be "scaled up," as policy rhetoric suggests it should be, or demanded from the poorest schools, without access to the necessary resources. Large-scale reform will require an overhaul of the intergovernmental school finance system that addresses the issues of equity, adequacy, and effective use.

Future legislation should include a new title to ensure that every school has adequate and equitable funding. This title would include a new interstate school equalization program and stronger fiscal equity targets for state-to-district funding. Features of Title I that exacerbate fiscal inequity should also be corrected. Because it serves an equity purpose by reimbursing local jurisdictions with tax-exempt federal property for the local revenue lost, the

Impact Aid program should be moved into this title. As in most of the other main areas of capacity, long-term state strategic plans should be negotiated that focus on the objectives of education finance adequacy, equity, and effective use and propose specific steps and timetables to meet them.

## CONCLUSION

If education reform is to be scaled up in the future, development of the capacity to access and apply new knowledge must become a top priority. Educational capacity involves an interconnected combination of human, social, and physical capital. Existing federal programs and policies are not well aligned with the dimensions of capacity. Past federal policy made little attempt to build comprehensive and systemic capacity. Instead, layer upon layer of uncoordinated federal, state, and local policies and programs have created an incoherent environment that overwhelms many schools. The burden is on local educators to repackage programs so they make educational sense.

The ESEA is potentially a tool for communicating learning-centered reform priorities and building capacity throughout the system. Future federal legislation should use the learning-centered framework as a strategic template to streamline and focus programs and policies on key areas where capacity needs to be developed throughout the education system. Each new title would specify long-term targets or objectives for capacity development. Within the areas of capacity defined by each title, states would submit strategic plans explaining how they will meet objectives for capacity development. Interagency committees would facilitate horizontal program coordination within the federal government. An outline of a new ESEA organized along these lines can be found in the Appendix.

The primary authorization for R&D functions in the U.S. Department of Education is in a separate statute, the Education Sciences Reform Act (ESRA) of 2002. Because learning-centered reform is knowledge-based, substantially increased investment in R&D and reorientation of research priorities are essential components of capacity. Change is needed in all aspects of research policy: the content of research priorities, research methods, and the theory of utilization. Future research agendas should focus on the educational core: learning, teaching, content, leadership, and effective educational contexts. A broad spectrum of research designs and methods should be encouraged, as well as innovative thinking about how research and practice connect. It is appropriate for federal legislation to encourage research-based practices, but it should not define the meaning of scientific research. Policymakers should defer to the research community on this point.

# CHAPTER 12

# Accountability
# and Improvement

The learning-centered framework described an alternative accountability theory that emphasized the principles of shared responsibility and reciprocity. In this chapter, I apply those principles to federal policy by recommending a hybrid system for the future that combines professional, bureaucratic, and public accountability. In the hybrid system, the goal of improved student outcomes is shared, but stakeholders play different roles in attaining it. Professional accountability emphasizes the collective responsibility of educators for establishing and maintaining high standards of practice. Bureaucratic accountability emphasizes the responsibility of administrators and policymakers for providing the necessary infrastructure and resources. The public is empowered to monitor both the inputs and the outputs.

Lessons from the states can also inform future national accountability policy. State experience prior to NCLB indicates that an accountability system composed of unrealistic goals, high pressure, and minimal support is counterproductive (Lee, 2006; Mintrop & Trujillo, 2005). A better national accountability system, like the more successful state systems, would combine goals that are challenging but attainable, strong support for system capacity, and a medium degree of pressure.

Previous chapters in this part addressed educational goals and capacity-building. In this chapter, I propose a combination of accountability strategies that would exert a medium degree of pressure throughout the system, not just on schools.

## PROFESSIONAL ACCOUNTABILITY AND TEACHING

Over a decade ago a blue-ribbon group called the National Commission on Teaching and America's Future (NCTAF) argued that strengthening professional accountability was an important strategy to improve teaching. NCTAF pointed out that most professions develop their own standards of practice and then use a three-legged stool to ensure quality control: accreditation of professional education, requirements for initial licensing, and certification of advanced expertise (NCTAF, 1996). The three-legged stool is underdeveloped in the education profession. Some of these standards-setting and evaluation functions are handled by the profession and some by the states. NCTAF recommended a shift in the locus of control from bureaucratic to greater professional accountability, and since then there has been some movement in that direction.

What is the rationale for this shift? Considerable authority is granted to most professions to set and enforce standards of practice because their practice is informed by specialized knowledge. In education the body of knowledge that can inform teaching has developed relatively recently (Cochran-Smith & Zeichner, 2005; Darling-Hammond & Bransford, 2005; Richardson, 2001). Professional accountability is an important strategy to improve teaching because the tasks associated with it serve to develop and disseminate new knowledge within the profession. For example, the development of teaching standards that draw upon research and best practice applies and extends theory. Also, new knowledge is disseminated when it is embedded in accreditation criteria and in exams for licensing and certification (Darling-Hammond et al., 2005). The more the knowledge base in education grows, the more important strengthening professional accountability becomes as a strategy to improve teaching and learning.

Therefore, in addition to the capacity objectives discussed in Chapter 11, legislative objectives for building a comprehensive and systemic infrastructure to improve teaching and leadership should include the objective of strengthening professional accountability. This can be accomplished by requiring states to establish professional standards boards for teaching and school leadership. As in other professions, these boards would develop and enforce rigorous professional standards, licensing requirements, and evaluation systems that include peer review. In establishing partnerships for education reform, no partners are more important than practicing teachers and administrators themselves.

Advanced teacher certification is the most developed of the potential mechanisms for professional accountability. The National Board for Professional Teaching Standards (NBPTS), an independent professional organization, has since 1993 offered teachers the opportunity for advanced certification. The operational phase of NBPTS was preceded by multiyear research projects at Stanford and the University of North Carolina that synthesized research on teaching, developed a vision of advanced teaching, studied certification processes in other professions, and developed measurement methodology. As of 2009, about 74,000 teachers have earned advanced certification.

A recent study by the National Academies found that students of board-certified teachers have higher achievement test gains than those taught by non-board-certified teachers, that teachers found the certification process to be a valuable professional development experience, and that the well-regarded standards- and performance-based certification process has had a positive influence on processes for initial teacher certification and accreditation of schools of education (Hakel, Koenig, & Elliott, 2008). The NBPTS is a successfully functioning national institution advancing education reform that probably could not have been developed without federal government subsidy. It is a good example of government support without control.

The initial licensure of teachers and other professionals is intended to ensure that they demonstrate the knowledge, skills, and disposition needed to practice responsibly. Individual states are responsible for licensing teachers, and their requirements vary considerably. According to a recent study (Wilson & Youngs, 2005), most states award an initial license after candidates complete an approved teacher education program. Forty-two states also require some form of teacher testing. However, 45 states have alternative licensing programs that usually require only a bachelor's degree. Most states have a staged licensing process: the initial license is good for 3 to 5 years, and a permanent license may be granted when additional requirements are fulfilled. To earn a permanent license, some states require performance-based assessments of actual teaching.

Systems of teacher and administrator licensure in education are beginning to change. Some states have established professional standards boards similar to those in other professions. Connecticut has invested over 2 decades of effort to establish a model standards-based licensing system for teachers and administrators. Connecticut's comprehensive teaching quality agenda involved developing aligned standards for students, teachers, and administrators and linking these to more demanding performance-based licensing and recertification requirements, as well as to evaluation and professional development policies (Wilson, Darling-Hammond, & Berry, 2001).

Other states are moving in a similar direction. In 2002, an interstate consortium published teaching standards for beginning teachers that presently serve as the basis for licensing in 38 states. The consortium, now known as the Interstate Teacher Assessment and Support Consortium (InTASC), is currently updating and expanding their teaching standards to provide a basis for professional practice that can apply at different levels of sophistication throughout a teachers' career (Darling-Hammond, 2001; InTASC, 2010). A similar interstate consortium, the Interstate School Leaders Licensure Consortium (ISLLC), developed a broad set of national guidelines for administrators and encouraged states to use them to update and improve their own licensing standards (ISLLC, 2008).

Federal policy can advance reform in teacher and administrator licensing. First, policymakers should retain the NCLB requirement that teachers be fully licensed. In addition, they should consider strengthening professional accountability by requiring every state to establish a professional state standards and licensing board, a recommendation made over a decade ago to the states by NCTAF but unevenly implemented (1996). Finally, policymakers should invest in R&D related to assessment and licensing of educators (Wilson & Youngs, 2005) as well as evaluation of model systems such as the one in Connecticut.

In other professions candidates must graduate from an accredited professional school before taking the state licensing examination, but this is not so in education. There is an independent professional organization, the National Council for the Accreditation of Teacher Education (NCATE), which accredits schools of education. About 10 years ago NCATE revised its standards to make them compatible with NBPTS, InTASC, and national student content standards. NCATE is now in the process of updating its standards again. However, only about half the nation's schools of education are NCATE-accredited. The others may be accredited by the Teacher Education Accreditation Council (TEAC), which uses a generic self-study approach; state accrediting agencies whose standards vary considerably; or not at all. To complicate the picture further, many alternate routes outside the university systems prepare teachers, such as Teach for America.

A consensus about how to improve teacher preparation is clearly lacking and the debate is highly politicized. The argument is often framed around traditional versus alternative routes, but research suggests that the terms of this debate are unproductive. There is as much variation within these categories as there is between them. The real issue is defining the substantive components of a high quality program. Several sequential steps are needed to resolve the political debate and strengthen teacher preparation. First, the government should support a new generation of research to determine the actual substantive characteristics of effective preparation programs (Zeichner & Conklin, 2005). Later, if this research yields clarification, accreditation criteria should be made consistent with the findings. As a third step, federal policy should require (or at least provide incentives for) professional accreditation of all preservice programs, whether they are within or outside schools of education. A long-term perspective is needed in this area because the third step might be a decade in the future.

## TEACHER EVALUATION AND COMPENSATION

Teacher evaluation can serve as a tool for both accountability and instructional improvement. In most places today, however, teacher evaluation does not serve either of these purposes very well. Sometimes described as "drive-bys," typical teacher evaluations consist of a single classroom visit by an administrator, untrained in evaluation, with a superficial checklist (Toch & Rothman, 2008). According to a recent study of 12 school districts, 99% of teachers receive satisfactory or better ratings (Weisberg, Sexton, Mulhern, & Keeling, 2009). Clearly, teacher evaluation fails to distinguish differences in teaching quality, and the process needs to be improved.

Some states and school districts have developed promising models that have common characteristics. They usually are consistent with research-based teaching standards (such as NBPTS and InTASC), involve multiple observations, combine peer review and supervisory review, provide training for evaluators, encourage teacher self-assessment and reflection, and include analysis of varied types of student work (Porter, Youngs, & Odden, 2001; Toch & Rothman, 2008). A growing number of "Peer Assistance and Review Programs" engage master teachers in the evaluation process. Participating teachers are competitively selected, provide extensive advice to novices or struggling veterans, and make recommendations for retention or dismissal (Johnson & Papay, 2009).

Some reformers advocate teacher pay-for-performance. However, evidence from decades of experiments along these lines in education, government, and business shows that these schemes have proven disappointing (Adams, Heywood, & Rothstein, 2009; Cohen & Murnane, 1985). The U.S. Department of Defense recently suspended its pay-for-performance plan (Vogel, 2009). The prerequisites for such a plan do not exist in education. Most schools lack a credible teacher evaluation system, and, moreover, there is no valid and reliable way to measure results. Some advocates of this approach favor using student outcomes as a measure of performance (especially value-added models). However, the research shows that the technical problems with value-added models are substantial and warns that they should not be used for making high-stakes decisions (Board on Testing and Assessment [BOTA], 2009; Braun, 2005). Even if the technical obstacles could be eliminated, a pay-for-performance strategy is based on last-century motivation theory and, moreover, it only serves to reward pre-existing teaching capacity.

The research on teacher compensation encourages other alternatives that build capacity for improved teaching or pay teachers for extra work. An option of the first type is "knowledge- and skill-based pay." These plans reward teachers for acquiring and demonstrating specific knowledge and skills to meet educational goals. It is assumed that improvements in teaching practice will have positive effects on student outcomes (Odden et al., 2001). Pay increases for obtaining advanced NBPTS certification fall into this category. An option of the second type is to pay teachers more to teach in hard-to-staff schools, recognizing that more work is involved. Research has found that substantial increments are needed to attract candidates. Even these, however, are insufficient because teachers will not stay without improved working conditions and other supports for teaching such as good management, social support, and induction or mentoring programs for new teachers (David, 2008). Both pay incentives and improved working conditions are necessary to attract and retain teachers in low-performing schools.

There has been experimentation with career ladder compensation plans for some time. This approach rewards teachers for assuming additional roles and responsibilities. One difficulty with these plans in the past was insufficient opportunity for real role differentiation. However, as teacher professionalism and job-embedded professional development grow, varied roles for teachers as participants on state licensing boards, peer reviewers, coaches, and the like will continue to open up. Meaningful role differentiation is becoming more common. A comprehensive alternative teacher compensation plan called the "Tiered-Pay-and-Career-Structure" was recently proposed by Johnson and Papay (2009). It combines rewards for demonstrated knowledge and skills with incentives for assuming leadership roles. Research-based compensation plans are more likely to work because, consistent with contemporary motivation theory, they build teacher competence and preserve autonomy.

Future federal policy should support more rigorous teacher evaluations that differentiate performance and provide useful feedback to teachers. Teachers not rated satisfactory should receive assistance from more expert colleagues and other opportunities for professional development to improve their teaching. However, teachers unable or unwilling to improve should be counseled out or dismissed. The evidence suggests that pay systems that reward teachers for measurable objectives related to reform, such as increased knowledge and skills, service in low-performing schools, progress up a career ladder, and professional leadership are also worth considering. However, federal policy should avoid simplistic pay-for-test-scores proposals. Policymakers should heed the expert advice against premature use of value-added assessments for high-stakes decisions related to teacher evaluation or compensation.

## SCHOOL ACCREDITATION AND IMPROVEMENT

To improve accountability in schools, educators need support for building structures and processes that foster a sense of collective responsibility for student learning and commitment to continuous improvement that mediates between individual and external accountability. The education system needs–but currently lacks–the capacity to identify where a school is on a complex continuum of improvement in order to provide an appropriate level and type of support for capacity-building tailored to the unique circumstances of each school (Elmore, 2005).

A system of school review and accreditation is a promising strategy to build a culture of improvement and accountability within schools, to array schools on a continuum of improvement, and to provide individualized feedback to schools on how they can improve practice. Many other countries have systems of school inspection operated by the government that serve both accountability and improvement purposes, for example the United Kingdom, Denmark, and Australia. During the standards era, some states and school districts experimented with school review processes, for example New York, Rhode Island, and Chicago (Cuttance, 2005; Luginbuhl, Webbink, & deWolf, 2009; Rothstein, Jacobsen, & Wilder, 2008; Wilson, 1996). However, NCLB's myopic emphasis on test scores undermined these innovations.

In the United States, there is a system of voluntary evaluation and accreditation operated by professional Regional Accreditation Agencies and funded by the member dues of participating schools. Participation varies widely from state to state. Overall, only about one-fifth of schools in the United States are accredited (mostly high schools). Using the accreditation process in the Midwest and South as an example, the cycle begins with a school self-assessment based upon school quality standards. Every 5 years, a "Quality Assurance Review Team" visits each school and prepares a report with a recommendation regarding accreditation as well as steps for school improvement. Within 2 years, the school must submit a progress report documenting action on the team's recommendations. Every year, the school is expected to engage in an ongoing process of continuous improvement, such as their state's school improvement planning model (AdvancED, 2009).

Some researchers have suggested that the United States consider adopting a system of school review (Rothstein, Jacobsen, & Wilder, 2008; Wilson, 1996). If this were done, school accountability could be based on a more complete picture of the school, not just its test scores. There are two options for implementation: one is a government-run system and the other is mandatory, independent professional accreditation. There are pros and cons to each perspective, but the arguments in favor of strengthening professional accreditation seem more convincing.

As with teacher accountability, one of the advantages of the professional accountability route is that the necessary knowledge of best practice resides in the profession and in the research community. The accrediting agencies have developed considerable knowledge of best practices over the years, and building on those resources makes more sense than trying to build another system from scratch. Independence from political interference has been an issue abroad, where the review process is bureaucratically controlled (Cuttance, 2005). In the United States, accrediting agencies have been responsive to trends in education (e.g., greater emphasis on standards), but have resisted simplistic political agendas (e.g., judging schools only by standardized test scores) (Gray-Bennett, 2003). Stability has been a problem both with foreign government-run systems and with state and local experiments in the United States (Cuttance, 2005), but the system of professional accreditation has persisted for a century.

Criticisms of the existing accreditation process (e.g., that it is voluntary, underresourced, and needs more rigorous criteria and better reviewer training) could be addressed through limited government funding (Rothstein, Jacobsen, & Wilder, 2008). National policymakers should consider making accreditation mandatory for all schools and partnering with the existing accreditation agencies to enable them to scale up and improve the process. Support could be provided through hands-off subsidies (like those given to NBPTS).

One important improvement would be to make the criteria more rigorous and systematically grounded in current research on learning, teaching, and classroom and school contexts. The *Technical Guide* that provides references to the research used in developing the criteria contains many references to older effective schools research, but few to the kinds of current research upon which the learning-centered framework was based (National Study of School Evaluation, 2004). Another criticism of the accreditation criteria is that they do not place sufficient emphasis on outcomes (Rothstein, Jacobsen, & Wilder, 2008). This could be remedied if the accreditation agencies were willing to consider revisions along the lines of the balanced scorecard discussed earlier in Chapter 8. In-depth research synthesis and consultation with research experts would be required to improve the criteria.

Other improvements in the accreditation process that have been suggested include better training for evaluators, inclusion of some full-time evaluators, and more in-depth reviews (Rothstein, Jacobsen, & Wilder, 2008). Coordination with school improvement planning processes that many states or districts require should be continued. The accreditation process might be strengthened by linking it more closely with other school improvement processes, such as benchmarking. Accreditation could facilitate benchmarking by giving out an exemplary rating. These schools would then become exemplars of best practices in a benchmarking process operated by the district or the state and perhaps receive small grants to host visits and share practices with other schools.

For the majority of schools, the external assistance they get from professional accreditation, opportunities to benchmark, and more options for networking may be enough, in combination with their own internal improvement planning process, to enable them to succeed. These enhanced opportunities to learn would fill a gap in assistance for schools in the middle range of performance whose needs for external assistance to improve tend to be overlooked. There will be a certain percentage of schools whose performance is unsatisfactory even with these supports. Persistently low-performing schools that cannot attain accreditation will require more comprehensive and intense intervention by the district or state. If intervention is needed, however, at least the accreditation process will provide a preliminary, independent assessment of each school's strengths and weaknesses.

## RECIPROCAL BUREAUCRATIC ACCOUNTABILITY

State and district education agencies play important roles in agenda-setting, monitoring the performance of the level below them, and providing services and resources. Case studies of effective districts indicate that they function as partners in a reciprocal relationship with schools in which they communicate expectations for results, but have a concomitant responsibility to provide an infrastructure of support (Hightower, 2002; McLaughlin & Talbert, 2003; Resnick & Glennan, 2002). Similarly, states viewed as models of reform see themselves in a reciprocal accountability relationship with districts where the key to success is not the accountability process by itself, but the web of supports it activates (Darling-Hammond, 2004).

A study that compared urban districts that were more and less successful in improving student achievement illustrates some important differences. The successful ones developed comprehensive and systemic reform strategies. They formulated explicit student achievement goals, held district- and building-level leadership personally responsible for results, provided supports in key areas suggested by the learning triangle, and focused on the lowest-performing schools. Less successful districts lacked a clear consensus on goals; failed to take responsibility for instructional improvement; did not have standards, plans, and timetables; had policies that were disconnected from the classroom; and gave schools multiple and conflicting signals (Snipes, Doolittle, & Herlihy, 2002).

Changes in federal policy can encourage reciprocal accountability at the state and district levels. In addition to the state strategic plans built around key aspects of capacity, as recommended in the previous chapter, future federal legislation could also require states to negotiate similar strategic plans with each of their districts. These plans would address the issue: How will federal, state, and district programs and funds be used in combination to accomplish key capacity and student outcome objectives? Exemplary districts have already developed strategic plans on their own; future federal legislation could scale up this best practice by requiring all of them to do it.

It is also instructive for national policymakers to consider how successful states and districts measure progress on their goals. Various systems of multiple measures are used formatively to track growth in capacity and resources, as well as different kinds of results (McLaughlin & Talbert, 2003; Togneri, 2003). For example, one case study described a district that developed a sophisticated data system of indicators to monitor the depth of implementation of its five key strategic goals, such as the implementation of "safety nets" for all students (Supovitz & Weathers, 2004). Many of these studies of balanced data systems were conducted prior to or about the time NCLB became law, and it is unclear whether they survived.

## PUBLIC ACCOUNTABILITY

Public accountability is an underdeveloped strategy that goes hand-in-hand with reciprocal bureaucratic accountability because both educators and policymakers are ultimately responsible to the public. Districts have the power to monitor school practices, but teachers and principals do not have the power to monitor district supports and resources. With better information and accountability processes, the public could be in a unique position to assess whether reciprocal responsibilities are being met. There is not much research on public accountability, but what there is suggests that it has several components: greater transparency, substantive public conversations, and public empowerment (Gold, Simon, & Brown, 2003; Mediratta & Fruchter, 2003; Rogers, 2006; Turnbull, 2006).

Transparency is currently not adequate to enforce reciprocal accountability. NCLB requires publication of test score and some teacher data, but the public deserves better information that will enable them to evaluate all aspects of schooling and hold the responsible parties accountable. As part of their improvement planning processes, every school, district, and state should be required annually to produce a balanced scorecard. This document should be designed to enable the public to assess inputs (including gaps in inputs), outcomes (including gaps in outcomes), and school practices and plans to improve them. School accreditation reports should also be public information, since they provide an independent perspective.

Public conversations are deliberative processes in which stakeholders examine information, engage in problem solving, and make commitments to work for solutions. These conversations might take place at periodic accountability events that include school staff, parents, school system and public representatives, and community organizations. District and state agencies should also be required to meet with stakeholders to develop plans for improvement. Action by the school, the district, the community, and the state should be expected to result from the public deliberation.

In low-income neighborhoods, where schools are often isolated from the community, extra efforts are needed to reach out not only to parents, but to community organizations. A case study of effective public accountability in two Los Angeles neighborhoods illustrates what it takes. Parents were dissatisfied with their schools, but did not know what to do. Some parent leaders attended courses at UCLA designed to teach parents about education reform, how to obtain and analyze information about conditions at their schools, and avenues for action. Parents mobilized in a group called Parent-U-Turn and eventually built a significant base of parental power in the community that enabled them to get changes in school, district, and even state policies (Rogers, 2006).

According to the author of this Los Angeles study, NCLB "reflects a failure of imagination." Its policies fundamentally misunderstand the systemic nature of inequality and the problems facing schools that serve poor and minority students (Rogers, 2006, p. 623). He recommends that future ESEA legislation make a greater investment in developing parents' understanding of education reform and their capacity to participate, require publication of data that show gaps in resources and capacity (not just test scores), and provide better ways to enforce existing legal requirements for parent involvement.

## CONCLUSION

National accountability policy is fundamentally flawed because it is not designed in a way that will improve education. An alternative future accountability system should be based on principles of shared responsibility and reciprocity. Education reform is a systemic enterprise. Schools should be one, but not the only, agent held responsible for performance. Other stakeholders outside the school have critical roles to play in improving educational outcomes. Therefore, a hybrid accountability system is needed that expands participation by combining professional, reciprocal bureaucratic, and public accountability. Implementing these philosophical changes requires a complete overhaul of NCLB accountability goals, strategies, and consequences.

Professional accountability focuses on the improvement of practice and is, therefore, the best way to build understanding of and collective commitment to higher standards of practice among educators, including teachers and administrators. Therefore, one objective of a new accountability system should be to expand and strengthen professional accountability for educators. This chapter recommended several strategies for strengthening professional accountability. The requirement in NCLB that teachers be licensed should be maintained. In addition, ESEA should require that states create professional standards boards for teaching and school leadership, develop professional standards and more rigorous licensing systems, and strengthen evaluation systems for teachers and principals. The federal government should conduct research on professional preparation to improve, and eventually provide a foundation for accrediting, all types of programs.

At the school level, the new ESEA should mandate professional accreditation for all elementary, middle, and secondary schools. It should subsidize professional school accreditation agencies to develop improved, research-based school assessment criteria, to train evaluators more rigorously, and, if necessary, to cover other expansion costs. The accreditation system should be designed so that it can also serve as the foundation for a system of benchmarking in which schools can learn from one another about best practices.

Federal policy should encourage shared, reciprocal bureaucratic accountability between the federal government and states, states and districts, and districts and schools. Most states or districts already require schools to have improvement planning processes that produce strategic plans. If required at all levels of the system, these strategic plans and improvement processes could become the basis for the kind of negotiation between different levels of the system about expected outcomes and necessary supports that characterizes reciprocal bureaucratic accountability. The purpose of systematic strategic planning is not to increase top-down control, but the opposite. The idea does presuppose a limited number of shared capacity and accountability objectives, but it also assumes that each level of the system should have considerable flexibility to decide how to meet those objectives, taking local contexts into account.

Public accountability complements reciprocal bureaucratic accountability. Federal legislation can place more emphasis on public accountability by requiring its basic elements, including transparency, public conversations, and incentives for public learning and empowerment, especially in communities serving large numbers of poor and minority students. Because experience with hybrid accountability is limited, any initiatives in this area should include a research and evaluation component.

# CHAPTER 13

# Turning Around Low Performance

In recent years, policy and research have been shining a spotlight on persistently low-performing schools. Transforming or turning them around has become a high priority and is likely to remain so in the future. Under NCLB, 10% of all public schools are in restructuring, the law's ultimate sanctions category (Jennings, Scott, & Kober, 2009). Researchers who study dropouts estimate that, depending on the criteria used, in 1,700 to 2,000 high schools, dubbed "dropout factories," less than two-thirds of students graduate year after year (Balfantz & Bridgeland, 2007).

This chapter begins by reviewing the evidence about the sanctions-driven strategies and the limited support strategies that have dominated state and federal school turnaround policy for the last decade. The remedies typically used have proven disappointing. However, there are some islands of success where reformers have substantially raised student achievement in high-poverty areas. Such cases demonstrate that change is possible. The last two sections of this chapter describe two strategically chosen case studies that illustrate more promising turnaround approaches for the future and discuss their implications for a substantial reframing of federal policy.

## SANCTIONS-DRIVEN STRATEGIES

This section synthesizes what we have learned about two of the most popular sanctions, school reconstitution and state or mayoral takeovers. Reconstitution is the wholesale replacement of the personnel in a school. This strategy implicitly assumes that the educators in the school are the problem and that there is a reserve pool of better qualified educators ready to take over. State or mayoral takeovers give control of school systems to political leaders. This strategy locates the problem in existing governance arrangements, usually an elected school board, and assumes that political leaders are more competent and accountable.

A recent synthesis of research on school reconstitution included studies of both schools on probation (threatened with reconstitution) and of schools

actually reconstituted (Malen & Rice, 2009). It found that schools on probation may receive some additional resources and external assistance, but the
help is often insufficient or not congruent with what they need. Assistance
tends to be offset by other negative factors such as faculty turnover in response to the stigma of failure, overly controlling behavior by principals,
and frenetic and unproductive efforts to raise test scores. When actual reconstitution takes place, the synthesis found that restaffing is problematic
because demand outstrips supply and schools must hire uncertified, novice
teachers. When several schools within a district are reconstituted, they hire
one another's rejects. After reconstitution, there is typically a growth in student discipline problems and a failure to improve test scores. The authors of
this synthesis concluded that school reconstitution "is, at best, a very risky
strategy" and that its effects may "harm rather than help struggling schools"
(Malen & Rice, 2009, p. 475).

There is less research about the effects of state or mayoral takeovers,
but the findings so far are mixed. Studies of state takeovers of districts have
found that state intervention can improve financial management (Mintrop
& Sunderman, 2009). When financial management is the problem, taking
over this aspect of district operations makes sense. However, the educational
effects of state or mayoral takeovers on schools are more ambiguous. The
takeover strategy often involves turning schools over to private educational
management organizations (EMOs) or establishing charters. Pennsylvania
took over the Philadelphia school system and instituted a diverse provider
model where some schools were operated by the district and others by for-
profit firms, nonprofit organizations, or universities. Overall student achievement improved, but the privately managed schools did not outperform the
district's schools (Gill, Zimmer, Christman, & Blanc, 2007).

Sanctions-driven accountability has been around long enough that some
low-performing schools and districts have gone through several rounds of
corrective action. These schools tend to be unstable anyway with high teacher
and administrator turnover. Many schools that already went through governance changes or reconstitution under state policies are now being subjected
again to NCLB's rigid schedule of sanctions. Ongoing application of state
and federal sanctions creates an atmosphere of unproductive turbulence in
low-performing schools (Mintrop & Sunderman, 2009).

Experience suggests that negative labels that stigmatize schools should be
avoided. Some educators and students internalize the underperforming label
and become demoralized (McQuillan & Salomon-Fernandez, 2008). Studies
of educational change emphasize that the opposite kind of atmosphere is
needed. Positive change begins when change agents build trust (Bryk et al.,
2010) and create a sense of hope and momentum for the faculty and the community (Fullan, 1993). Other research stresses the need to renew teachers'

commitment to the school and to the moral purpose of education (Mintrop & Trujillo, 2005).

## TYPICAL SUPPORT STRATEGIES

Studies of state capacity to assist districts (Laguarda, 2003) and district capacity to assist schools (Spillane, 2000; Spillane & Thompson, 1997) indicate that the capacity to turn around low performance is very limited. However, the evidence does suggest that a more positive approach emphasizing comprehensive supports is preferable.

Studies of school turnaround stress the need to build human and social capital within the school (Smylie & Evans, 2006). When intervention takes place, it is important to build a basis for real partnership and to gain buy-in for change. In a set of case studies of change, Fullan (1993) found that all the success stories were based upon strong ongoing relationships between external support groups and internal teams. Rather than fire everybody, it makes more sense to identify and mobilize previously hidden strengths and talents within the school and the community. Another challenge is to turn low-performing schools into learning communities (Fullan, 1993). Low-performing schools tend to be either atomistic or unified in their low expectations. To develop internal accountability, it is critical to build the internal structures and processes that encourage collective norms around high performance (Carnoy, Elmore, & Siskin, 2003).

States and districts responsible for turning schools around typically send in external consultants or intervention teams. A nine-state study found that external help ranged from one person who visited monthly (or less) to on-site teams consisting of several people who stayed for a year or more. Assistance took such forms as conducting audits, developing school improvement plans, coaching and professional development, and brokering extra services from other organizations (Laguarda, 2003). This study and others found that low-intensity external assistance was not very useful. Kentucky and North Carolina developed better external team models. Their teams were well trained and consisted of several people who stayed at least a year (Mintrop & Trujillo, 2005). States and districts generally required each low-performing school to develop a school improvement plan with external help. All too often, however, assistance and resources to fully implement the plan were lacking.

One of the most popular approaches for turning around low-performing schools is to encourage or require them to adopt an external school reform model. There are several types of potential models: curriculum-based programs, subject-specific innovations, school leadership models, and comprehensive school reform designs (Glazer, 2009). Most of the models were designed for use in a variety of schools, not specifically for failing schools, and may not be intense enough for the low-performing settings. Many models claim to be research-based and comprehensive, but are not strategically focused on all aspects of the learning triangle (Finnegan, Bitter, & O'Day, 2009). Although these models are often treated as panaceas, due to their limited scope, they might serve as part but not all of a solution.

Implementation research has also identified the problem of "fit" (Glazer, 2009). The issue is not whether a model "works," but for what purposes and in what contexts it works. For example, a recent study of three reform models showed that Success for All emphasized "skills-based" reading and had positive effects on reading achievement in the lower elementary grades. America's Choice emphasized "literacy-based" reading and had positive effects on reading achievement in the upper elementary grades (Rowan, Correnti, Miller, & Camburn, 2009). Adoption of a model might help a school solve a specific problem if it fits the school's needs and is used for an appropriate purpose, but none of them by themselves can turn around a persistently low-performing school.

A synthesis of "lessons learned" from first-generation accountability systems found that "the task of continuous school improvement requires a sophisticated school improvement infrastructure that goes beyond sanctions and incentives and comprehensively 'moves on all fronts'" (Mintrop & Trujillo, 2005, p. 20). Similarly, a more recent study of schools in restructuring under NCLB in five states found that the legally prescribed remedies were insufficient to turn these schools around. All the schools that raised achievement enough to exit restructuring used a combination of multiple, coordinated strategies over many years. The combination of external assistance and comprehensive support strategies were found to be crucial ingredients in successful turnaround efforts (Jennings, Scott, & Kober, 2009).

## TOWARD MORE PROMISING FUTURE STRATEGIES

Schools and the communities in which they are located interact in multiple and complex ways. Although the learning-centered framework clearly emphasizes these interactions, recent policy rhetoric has chosen to ignore them. The "no excuses" approach to school reform maintains that schools alone should be able to close the achievement gap and places blame for failure on school personnel. This mantra is being increasingly questioned by evidence that suggests that when low-performing schools are located in communities characterized by extremely dire circumstances, it may be necessary to transform the community as well as the school (Bryk et al., 2010; Tough, 2008), or to address even broader issues of growing social-class inequality (Rothstein, 2004) in order to achieve positive educational results.

A study of school reform in Chicago found that close examination of neighborhoods in a big city with low-performing schools reveals considerable variation. Urban neighborhoods in Chicago vary in family income, degree of racial isolation, level of social capital, incidence of crime and violence, and the density of children living under extreme circumstances (foster care, neglected and delinquent, child abuse, etc). Differences in these aspects of the community context account for much of the variation in rates of school improvement and virtually all of the differences in rates of school stagnation between neighborhoods. In other words, the neighborhood served by a school may present formidable barriers to school improvement (Bryk et al., 2010).

Two initiatives are worth considering as examples of better approaches to turning around low-performing schools in the future. The already-mentioned study of Chicago school reform provides strong empirical evidence that there are at least five essential, and interacting, elements involved in school transformation. This study helps define what comprehensive school transformation means (Bryk et al., 2010), but found that that may not be enough in the most disadvantaged neighborhoods. In New York, an initiative called the Harlem Children's Zone goes further; it has the dual objectives of school *and* community transformation. Studies of the Harlem approach illustrate what it may take in the most extremely disadvantaged neighborhoods to transform both school and community contexts (Dobbie & Fryer, 2009; Tough, 2008).

The Chicago study likened school reform to baking a cake: a set of essential ingredients, a certain oven temperature, and the right timing are necessary. If anything is missing, the product won't be a cake. The five essential school reform ingredients are all interrelated. The authors found that school leadership that is inclusive and facilitative, sets high standards, focuses on instructional improvement, is able to craft program coherence, and gets people involved in school reform is the driving force. Other essential ingredients are professional capacity developed through frequent, high-quality professional development, teacher professional community, and the capacity to recruit quality teachers and remove problematic ones; an aligned content infrastructure and teaching methods that engage and challenge students; a student-centered learning climate that provides safety, order, and the support students need to succeed; and, finally, strong parent–community–school ties (Bryk et al., 2010). These essential supports align closely with the components of the learning-centered framework because both are derived from the learning triangle (the learning-centered framework has only four key components because parent–school–community ties are treated as an extension of the student context).

Relational trust is important because people in a school are highly interdependent. Learning, for example, is co-constructed by students and teachers. Authors of the Chicago study likened trust to the oven temperature in their cake analogy: it provides the social energy for the hard work of improvement. This study also offers an important perspective on the timing of school turnarounds. It tracked a decentralized school reform initiative that began in 1988 for 7 years, through 1996. In 1992, 4 years into this initiative, there was little observable improvement overall or differences among schools. However, by 1996, clear trends could be distinguished. There was a group of schools with significantly positive trends and another group with flat to negative trends. This study clearly demonstrates that school reform takes time.

The Harlem Children's Zone is a 97-block area in New York where a comprehensive initiative to address the problems of poverty, minority isolation, and educational inequality has been under way since 2004. Recognizing that children learn both in and out of school, the goals of the Zone include both school and community transformation. The educational goal is to provide the children of Harlem with an education that is equal to what children in wealthier communities get and to close gaps in achievement and attainment. The goal for the community is to change child-rearing practices and other aspects of community life that impede the education and success of children (Tough, 2008).

Several strategies are being used to achieve these goals. One is the "conveyor belt," which seeks to provide each child with an unbroken sequence of student and family support services that begins before birth and continues through college. The idea is to never let a child fall behind, to never let an achievement gap materialize. The conveyor belt starts with Baby College, a parenting workshop for parents of children 0–3; a Get-Ready for Pre-K program; Harlem Gems (an all-day kindergarten); and then the Promise Academy college-preparatory charter school system. The schools are designed on the community schools model with extended day and year; numerous extra tutoring, enrichment, and college-oriented opportunities; free medical, dental, and mental health services; and student meals and family food baskets. Beyond the schools, the Zone makes additional community investments to support families such as crisis intervention services, foster care prevention, obesity programs, tenant associations, and drug and alcohol assistance (Tough, 2008).

As in Chicago, it took time to get results in Harlem. Student assessments in the early years of charter school operation were disappointing (Tough, 2008). However, recent eighth grade test results show that students have moved from the 50th to the 71st percentile in mathematics and from the 50th to the 58th percentile in English language arts on state accountability tests (Dobbie & Fryer, 2009; What Works Clearing House, 2010). According to one reanalysis of the data, however, results on a low-stakes assessment are less impressive (Pallas, 2009). More research is needed to establish outcome trends and to better understand the educational program in the schools. How would the Harlem Children's Zone schools rate if evaluated based on the learning-centered framework or the five essential supports identified in Chicago?

Taken together, these case studies in Chicago and New York suggest that policymakers would be wise to consider a continuum of intensity of positive support strategies to turn around low performance. In determining which strategy might fit a particular school, both school and community circumstances should be taken into account. The least intense strategy would be comprehensive school transformation, followed by community schools that extend services to the neighborhood, then by the more intense Harlem school and community transformation model. It is possible to imagine even bolder approaches that might combine education reform with major initiatives to reduce social-class inequality.

Better data about both a school and its community context are needed to determine what type of turnaround strategy might work in a particular school. School data should include not just test scores, but data on the school's strengths and weaknesses with regard to the key areas defined by the learning-centered framework that could be generated by a school accreditation or inspection system. School lunch data are inadequate as a measure of poverty in the school and its surrounding community. The authors of the Chicago study developed a more sophisticated SES indicator system using data from the census, the school system, and other local agencies that enabled them to make meaningful distinctions between neighborhoods (Bryk et al., 2010). More sophisticated school and neighborhood data systems are needed to ensure that interventions fit the local context.

These case examples have implications for the kinds of capacities needed by federal, state, and district agencies that provide external assistance to schools. These agencies need substantive expertise related to all components of the learning-centered framework (or the five essential ingredients, Bryk et al., 2010). Also, in the most truly disadvantaged communities, schools and education systems need the capacity to link with other institutions that can provide broader supports, such as law enforcement, social services, health, and job training, to mobilize and tailor community intervention. These findings underline the importance of the intergovernmental capacity-building initiative and horizontal coordination mechanisms suggested in Chapter 11.

A study of the Harlem Children's Zone estimated that they spent $19,272 per pupil. This is an additional $4,657 per pupil for in-school costs and $2,172 per pupil for afterschool and other programs above the $12,443 allowance that New York City provides for charter schools (and also $3,101 above the state median expenditure of $16,171) (Dobbie & Fryer, 2009). While the Harlem Children's Zone filled the funding gap with foundation grants and contributions, it is unrealistic to expect every high-poverty, low-performing school or district to raise substantial private capital. Clearly, the financial adequacy and equity issues discussed in Chapter 11 must be addressed if comprehensive and successful innovations like these are to be scaled up in the future.

## CONCLUSION

The evidence indicates that punitive sanctions have not been a successful strategy to turn around low-performing schools. There was no empirical evidence to support either the sequence or the specific components of the standardized schedule of increasingly severe sanctions that was enacted in NCLB. Since then, evidence has accumulated that repeated application of sanctions creates turmoil in targeted schools and that stigmatizing labels demoralize the educators whose active commitment and support is essential for change. The punitive approach to turning around low-performing schools should be abandoned. Sanctions should be a last resort, an option to be used when improvement strategies have failed over the long term, not a required or routine "solution."

The future focus should be on developing constructive solutions that are comprehensive, systemic, and research-based. Expectations about the time frame for school turnarounds should be adjusted to the 6- to 10-year range and the capacity to provide improved external support to schools throughout the change process should be developed. A range of approaches is needed, along with better information about each school and its context, so turnaround strategies can be adapted to fit different circumstances. If the school accreditation process recommended in Chapter 12 were implemented, approaches to school turnaround could be informed by these reviews.

A better future framework for federal policy might consist of three categories of strategies to turn around low performance: comprehensive school transformation, school and community transformation, and a "last resort" category.

The specifics of the school transformation model should reflect research knowledge about what successful school improvement actually involves (such as the five elements found to be important in Chicago or the components of the learning-centered framework). The second model, school and community transformation, might include strategies ranging from community schools to strategies that seek to transform both schools and the communities in which they are located, like the Harlem Children's Zone. Most existing interventions emphasize providing a variety of services to mitigate poverty, but the Chicago case study indicates that it may also be important to address more intangible problems, such as strengthening social capital in the most truly disadvantaged neighborhoods (Bryk et al., 2010). The third, last-resort model would include school reconstitution, charters, or closure. None of these last-resort approaches should be federally mandated; they might be retained only as allowable state or district options.

# CHAPTER 14

# Reframing
# Future National Policy

The learning-centered framework offers a research-based way of conceptualizing education reform. It provides a coherent, comprehensive, and systemic template for fundamental change. When used as a tool to analyze national policy, the learning-centered framework suggests that policy is deeply flawed. For national policy to succeed in the future, goals, strategies, and outcome measures all need to be reframed. Beyond that, a new spirit of trust, collaboration, and partnership among stakeholders should replace top-down policy direction. In this chapter, I do two things. First, I summarize a learning-centered vision of future national policy. Second, I offer an interim assessment of the Obama administration's emerging education policies in comparison to his campaign promises as well as the learning-centered framework.

## LEARNING-CENTERED NATIONAL POLICY

Current policy makes raising student achievement and attainment, and closing gaps between more and less advantaged groups of students, central policy objectives. Research offers new knowledge that makes these objectives more feasible than ever before. However, oblivious to both recent theoretical breakthroughs related to learning and achievement and to the rich tradition of goals that public education has traditionally served in America, NCLB has narrowed and trivialized educational achievement by equating it with standardized test scores. There is not a clear consensus on what attaining a high school diploma should mean. Future policy must begin with a better sense of what it means to be an educated person in today's world.

Even before NCLB, Americans were prone to equate student achievement with standardized test scores, but these obscure the most important new dimensions—such as higher-order thinking skills, more advanced disciplinary knowledge, applications of knowledge, and noncognitive development—that research says should be incorporated into our concept of achievement in the future. National policy should be promoting, not constraining, public understanding of the multiple facets of student achievement. The NCLB approach to defining and measuring educational outcomes is counterproductive and its overemphasis on testing, unrealistic proficiency targets, and AYP requirements should be eliminated.

There are more effective ways to express education goals and national policy objectives. A future statute should affirm the many important purposes that education serves in American life that make it worthy of public support. It should state that raising achievement and attainment and reducing gaps in outcomes, capacity, and resources are national policy objectives. However, lawmakers should eschew the temptation to reduce educational outcomes to a simplistic, quantitative statutory formula. Instead, Congress should support participatory, deliberative processes to produce documents that might capture more fully the aspirations for student achievement and attainment that are now possible. A high-profile activity to promote public deliberation about educational goals and content standards that incorporate important disciplinary knowledge and skills as well as advances in knowledge about learning are two options. In combination, these strategies might promote a shared sense of purpose and build public commitment to education reform.

Despite a longstanding tradition of limited control, national policy has become increasingly top-down. In the future, a real partnership among stakeholders, one that is characterized by collaborative, knowledge-based problem-solving and capacity-building, needs to be formed. This would involve distributing leadership responsibility in a way that activates stakeholders and gives them a sense of membership in a common cause. No existing institution has the right combination of legitimacy and expertise to carry out the goal- and standards-setting activities just discussed. Partnerships of particular importance in a shift to more knowledge-based policy are with educators, disciplinary experts, and education researchers, who have had little influence on policy in recent years. Therefore, a new independent leadership consortium that includes states, educators, and researchers as co-equal partners is needed.

Future progress depends on getting not only educational goals and the federal role right, but the strategies of reform right, too. The key to success in education reform is recognizing the value of and effectively using new knowledge. Changes in R&D policy are essential. Research priorities must be refocused on the educational core, methods must be expanded, and more emphasis placed on development. Compared to providing services, R&D is a relatively inexpensive strategy that can have a high impact. Future federal policy should invest substantially more in the kind of basic research, and especially development, that has already demonstrated the potential to improve practice.

The relative emphasis on capacity and accountability that has characterized the NCLB era should be reversed. Building the capacity for high performance should become the top national priority in education. In the future, ESEA should be reframed to focus on the key elements of capacity and to communicate clear objectives for comprehensive, systemic, intergovernmental reform. If this recommendation were implemented, the titles and main objectives of a future ESEA might look something like the outline in the Appendix. Strategic plans, tailored to the circumstances of each state and district, would provide both flexibility and accountability in meeting these capacity objectives.

A U-turn is needed in national accountability strategies. Future accountability policies should be based on the principles of shared responsibility and reciprocity. Top-down compliance should be replaced with a hybrid system of professional, reciprocal bureaucratic, and public accountability. Greater reliance on professional accountability would be achieved by mandating state professional standards and licensing boards and giving educators the responsibility for setting and enforcing high standards of practice. A system of school review, established in partnership with the regional accreditation agencies, would provide accountability oversight as well as opportunities for professional learning and dissemination of best practices.

The lowest-performing schools, presumably those that could not get accredited, would receive assistance from well-trained, experienced state or district intervention teams. Three intervention models should be considered for the future. The first model would be a school transformation model that comprehensively addresses all aspects of the learning-centered framework with research-based strategies. The second model would be a school and community transformation model that, recognizing the interaction of schools and their environments, would seek to transform both in the most disadvantaged neighborhoods. Finally, a last-resort model would include school reconstitution, charters, or closure. None of the last-resort strategies would be mandated, but they would be available for use at state or district discretion. States and districts should have flexibility to choose among and adapt these models.

High-stakes testing should be eliminated and replaced with a low-stakes system of multiple measures that can serve a variety of purposes and audiences. This system would shift emphasis from summative to formative assessment, evaluate status and growth on the multiple dimensions of student achievement, and provide a balanced scorecard for accountability purposes that would track progress in closing gaps in capacity and resources as well as student outcomes. The balanced scorecard would be published and designed to serve as a basis for public accountability. In addition to this kind of transparency, policy would require state and local public events to encourage substantive discussion and would provide assistance for public learning about education reform.

NCLB assumed that suboptimal performance was a failure of individual students, teachers, and schools and prescribed sanctions-driven accountability as a cure. However, when we look at the problem through the learning-centered lens, we see a more complex system failure. Blame can just as well be assigned to U.S. national policymakers for their failure to recognize the value of new knowledge and develop the grassroots capacity to use it, to build an infrastructure of supports for improved practice, and to grasp the importance of school–community interactions, especially in the poorest areas. It takes capacity to get results. NCLB-style accountability should be abandoned because it is both impractical and unethical to punish students, teachers, and schools for a systemwide failure. NCLB's ineffective strategies detract energy and resources from better ones.

The focus of this book has been on education reform—what can be done to improve the multi-level education system. The analysis in Part III applied the learning-centered reform framework to national education policy. Table 14.1 summarizes an alternative federal role conception and a coherent set of national policies that are more consistent with research. With some adaptation, policymakers at state and local levels, practitioners, and other stakeholders can use the learning centered framework to frame their own policies or practices.

With the significant changes in education reform and national policy suggested by the learning-centered framework, there is much that can be done to improve educational outcomes, but the limitations of education reform must also be recognized. The learning-centered framework clearly illustrates that the education system itself is embedded in the larger U.S. social, political, and economic environment and that these broader contexts also influence educational outcomes. During the latest period of education reform, from the mid-1980s to today, there has been a tremendous growth of economic inequality in the United States (Bartels, 2008). The United States is now one of the most unequal of all industrialized nations, ranking 22 out of 23 on income inequality. The evidence is accumulating that the degree of income equality in industrialized societies is related to many important outcomes in areas such as education, health, and social mobility. The least equal of these societies have the lowest educational achievement and attainment outcomes; the most equal have the best educational achievement and attainment outcomes (Wilkinson & Pickett, 2009).

The nations that rank high on measures of educational performance today have invested in building the capacity of their education systems and they are at or near the top of the international scale on equality. Experts on education reform in Finland, for example, attribute their success both to their longstanding commitment to social justice and equality as well as to their more recent investments in education capacity, especially improvements in the quality of teacher preparation and greater teacher autonomy (Estola, Lauriala, Nissilä, & Syrjälä, 2007). In recent years, education reform in the United States has not only been hampered by misguided assumptions and strategies, it has also faced the headwinds of growing inequality. Although

**Table 14.1. Future National Policy Reframed**

| | |
|---|---|
| **Federal Role in Education** | Continue higher student achievement and attainment as central policy objectives, but reconceptualize them.<br><br>Reduce gaps not only in achievement and attainment, but also in capacity and resources. |
| **Leadership, Goals, and Standards** | Distribute leadership roles and build a partnership committed to knowledge-based education reform.<br><br>Emphasize a broad and balanced set of educational goals and recognize the multifaceted nature of achievement.<br><br>Use standards as tools to translate advances in knowledge about the disciplines and learning into a visible and usable form. |
| **Capacity-Building** | Make comprehensive, systemic capacity building *the* top priority. |
| *Research and Development* | Reorient substantive research priorities, emphasize strategic development work, and substantially increase R&D investment. |
| *Learning-Centered Grant Programs* | Strategically organize the federal program infrastructure around the key elements of capacity–strengthening content, supporting teachers and leaders, improving student support services. |
| *Social Networks* | Support a new initiative to strengthen SEA and LEA capacity and build a network of learning communities throughout the system. |
| *Resource Adequacy and Equity* | Create a new program for interstate adequacy and equity, set more specific targets for state-to-district equalization, and better target compensatory funding. |
| **Accountability and Improvement** | Strengthen shared accountability through a hybrid system that combines professional, bureaucratic, and public approaches.<br><br>Recognize the reciprocal nature of accountability by emphasizing both capacity and results.<br><br>Measure what matters–invest in a system of low-stakes multiple assessments. Eliminate high-stakes testing.<br><br>Develop the systemic capacity to more accurately identify and turn around low-performing schools with positive, constructive approaches. Use sanctions only as a last resort. |

contexts beyond the education system are outside the scope of this book, we cannot afford to ignore the fact that future education reform is best pursued within the larger context of a broad commitment to greater equality and social justice.

## OBAMA'S INTERIM ASSESSMENT

After almost 2 years in office, the Obama administration's education policies are beginning to take shape. Despite many other pressing problems related to the economy, energy, and health care, it seems clear that this administration is committed to making education a priority too. Education received generous funding in the stimulus package, and at a time when other domestic programs were level-funded, the administration requested $49.7 billion for education in the 2011 budget, an increase of about 7.5% (Klein, 2010; USDE, 2010a). The scope of action for administration initiatives is wide, including preschool, elementary and secondary, and postsecondary education.

We know from long experience in education policy, however, that good intentions and increased funding are not enough to improve education outcomes. Money matters only when it is used well. Therefore, it is important to probe more deeply into the emerging substance of the administration's policies using key documents, including the Race to the Top Fund regulation (2009); the *Blueprint for Reform*, a summary of ESEA reauthorization proposals (USDE, 2010b); a School Improvements Grants regulation (2009); and the 2011 budget (USDE, 2010a). The President's two campaign promises provide useful criteria for an interim assessment: (1) his promise of substantive policy change, and (2) his commitment to use research knowledge rather than ideology as a foundation for policy. I use these, along with the learning-centered framework, as a basis for evaluation.

Some adjustments in concepts of educational goals and achievement have been forthcoming, but not fundamental change. Rhetoric about goals still focuses on economic competitiveness and workforce preparation. There is little evidence of an interest in thinking more deeply about the role of education in a democracy or in an increasingly diverse and unequal society. Improved attainment has been added to achievement as a national policy objective. In lieu of NCLB's mandated proficiency and AYP requirements (these are eliminated), the Blueprint proposes an "aspirational" objective that by 2020 all students should graduate from high school "College and Career Ready." Since less than a quarter of U.S. students graduate college-ready today (ACT, 2009), the Obama objective, like Bush's, seems unrealistic.

In terms of the federal role and strategies, the administration is still in the top-down accountability mode and will continue the carrot-and-stick approach that has characterized education policy for the last half-century.

Secretary of Education Arne Duncan promised more emphasis on positive incentives in a new ESEA. He says he wants to "reward excellence" (Klein, 2009). Although it gets less rhetorical emphasis, there are also more sanctions for low-performing schools, principals, and teachers.

Two problems with rewards and sanctions have already been identified. The first is that they do not automatically build capacity. Grantees respond based on their preexisting capacity. Capacity-building does not appear to be getting any more emphasis in the Obama administration than it did under Bush. The second problem is that reinforcement techniques are not used in ways that are consistent with contemporary motivation theories. Carrots and sticks can induce people to comply with relatively straightforward directives, but they do not work well to motivate high performance in complex situations. Overemphasis on extrinsic motivation is likely to drive out intrinsic motivation. A quick look at three of the administration's priorities, enhancing standards and assessments, increasing teacher effectiveness, and turning around struggling schools, illustrates these points.

The administration's strategy for enhancing standards and assessments is to encourage states to adopt the common core standards already developed in English language arts and mathematics by the NGA/CCSSO consortium and to fund aligned assessment systems. The administration is investing $350 million of Race to the Top funds in improved assessments. About 90% of the funds will go to develop comprehensive assessment systems in mathematics and English language arts, and the remaining 10% to high school course assessments. The new assessments must measure both status and growth, covering the full range of the performance continuum, including complex student demonstrations and applications of knowledge and skills (Comprehensive Assessment Systems, 2010). On the positive side, these specifications are likely to produce assessments in some content areas that will be superior to the NCLB-era multiple-choice tests. However, on the negative side, the specifications ignore cautions from assessment experts and require that the new system produce data that can be used to make determinations of individual school, teacher, and principal effectiveness.

While accountability goals, standards, and assessments will change somewhat, there is no change in the frequency of testing. NCLB requirements that students be tested every year in reading and math in grades 3 through 8 and once in high school are continued. A focus on standards and assessments is less sophisticated than the concept of a fully aligned content infrastructure that was held up as an ideal during the early standards movement. Plans to develop the curricula and materials that teachers use every day in their classrooms are missing. This is not a plan for a broad and balanced curriculum—plans to develop content infrastructures for most school subjects are also missing. The development of both standards and assessments are on quick turnaround schedules. This will make it difficult to take advantage of scientific opportunities, for example, developing empirical learning progressions that provide pathways to meet the standards. The administration's initiatives related to content are a somewhat mixed beginning, but a broader and deeper long-term plan is needed to significantly improve school content. The overall approach to content improvement is too short term and too *ad hoc.*

What is being done to develop teacher and principal capacity to meet higher demands? The *Blueprint* focuses on evaluating and labeling educators. States must (in order to receive formula grants) develop definitions of "highly effective" teachers and principals and "effective" teachers and principals. Despite pleas for caution from researchers, definitions of effectiveness must be based in significant part on student growth measures. These definitions are to form the basis of evaluation systems that will differentiate performance into at least three categories, provide performance feedback to educators, and inform professional development. At least every 2 years, states and districts must publish "report cards." Data on teacher and principal credentials and effectiveness are recommended for inclusion. Improved teacher and principal evaluation systems are needed, but systems that use simplistic, extrinsic motivation techniques; rely on student-outcome data of questionable quality; and label professionals are not better.

Merit pay for teachers and principals, based on the new evaluation systems, is encouraged. It does not take much foresight to predict that the test prep frenzy will become even more intense if the reputations and salaries of individual educators are largely determined by test scores. Teachers' intrinsic motivation to teach well in accordance with professional norms is likely to be driven out by extrinsic pressure. The Obama administration's *Blueprint* extends the Bush strategy of assess, label, reward, and punish from schools to individual educators. High-states testing continues in a stepped-up form.

While the *Blueprint* states that "elevating the profession" is one of its goals, it fails to pursue paths that might accomplish this and instead follows paths that do the opposite. Effectively strengthening the profession would involve displaying trust and devolving to the profession the kind of authority for professional preparation, licensing, evaluation (emphasizing peer review), and advanced certification that other professions have. These professional activities build capacity as well as accountability. Instead of strengthening educators' professional role in these areas, the Blueprint strengthens the top-down bureaucratic role of the federal government and the states. Activities such as ongoing, job-embedded professional development that would serve to build professional capacity are allowable or funded through discretionary grants, but not required.

Despite the research, the Obama administration has issued a list of four required interventions for low-performing schools, all of them punitive to some degree, that apply to recipients of Race to the Top, State Fiscal Stabilization Fund, and Title I School Improvement grants (School Improvement Grants,

2009). The intervention choices are "turnaround," a form of reconstitution; "restart" conversion to a charter or private EMO; "closure"; or "transformation," firing the principal and implementing a prescribed list of changes. Districts with more than nine persistently low-performing schools cannot use the transformation model in more than 50% of their schools. These categories of sanctions apply to the bottom 5% of schools. The policy of negative labeling continues, with the bottom 5% labeled "challenge" schools and the next 5% placed in a "warning" category. Since the bottom 5 to 10% of schools are likely to serve poor and minority students, this approach effectively exempts middle class schools from sanctions.

The Obama administration has created another program called "Promise Neighborhoods" that will replicate the Harlem Children's Zone in 20 neighborhoods. The Promise Neighborhoods initiative emphasizes extensive school and community supports. In combination with school turnaround policies that require punitive sanctions, the result is an illogical and inequitable policy environment where similar schools will be treated very unevenly. We need variation to study a range of approaches to address persistent low performance, but the range should include different approaches that research has found to be promising. However, in the Obama framework, much of the variation includes approaches already found to be ineffective or harmful. The Obama approach should be replaced with a positive, constructive framework of options such as the three-part school transformation (redefined in accordance with evidence), school and community transformation, and last resort models recommended in Chapter 13.

The administration's 2011 budget proposes a significantly stepped-up emphasis on competition, specifically by devoting billions of new ESEA dollars (in addition to Race to the Top) to competitive, discretionary grants rather than formula grants. The federal government has always made competitive grants, but the amounts were small enough so that they did not have significant school finance implications. What effects will this proposal have on interstate education finance equity? Winning a competitive grant requires preexisting capacity. Devoting big bucks to competitive grants may increase rather than reduce existing gaps in state, district, and school capacity. How can a funds allocation policy that increases capacity gaps serve at the same time to reduce outcome gaps? The equity implications of this proposal should be seriously considered, as well as whether other options, such as interstate school finance equalization, would be more consistent with the traditional federal commitment to equity and more effective in reaching outcome goals.

It does not appear that the administration is using either basic education research or even program evaluation as a foundation for its policy initiatives. Their overall vision of reform is not framed and conceptualized in a way that is compatible with research. Many of their signature elementary and secondary education policies, such as school reconstitution, charter schools, and performance pay, either have little research support or run counter to the research evidence. The lack of research knowledge behind key policies has been noted in press reports (Maxwell, 2009; Viadero, 2009; Weiner, 2009) and in many critical research-based comments on proposed program regulations (e.g., Board on Testing and Assessment, 2009; Pennsylvania State Education Association, 2009). The problem is not just the probability that opinion-based panaceas will fail, but the opportunity costs of ignoring research-based alternatives that are more likely to succeed, especially with so much money at stake.

The Obama education agenda is not based on research. It does not reflect the views of most practicing educators. Where did these ideas come from? The Obama administration's education agenda matches the agenda of the Billionaire Boys Club, a constellation of corporate entrepreneurs acting through their foundations, education advocacy groups funded by those foundations, and allied politicians of both parties. This iron triangle gained ascendancy as a force in education policy during the Bush era. Now the Obama administration is acting to elaborate and extend the same agenda. Ravitch (2010), who described the club in her recent critique of national policy, argued that the corporate agenda, if it continues unchecked, will ultimately destroy public education in America by transforming it from a public good into a commodity and replacing civic and educational values with top-down accountability and market competition.

The bottom line of this interim assessment is that the Obama administration urgently needs a midcourse correction in its education policies. Good intentions notwithstanding, the administration has not lived up to its promises to bring fundamental change to education or to use research as a basis for policy formulation. Recognizing the value of new knowledge and using it to transform policy and practice is a prerequisite for achieving the kind of results policymakers seek. Breakthrough progress cannot be achieved without using new knowledge and technology as a basis for change.

A president, whether this one or the next, who is serious about research-based change needs a scholar-educator to lead his education team. This means someone with a deep understanding of the scientific opportunities, someone who can articulate a research-based vision of change, and someone who also knows education practice and how to apply new knowledge. A leader of real change must also have the ability and courage to shift the balance of power in education reform. It must be someone who regards partnership as a necessity, not just a rhetorical flourish. Corporate interests deserve a place at the education policy table, but success will be elusive if they continue to dominate. Educators and researchers must be brought back in as senior partners. Education reform will not reach every classroom in America until educators themselves are inspired by a framework of ideas that makes educational sense and empowered to lead reform.

# A New Framework for ESEA

In the future, ESEA should be reframed to communicate a new message about education reform. The mission statement should affirm the many important purposes that education serves in American life that make it worthy of public support. It should state national policy objectives in education:

- To improve student achievement and close achievement gaps
- To improve student attainment and close attainment gaps
- To build the capacity of the education system and to encourage the shared, reciprocal responsibility necessary to meet these goals and student performance objectives

If ESEA focused on capacity and took a more constructive approach to accountability, its titles and their main objectives might look something like this:

### Title I—Supports for Student Learning, Achievement, and Attainment

- Build a comprehensive and systemic infrastructure of academic and other supports matched to the needs of each student that will enable them to meet high standards and reach their full potential and that will enable schools and school systems to narrow achievement and attainment gaps among groups. Group programs that focus on student supports in this title and encourage more coordination.

### Title II—Accountability and Supports for Teaching and Leadership

- Expand and strengthen professional accountability for educators by requiring states to establish professional standards boards for teaching and school leadership. These boards will develop and enforce rigorous professional standards, licensing requirements, and evaluation systems that include peer review.
- Develop an infrastructure of high-quality professional learning opportunities for teachers and administrators that begins with preservice education, continues with a combination of job-embedded and external opportunities throughout their careers, and enables them to meet high standards.

- Require states to create incentive systems to ensure that poor and minority students are not taught by inexperienced, out-of-field, or otherwise unqualified teachers at higher rates than are other students.

## Title III—Challenging Content and Improved Assessment

- Create an independent entity—including state organizations, teacher-content associations, and research and assessment organizations—to collaborate in partnership to improve the education content infrastructure. (This entity might also be given the responsibility to convene a national, grassroots dialogue about educational goals, achievement, and the meaning of a high school diploma.)
- Proceed simultaneously on two tracks to create a complete content infrastructure in each subject area, including curriculum, textbooks, materials, and assessments aligned with challenging goals and standards. A short-term track would continue the ongoing work on common standards and related assessments, but would expand to other components of a content infrastructure and other subjects. A long-term track would plan and conduct the R&D necessary to go beyond the existing state of the art in the next round.
- Develop a system of multiple measures to assess progress that can serve a variety of purposes and audiences. This system would shift emphasis from summative to formative assessment, evaluate status and growth on the multiple dimensions of student achievement, and provide a balanced scorecard for accountability purposes that would track progress in closing gaps in capacity and resources as well as student outcomes.
- Move the many small grant programs related to educational content to this title, remove overly prescriptive language, group programs under major disciplinary categories and streamline them to the extent possible, fund the major disciplinary categories more equally to encourage a balanced curriculum.

## Title IV—Networks for Knowledge-Based Reform

- Support the development of human and social capacity for high performance in state and district education agencies, including knowledge of learning-centered reform and capacity to assist and intervene in low-performing schools.
- Support external professional networks to enable practitioners to learn about best practices from one another and to link them in partnerships with sources of formal research knowledge.

## Title V—Adequate and Equitable Funding

• Make a commitment to adequate and equitable funding for each school by creating a new federally funded interstate school finance equity program, requiring states to set more specific targets for state-to-district equity, and correcting the disequalizing aspects of the Title I comparability requirement.

## Title VI—School System Accountability and Improvement

• Create a new hybrid accountability system that combines professional, reciprocal bureaucratic, and public accountability.
• Require professional accreditation for all elementary, middle, and secondary schools. Subsidize improvements in the regional accreditation system to make criteria more research-based and improve evaluator training. Tie the accreditation process to a system of school-level benchmarking so that schools can learn about best practices from one another.
• Encourage reciprocal bureaucratic accountability with a system of state and district strategic plans addressing key objectives in each main area of capacity and accountability (i.e., each title) in a new ESEA. Use a balanced scorecard to track progress and gap reduction in capacity, resources, and student outcomes.
• Encourage public accountability by requiring greater transparency in documents available to the public and by requiring substantive public conversations, at least every 2 years, at the school, district, and state levels. Provide assistance for public learning about education reform and opportunities to become involved, especially in poor and/or minority communities.
• Support positive, constructive strategies to turn around low-performing schools emphasizing three models: (1) comprehensive school transformation, (2) school and community transformation, and (3) a "last-resort" model allowing reconstitution, charters, or closure as state or district options.

# References

Abelmann, C., & Elmore, R. (1999). *When accountability knocks, will anyone answer?* Philadelphia: Consortium for Policy Research in Education.

ACT. (2009). *Measuring college and career readiness: The class of 2009.* Retrieved June 19, 2010, from http://www.act.org/news/data/09/pdf/output/NationalOverview.pdf

Adams, J. E., & Kirst, M. W. (1999). New demands and concepts for educational accountability: Striving for results in an era of excellence. In J. Murphy & K. S. Louis (Eds.), *Handbook of research on educational administration* (2nd ed., pp. 463–489). San Francisco: Jossey Bass.

Adams, S., Heywood, J., & Rothstein, R. (2009). *Teachers, performance pay and accountability: What education should learn from other sectors.* Washington, DC: Economic Policy Institute.

Adler, M. (1982). *The paideia proposal: An educational manifesto.* New York: Macmillan.

AdvancED. (2009). *Overview of the AdvancED standards and accreditation process for schools.* Retrieved November 2, 2009, from http://www.advanced.org/accreditation/school_accreditation/accreditation_process/

Alexander, P. A. (2003). The development of expertise: The journey from acclimation to proficiency. *Educational Researcher, 32*(8), 10–14.

Allensworth, E. M., & Easton, J. Q. (2005). *The on-track indicator as a predictor of high school graduation.* Chicago: Consortium on Chicago School Research.

American Association for the Advancement of Science (AAAS). (1999). *Heavy books light on learning: Not one middle grades science text rated satisfactory by AAAS's Project 2061* [Press Release]. Washington, DC: Author.

American Federation of Teachers (AFT). (2001). *Making standards matter 2001.* Washington, DC: Author.

Ancess, J. (1995). *An inquiry high school: Learner-centered accountability at the urban academy.* New York: National Center for Restructuring Education, Schools, and Teaching.

Anderson, L. W., et al. (2001). *A taxonomy for learning, teaching, and assessing: A revision of Bloom's taxonomy of educational objectives.* New York: Longman.

Anderson, L. W., & Sosniak, L. A. (1994). *Bloom's taxonomy: A forty-year retrospective.* Chicago: University of Chicago Press.

Atkinson, R. C., & Jackson, G. B. (1992). *Research and education reform.* Washington, DC: National Academies Press.

Australian Council for Educational Research (ACER). (2007). *Index of school tests.* Retrieved March 19, 2007, from http://www.acer.edu.au/tests/school/index.html

Ayoub, C. C., & Fischer, K. W. (2006). Developmental pathways and intersections among domains of development. In K. McCartney & D. Phillips (Eds.), *Handbook of early child development* (pp. 62–82). Oxford, UK: Blackwell.

Bailey, S. K., & Mosher, E. K. (1968). *ESEA: The Office of Education administers a law.* Syracuse, NY: Syracuse University Press.

Baldi, S., et al. (2000). *International education indicators: A time–series perspective, 1985–1995.* Washington, DC: National Center for Education Statistics.

Baldrige National Quality Program. (2002). *Education criteria for performance excellence.* Gaithersberg, MD: National Institute of Standards and Technology.

Balfantz, R., & Bridgeland, J. (2007). *A plan to fix dropout factories.* Retrieved October 14, 2009, from http://www.csmonitor.com/2007/1123/p09s01-coop.html

Balfantz, R., Herzog, L., & MacIver, D. (2007). Preventing student disengagement and keeping students on the graduation path in urban middle-grades schools: Early identification and effective interventions. *Educational Psychologist, 42*(4), 223–235.

Ball, D. L., & Cohen, D. K. (1996). Reform by the book: What is–or might be–the role of curriculum materials in teacher learning and instructional reform? *Educational Researcher, 25*(9), 6–8.

Ball, D. L., & Forzani, F. M. (2007). What makes education research "educational"? *Educational Researcher, 36*(9), 529–540.

Banicky, L. A., & Foss, H. K. (1999). *The challenges of accountability.* Newark, DE: Delaware Education Research and Development Center.

Banicky, L. A., & Noble, A. J. (2001). *Detours on the road to reform: When standards take a back seat to testing.* Newark, DE: Delaware Education Research and Development Center.

Barnett, W. S. (1995). Long-term effects of early childhood programs on cognitive and school outcomes. *The Future of Children, 5*(3), 25–50.

Bartels, L. M. (2008). *Unequal democracy: The political economy of the new gilded age.* Princeton, NJ: Princeton University Press.

Barton, P. E. (2009a). *Chasing the high school graduation rate: Getting the data we need and using it right.* Princeton, NJ: Educational Testing Service.

Barton, P. E. (2009b). *National education standards: Getting beneath the surface.* Princeton, NJ: Educational Testing Service.

Battistich, V., Solomon, D., Watson, M., & Schaps, E. (1997, Fall). Caring school communities. *Educational Psychologist, 32*(3), 137–151.

Belfield, C. R., & Levin, H. M. (2009). Market reforms in education. In G. Sykes, B. Schneider, & D. N. Plank (Eds.), *Handbook of education policy research* (pp. 513–527). Washington, DC: American Educational Research Association & New York: Routledge.

Benavot, A. (2007). Instructional time and curricular emphases: U.S. state policies in comparative perspective. In C. E. Finn & D. Ravitch (Eds.), *Beyond the basics: Achieving a liberal education for all children* (pp. 149–183). Washington, DC: Thomas B. Fordham Institute.

Bensman, D. (2000). *Central Park East and its graduates.* New York: Teachers College Press.

Birman, B., et al. (2007). *State and local implementation of the No Child Left Behind Act: Volume II– Teacher quality under NCLB.* Washington, DC: American Institutes for Research.

Black, P., Harrison, C., Lee, C., Marshall, B., & Wiliam, D. (2002). *Working inside the black box: Assessment for learning in the classroom.* London: Kings College.

Black, P., & Wiliam, D. (1998). Inside the black box: Raising standards through classroom assessment. *Phi Delta Kappan, 80*(2), 139–148.

Blank, R. (2010, April). *States' growth models for school accountability: Progress on developing and reporting measures of student growth.* Paper presented at the annual meeting of the American Educational Research Association, Denver, CO.

Blank, R. K., & de las Atlas, N. (2009). *Effects of teacher professional development on gains in student achievement.* Washington, DC: Council of Chief State School Officers.

Board on Testing and Assessment (BOTA). (2009, October 5). *Comments on the Department of Education's proposal on the Race to the Top Fund.* Retrieved November 30, 2009, from http://books.nap.edu/openbook.php?record_id=12780&page=1

Bogan, C. E., & English, M. J. (1994). *Benchmarking for best practices: Winning through innovative adaptation.* New York: McGraw-Hill.

Bransford, J. D., Brown, A. L., & Cocking, R. R. (Eds.). (2000). *How people learn: Brain, mind, experience, and school.* Washington, DC: National Academies Press.

Braun, H. I. (2005). *Using student progress to evaluate teachers: A primer on value-added models.* Princeton, NJ: Educational Testing Service.

Braun, H., Chudowsky, N., & Koenig, J. (Eds.). (2010). *Getting value out of value-added: Report of a workshop.* Washington, DC: National Academies Press.

Bridgeland, J. M., Dilulio, J. J. Jr., & Morison, K. B. (2006). *The silent epidemic: Perspectives of high school dropouts.* Washington, DC: Civic Enterprises.

Bronfenbrenner, U. (1981). *The ecology of human nature: Experiments by nature and design.* Cambridge, MA: Harvard University Press.

Brophy, J., Alleman, J., & O'Mahoney, C. (2000). Elementary school social studies: Yesterday, today, and tomorrow. In T. Good (Ed.), *American education: Yesterday, today, and tomorrow* (pp. 256–311). Chicago: University of Chicago Press.

Brown, A. L., & Campione, J. C. (1996). Psychological theory and the design of innovative learning environments: On procedures, principles, and systems. In L. Schauble & R. Glaser (Eds.), *Innovations in learning* (pp. 289–325). Mahwah, NJ: Lawrence Earlbaum.

Bryk, A. S. (2008). *The future of education research.* [Speech at the American Enterprise Institute]. Retrieved January 1, 2008, from http://www.aei.org/events/filter.all,eventID.1823/transcript.asp

Bryk, A. S., & Driscoll, M. E. (1988). *The high school as community: Contextual influences and consequences for students and teachers.* Madison, WI: National Center on Effective Secondary Schools.

Bryk, A. S., Sebring, P. B., Allensworth, E., Luppescu, S., & Easton, J. Q. (2010). *Organizing schools for improvement: Lessons from Chicago.* Chicago: University of Chicago Press.

Carey, K., & Roza, M. (2008). *School funding's tragic flaw.* Washington, DC: Education Sector & Seattle: Center on Reinventing Public Education.

Carnoy, M., Elmore, R., & Siskin, L. S. (2003). *The new accountability: High schools and high stakes testing.* New York: RoutledgeFalmer.

Carnoy, M., Jacobsen, R., Mishel, L., & Rothstein, R. (2005). *The charter school dust-up: Examining the evidence on enrollment and achievement.* Washington, DC: Economic Policy Institute & New York: Teachers College Press.

Center for Information and Research on Civic Learning and Engagement (CIRCLE) & Carnegie Corporation. (2003). *The civic mission of schools.* New York: Carnegie Corporation of New York.

Center for Research on Education Outcomes (CREDO). (2009). *Multiple choice: Charter school performance in 16 states.* Stanford, CA: Author.

Center on Education Policy. (2006). *From the capital to the classroom: Year 4 of the No Child Left Behind Act.* Washington, DC: Author.

Center on Education Policy. (2007). *Educational architects: Do state educational agencies have the tools necessary to implement NCLB?* Washington, DC: Author.

Chabott, C., & Elliott, E. J. (2003). *Understanding others, educating ourselves: Getting more from international comparative studies in education.* Washington, DC: National Academies Press.

Clotfelder, C. T., Ladd, H. F., Vigdor J. L., & Diaz, R. A. (2004). Do accountability systems make it more difficult for low-performing schools to attract and retain high-quality teachers? *Journal of Policy Analysis and Management, 23*(2), 251–271.

Cobb, P., & Bowers, J. (1999). Cognitive and situated learning perspectives in theory and practice. *Educational Researcher, 28*(2), 4–15.

Coburn, C. E., & Stein, M. K. (2006). Communities of practice theory and the role of teacher professional community in policy implementation. In M. I. Honig (Ed.), *New directions in education policy implementation* (pp. 25–46). New York: State University of New York Press.

Coburn, C. E., & Talbert, J. E. (2006). Conceptions of evidence use in districts: Mapping the terrain. *American Journal of Education, 112*(4), 469–495.

Cochran-Smith, M., & Zeichner, K. M. (2005). *Studying teacher education: The report of the AERA Panel on Research and Teacher Education.* Washington, DC: American Educational Research Association & New York: Lawrence Erlbaum.

Cohen, D. K. (1990). A revolution in one classroom: The case of Mrs. Oublier. *Educational Evaluation and Policy Analysis, 12*(3), 327–345.

Cohen, D. K. (1995). What standards for national standards? *Phi Delta Kappan, 76*(10), 751–757.

Cohen, D. K., & Ball, D. L. (1990). Policy and practice: An overview. *Educational Evaluation and Policy Analysis, 12*(3), 347–353.

Cohen, D. K., & Hill, H. C. (2001). *Learning policy: When state education reform works.* New Haven, CT: Yale University Press.

Cohen, D. K., & Murnane, R. J. (1985). The merits of merit pay. *Public Interest, 80*(3), 3–30.

Cohen, D. K., Raudenbush, S. W., & Ball, D. L. (2000). *Resources, instruction, and research.* Seattle, WA: Center for the Study of Teaching and Policy.

Cohen, J. (2006). Social, emotional, ethical, and academic education: Creating a climate for learning, participation in democracy, and well-being. *Harvard Educational Review, 76*(2), 201–237.

Cole, N. S. (1990, April). Conceptions of educational achievement. *Educational Researcher, 19*(3), 2–7.

Comprehensive Assessment Systems, Race to the Top Assessment Program, Application for New Grants (CFDA Number 84.395B). (2010).

Consortium for Policy Research in Education (CPRE). (1991). *Equality in education: Progress, problems, and possibilities.* [*CPRE Policy Briefs*]. Philadelphia: Author.

Corcoran, T., Mosher, F. A., & Rogat, A. (2009). *Learning progressions in science: An evidence-based approach to reform.* Philadelphia: Consortium for Policy Research in Education.

Cornelius-White, J. (2007). Learner-centered teacher-student relationships are effective: A meta-analysis. *Review of Educational Research, 77*(1), 113–143.

Cuttance, P. (2005). Quality assurance reviews as a catalyst for school improvement in Australia. In D. Hopkins (Ed.), *The practice and theory of school improvement* (pp. 101–128). New York: Springer.

Darling-Hammond, L. (2001). Standard setting in teaching: Changes in licensing, certification, and assessment. In V. Richardson (Ed.), *Handbook of research on teaching* (4th ed., pp. 751–776). Washington, DC: American Educational Research Association.

Darling-Hammond, L. (2004). Standards, accountability, and school reform. *Teachers College Record, 106*(6), 1047–1085.

Darling-Hammond, L. (2006). No Child Left Behind and high school reform. *Harvard Educational Review, 76*(4), 642–667.

Darling-Hammond, L., & Ball, D. L. (2004). *Teaching for high standards: What policymakers need to know and be able to do.* Philadelphia: Consortium for Policy Research in Education and National Commission on Teaching and America's Future.

Darling-Hammond, L., & Bransford, J. (Eds.). (2005). *Preparing teachers for a changing world.* San Francisco: Jossey-Bass.

Darling-Hammond, L., & Wentworth, L. (2010). *Benchmarking learning systems: Student performance assessment in international context.* Stanford, CA: Stanford University, Stanford Center for Opportunity Policy in Education.

Darling-Hammond, L., et al. (2005). Implementing curriculum renewal in teacher education: Managing organizational and policy change. In L. Darling-Hammond & J. Bransford (Eds.), *Preparing teachers for a changing world* (pp. 442–479). San Francisco: Jossey-Bass.

David, J. L. (2008). Teacher recruitment incentives. *Educational Leadership, 65*(7), 84–86.

DeBray, E. H. (2005). Partisanship and ideology in the ESEA reauthorization in the 106th and 107th Congresses: Foundations for the new political landscape of federal education policy. In L. Parker (Ed.), *Review of Research in Education* (pp. 29–50). Washington, DC: American Educational Research Association.

DeBray, E. H., Parson, G., & Woodworth, K. (2001). Patterns of response in four high schools under state accountability policies in Vermont and New York. In S. H. Fuhrman (Ed.), *From the capitol to the classroom: Standards-based reform in the states* (pp. 170–192). Chicago: University of Chicago Press.

Delpit, L. (2006). *Other people's children: Cultural conflict in the classroom.* New York: New Press.

Diamond, J. B., & Spillane, J. (2005). High-stakes accountability in urban elementary schools: Challenging or reproducing inequality? *Teachers College Record, 106*(6), 1140–1171.

Dobbie, W., & Fryer, R. G. (2009). *Are high quality schools enough to close the achievement gap? Evidence from a social experiment in Harlem* [NBER Working Paper Series]. Retrieved November 4, 2009, from http://www.nber.org/papers/w15473

Dotterer, A. M., Burchinal, M., Bryant, D. M., Early, D. M., & Pianta, R. C. (2009). Comparing universal and targeted prekindergarten programs. In R. C. Pianta & C. Howes (Eds.), *The promise of pre-K* (pp. 65–76). Baltimore: Paul H. Brookes.

Eccles, R. G. (1991). The performance measurement manifesto. *Harvard Business Review, 69*(1), 131–137.

Eccles, J. S., & Templeton, J. (2002). Extracurricular and other after-school activities for youth. In W. C. Secada (Ed.), *Review of research in education* (pp. 113–180). Washington, DC: American Educational Research Association.

Eisenhart, M. (1998). On the subject of interpretive reviews. *Review of Educational Research, 68*(4), 391–399.

Eisenhart, M., & Towne, L. (2003). Contestation and change in national policy on "scientifically based" education research. *Educational Researcher, 32*(7), 31–38.

Elam, S. M., Rose, L. C., & Gallup, A. M. (1994). The 26th annual Phi Delta Kappa/Gallup poll of the public's attitudes toward the public schools. *Phi Delta Kappan, 76*(1), 41–56.

Elmore, R. F. (2003a). Accountability and capacity. In M. Carnoy, R. F. Elmore, & L. S. Siskin (Eds.), *The new accountability: High schools and high stakes testing* (pp. 195–209). New York: RoutledgeFalmer.

Elmore, R. F. (2003b). *Knowing the right thing to do: School improvement and performance-based accountability.* Washington, DC: NGA Center for Best Practices.

Elmore, R. F. (2004). Conclusion: The problem of stakes in performance-based accountability systems. In S. H. Fuhrman & R. F. Elmore (Eds.), *Redesigning accountability systems for education* (pp. 274–296). New York: Teachers College Press.

Elmore, R. F. (2005). Building new knowledge: School improvement requires new knowledge, not just goodwill. *American Educator, 29*(1), 20–27.

Elmore, R. F., & Burney, D. (1997). *Investing in teacher learning.* New York: National Commission on Teaching and America's Future and Consortium for Policy Research in Education.

Elmore, R. F., & Burney, D. (1998). *Continuous improvement in Community District #2, New York City.* Pittsburgh, PA: Learning Research and Development Center.

Elshtian, J. B. (2001). Civil society, religion, and the formation of citizens. In D. Ravitch & J. P. Viteritti (Eds.), *Making good citizens: Education and civil society* (pp. 263–278). New Haven, CT: Yale University Press.

Epstein, J. L., Sanders, M. G., Simon, B. S., Salinas, K. C., Jansorn, N. R., & Van Voorhis, F. L. (2002). *School, family, and community partnerships: Your handbook for action* (2nd ed.). Thousand Oaks, CA: Corwin Press.

Estola, E., Lauriala, A., Nissilä, S., & Syrjälä, L. (2007). The antecedents of success: The Finnish miracle of PISA. In L. F. Deretchin & C. J. Craig (Eds.), *International research on the impact of accountability systems* (pp. 189–206). Lanham, MD: Rowman & Littlefield Education.

Evertson, C. M., & Neal, K. W. (2006). *Looking into learning-centered classrooms: Implications for classroom management.* Washington, DC: National Education Association.

Farkas, G. (2009). Closing achievement gaps. In G. Sykes, B. Schneider, & D. N. Plank (Eds.), *Handbook of education policy research* (pp. 661–670). Washington, DC: American Educational Research Association & New York: Routledge.

Feiman-Nemser, S. (2001). From preparation to practice: Designing a continuum to strengthen and sustain teaching. *Teachers College Record, 103*(6), 1013–1055.

Fenstermacher, G. D. (1995). The absence of democratic and educational ideals from contemporary educational reform initiatives. *Educational Horizons, 73*(2), 70–80.

Fermanich, M., Mangan, M., Odden, A., Picus, L. O., Gross, B., & Rudo, Z. (2006). *Washington learns: Successful district study.* North Hollywood, CA: Lawrence O. Picus and Associates.

Filer, A., & Pollard, A. (2000). *The social world of pupil assessment.* London: Continuum Books.

Finn, C. E. Jr., & Ravitch, D. (2007). Why liberal learning. In C. E. Finn Jr. & D. Ravitch (Eds.), *Beyond the basics: Achieving a liberal education for all children* (pp. 1–10). Washington, DC: Fordham Institute.

Finnegan, K. S., Bitter, C., & O'Day, J. (2009). Improving low performing schools through external assistance: Lessons from Chicago and California. *Education Policy Analysis Archives, 17*(7), 1–27.

Forster, M., & Masters, G. (2004). Bridging the conceptual gap between classroom assessment and system accountability. In M. Wilson (Ed.), *Towards coherence between classroom assessment and accountability* (pp. 51–73). Chicago: University of Chicago Press.

Friedman, M. (2002). *Capitalism and freedom* (40th anniversary ed.). Chicago: University of Chicago Press.

Fuhrman, S. H. (Ed.). (1993). *Designing coherent education policy.* San Francisco: Jossey-Bass.

Fuhrman, S. H. (2001). Introduction. In S. H. Fuhrman (Ed.), *From the capitol to the classroom: Standards-based reform in the states* (pp. 1–12). Chicago: University of Chicago Press.

Fuhrman, S. H., Goertz, M. E., & Duffy, M. C. (2004). "Slow down, you move too fast": The politics of making changes in high stakes accountability policies for students. In S. H. Fuhrman & R. F. Elmore (Eds.), *Redesigning accountability systems for education* (pp. 245–273). New York: Teachers College Press.

Fullan, M. (1993). *Change forces: Probing the depths of educational reform.* London: Falmer.

Fuller, B., Wright, J., Gesiki, K., & Kang, E. (2007). Gauging growth: How to judge No Child Left Behind. *Educational Researcher, 36*(5), 268–278.

Gallimore, R., & Tharp, R. E. (1990). Teaching mind in society: Teaching schooling and literate discourse. In L. C. Moll (Ed.), *Vygotsky and education* (pp. 175–205). New York: Cambridge University Press.

Gardner, H. (1985). *Frames of mind: The theory of multiple intelligences.* New York: Basic Books.

Gardner, H. (1993). *Multiple intelligences: The theory in practice.* New York: Basic Books.

Gardner, H. (1999). *Intelligence reframed: Multiple intelligences for the 21st century.* New York: Basic Books.

Gardner, H., Feldman, D. H., & Krechevsky, M. (1998). *Building on children's strengths: The experience of Project Spectrum.* New York: Teachers College Press.

Gill, B. P., Zimmer, R., Christman, J. B., & Blanc, S. (2007). *State takeover, school restructuring, private management, and student achievement in Philadelphia.* Santa Monica, CA: RAND.

Gipps, C. (1999). Socio-cultural aspects of assessment. In A. Iran-Nejad & P. D. Pearson (Eds.), *Review of research in education* (pp. 355–392). Washington, DC: American Educational Research Association.

Glaser, R., & Silver, E. (1994). Assessment, testing, and instruction: Retrospect and prospect. In L. Darling-Hammond (Ed.), *Review of research in education* (pp. 393–419). Washington, DC: American Educational Research Association.

Glazer, J. L. (2009). How external interveners leverage large scale change: The case of America's Choice, 1998–2003. *Educational Evaluation and Policy Analysis, 31*(3), 269–297.

Goertz, M. E. (2001). Standards-based accountability: Horse trade or horse whip? In S. H. Fuhrman (Ed.), *From the capitol to the classroom: Standards-based reform in the states* (pp. 39–59). Chicago: University of Chicago Press.

Goertz, M. E., Floden, R. E., & O'Day, J. (1995). *Studies of education reform: Systemic reform* (Vol. 1). Philadelphia: Consortium for Policy Research in Education.

Goertz, M. E., & Odden, A. (1999). *School-based financing.* Thousand Oaks, CA: Corwin Press.

Gold, E., Simon, E., & Brown, C. (2003). *Reframing accountability for urban public schools.* Retrieved November 20, 2009, from http://www.hfrp.org/evaluation/the-evaluation-exchange/issue-archive/evaluating-education-reform/reframing-accountability-for-urban-public-schools

Goleman, D. (1997). *Emotional intelligence: Why it can matter more than IQ.* New York: Bantam Books.

Goleman, D. (2006). *Social intelligence: The new science of human relationships.* New York: Bantam Books.

Goodlad, J. I. (1994). *What are schools for?* (2nd ed.). Bloomington, IN: Phi Delta Kappa Educational Foundation.

Goodlad, J. I. (1999). Individuality, commonality, and curricular practice. In M. J. Early & K. J. Rehage (Eds.), *Issues in curriculum: A selection of chapters from past NSSE yearbooks* (pp. 29–47). Chicago: University of Chicago Press.

Gray-Bennett, P. (2003). Focused thinking: Aiming school accreditation toward improved learning. In J. DiMartino, J. Clarke, & D. Wolk (Eds.), *Personalized learning: Preparing high school students to create their futures* (pp. 286–308). Lanham, MD: Scarecrow Press.

Greene, J. P., & Winters, M. A., (2005). *Public high school graduation and college-readiness rates: 1991–2002* [Education Working Paper No. 8]. Retrieved October 25, 2007, from http://www.manhattan-institute.org/cgi-bin/apMI/print.cgi

Hakel, M. D., Koenig, J. A., & Elliott, S. W. (Eds.). (2008). *Assessing accomplished teaching: Advanced-level certification programs.* Washington, DC: National Academies Press.

Hannaway, J., & Woodroffe, N. (2003). Policy instruments in education. In R. E. Floden (Ed.), *Review of research in education* (pp. 1–24). Washington, DC: American Educational Research Association.

Hargreaves, A. (2003). *Teaching in the knowledge society: Education in the age of insecurity.* New York: Teachers College Press.

Hart, B., & Risley, T. (1995). *Meaningful differences in the everyday experiences of young American children.* Baltimore, MD: Brookes Publishing.

Hatch, T. (2001, February 14). It takes capacity to build capacity. *Education Week,* pp. 44, 47.

Hatch, T. (2002). When improvement programs collide. *Phi Delta Kappan, 83*(8), 626–634.

Heckman, J. J., & Krueger, A. B. (2003). *Inequality in America: What role for human capital policies?* Cambridge, MA: MIT Press.

Herman, J. I. (2004). The effects of testing on instruction. In S. H. Fuhrman & R. F. Elmore (Eds.), *Redesigning accountability systems for education* (pp. 141–166). New York: Teachers College Press.

Heubert, J. P., & Hauser, R. M. (1999). *High stakes: Testing for tracking, promotion, and graduation.* Washington, DC: National Academy Press.

Hightower, A. M. (2002). *San Diego's big boom: District bureaucracy supports culture of learning.* Seattle, WA: Center for the Study of Teaching and Policy.

Honig, M. I. (Ed.). (2006a). *New directions in policy implementation.* New York: State University of New York Press.

Honig, M. I. (2006b). Building policy from practice: Implementation as organizational learning. In M. I. Honig (Ed.), *New directions in policy implementation* (pp. 125–148). New York: State University of New York Press.

Honig, M., & Coburn, C. (2008). Evidence-based decision making in school district central offices. *Educational Policy, 22*(4), 578–608.

Honig, M. I., & Hatch, T. C. (2004). Crafting coherence: How schools strategically manage multiple, external demands. *Educational Researcher, 33*(8), 16–30.

Honig, M. I., & Ikemoto, G. S. (2008). Adaptive assistance for learning improvement efforts: The case of the Institute for Learning. *Peabody Journal of Education, 83*, 328–363.

Honig, M. I., Kahne, J., & McLaughlin, M. W. (2001). School–community connections: Strengthening opportunity to learn and opportunity to teach. In V. Richardson (Ed.), *Handbook of research on teaching* (4th ed., pp. 998–1028). Washington, DC: American Educational Research Association.

Hoxby, C. M., Muraka, S., & Kang, J. (2009). *How New York City's charter schools affect achievement.* Cambridge, MA: New York City Charter Schools Evaluation Project.

Ingersoll, R. (2001). *Teacher turnover, teacher shortages, and the organization of schools.* Seattle, WA: Center for the Study of Teaching and Policy.

Ingersoll, R. (2004). *Why do high-poverty schools have difficulty staffing their schools with qualified teachers?* Washington, DC: Center for American Progress.

Interstate School Leaders Licensure Consortium. (2008). *Educational leadership policy standards.* Washington, DC: Author/Council of Chief State School Officers.

Interstate Teacher Assessment and Support Consortium (InTASC). (2010). *Model core teaching standards: A resource for state dialogue* (Draft for public comment). Washington, DC: Author/Council of Chief State School Officers.

Jennings, J., Scott, C., & Kober, N. (2009). Lessons learned from five states over five years. *Education Week, 28*(31), 30, 36.

Johnson, S. M. (2006). *The workplace matters: Teacher quality, retention, and effectiveness.* Washington, DC: National Education Association.

Johnson, S. M., & Papay, J. P. (2009). *Redesigning teacher pay: A system for the next generation of educators.* Washington, DC: Economic Policy Institute.

Kaestle, C. F. (2000). Toward a political economy of citizenship: Historical perspectives on the purpose of common schools. In L. M. McDonnell, P. M. Timpane, & R. Benjamin (Eds.), *Rediscovering the democratic purposes of education* (pp. 47–72). Lawrence: University Press of Kansas.

Kantor, H., & Lowe, R. (2006). From new deal to no deal: No Child Left Behind and the devolution of responsibility for equal opportunity. *Harvard Educational Review, 76*(4), 474–502.

Kaplan, R. S., & Norton, D. P. (1992). The balanced scorecard–Measures that drive performance. *Harvard Business Review, 70*(1), 71–79.

Klein, A. (2009). Duncan aims to make incentives key element of ESEA. *Education Week, 29*(14), 1, 13.

Klein, A. (2010). Education budget plan welded as policy lever. *Education Week, 29*(21), 1, 18–19.

Knapp, M. S. (1997). Between systemic reforms and the mathematics and science classroom: The dynamics of innovation, implementation, and professional learning. *Review of Educational Research, 67*(2), 227–266.

Koppich, J. E., & Knapp, M. S. (1998). *Federal research investment and the improvement of teaching 1980–1997.* Seattle, WA: Center for the Study of Teaching and Policy.

Kuhn, T. S. (1970). *The structure of scientific revolutions* (2nd ed.). Chicago: University of Chicago Press.

Labaree, D. F. (1997). Public goods, private goods: The American struggle over educational goals. *American Educational Research Journal, 34*(1), 39–81.

Lagemann, E. C. (2000). *An elusive science: The troubling history of education research.* Chicago: University of Chicago Press.

Laguarda, K. G. (2003). *State-sponsored technical assistance to low-performing schools: Strategies from nine states.* Washington, DC: Policy Studies Associates.

Lam, W. S. E. (2006). Culture and learning in the context of globalization: Research directions. In J. Green & A. Luke (Eds.), *Review of research in education: Rethinking learning: What counts as learning and what learning counts* (pp. 213–237). Washington, DC: American Educational Research Association.

Learning First Alliance. (2005). *Values, vision, and performance: Americans' hopes for their public schools.* Washington, DC: Author.

Lee, J. (2006). Input-guarantee versus performance-guarantee approaches to school accountability: Cross-state comparisons of policies, resources, and outcomes. *Peabody Journal of Education, 81*(4), 43–64.

Lee, J. (2008). Is test-driven external accountability effective? Synthesizing the evidence from cross-state causal comparative and correlational studies. *Review of Educational Research, 78*(3), 608–644.

Lee, V. E., & Burkam, D. T. (2002). *Inequality at the starting gate: Social background differences in achievement as children begin school.* Washington, DC: Economic Policy Institute.

Lee, V. E., & Ready, D. D. (2009). U.S. high school curriculum: Three phases of contemporary research and reform. *The Future of Children, 19*(1), 135–156.

LeMahieu, P. G. (1996). *From authentic assessment to authentic accountability.* Paper from a briefing book for the 1996 education summit. Retrieved October 17, 2007, from http://electronicportfolios.org/afl/LeMahieuAuthentic.pdf

Lickona, T. (1997). Educating for character: A comprehensive approach. In A. Molnar & K. J. Rehage (Eds.), *The construction of children's character* (pp. 45–62). Chicago: University of Chicago Press.

Lieberman, A., & Grolnick, M. (1996). Networks and reform in American education. *Teachers College Record, 98*(1), 7–45.

Lieberman, A., & McLaughlin, M. (1992). Networks for educational change: Powerful and problematic. *Phi Delta Kappan, 73*(9), 573–578.

Lieberman, A., & Wood, D. R. (2003). *Inside the National Writing Project.* New York: Teachers College Press.

Linn, R. L. (2003). Accountability: Responsibility and reasonable expectations. *Educational Researcher, 32*(7), 3–11.

Little, J. W. (2006). *Professional community and professional development in the learning-centered school.* Washington, DC: National Education Association.

Luginbuhl, R., Webbink, D., & deWolf, I. (2009). Do inspections improve primary school performance? *Education Evaluation and Policy Analysis, 31*(3), 221–237.

Madaus, G. F. (1999). The influence of testing on the curriculum. In M. J. Early & K. J. Rehage (Eds.), *Issues in curriculum: A selection of chapters from past NSSE yearbooks* (pp. 71–111). Chicago: University of Chicago Press.

Malen, B., & Rice, J. K. (2009). School reconstitution and school improvement. In G. Sykes, B. Schneider, & D. Plank (Eds.), *Handbook of education policy research* (pp. 464–476). Washington, DC: American Educational Research Association & New York: Routledge.

Manna, P. (2008). *Federal aid to elementary and secondary education: Promises, effects, and major lessons learned.* Paper commissioned by the Center on Education Policy. Retrieved December 1, 2009, from http://www.cep-dc.org/_data/n_0001/resources/live/RethinkingFederalRole/Federal%20Aid%20to%20Elementary%20and%20Secondary%20Education.pdf

Manna, P., & Petrilli, M. J. (2008). Double standard? "Scientifically based research" and the No Child Left Behind Act. In F. M. Hess (Ed.), *When research matters: How scholarship influences education policy* (pp. 63–88). Cambridge, MA: Harvard University Press.

Marsh, J. A. (2000). *Connecting districts to the policy dialog.* Seattle, WA: Center for the Study of Teaching and Policy.

Marsh, J. A., et al. (2005). *The role of districts in fostering instructional improvement: Lessons from three urban districts partnered with the Institute for Learning.* Santa Monica, CA: RAND.

Marshall, H. H. (1994). Seeing, redefining, and supporting student learning. In H. H. Marshall (Ed.), *Redefining student learning: Roots of educational change* (pp. 1–32). Norwood, NJ: Ablex.

Martinez, M. E. (2000). *Education as the cultivation of intelligence.* Mahwah, NJ: Lawrence Erlbaum.

Massell, D. (1998). *State strategies for building capacity in education: Progress and continuing challenges.* Philadelphia: Consortium for Policy Research in Education.

Maxwell, L. A. (2009). Text experts wary on "race to top" rules. *Education Week, 29*(7), 16.

McDonnell, L. M., & Elmore, R. F. (1987). Getting the job done: Alternative policy instruments. *Educational Evaluation and Policy Analysis, 9*(2), 133–152.

McGuinn, P. J. (2006). *No Child Left Behind and the transformation of federal education policy, 1965–2005.* Lawrence: University of Kansas Press.

McLaughlin, M. W. (1990). The Rand change agent study revisited: Macro perspectives and micro realities. *Educational Researcher, 19*(9), 11–16.

McLaughlin, M. W., & Talbert, J. E. (1993). *Contexts that matter for teaching and learning.* Stanford, CA: Center for Research on the Context of Teaching.

McLaughlin, M. W., & Talbert, J. E. (2001). *Professional communities and the work of high school teaching.* Chicago: University of Chicago Press.

McLaughlin, M. W., & Talbert, J. E. (2003). *Reforming districts: How districts support school reform.* Seattle, WA: Center for the Study of Teaching and Policy.

McLaughlin, M. W., & Talbert, J. E. (2006). *Building school-based teacher learning communities.* New York: Teachers College Press.

McQuaide, J. (1996). *The school principal and character education.* Unpublished dissertation. Pittsburgh, PA: University of Pittsburgh.

McQuillan, P. J., & Salomon-Fernandez, Y. (2008). The impact of state intervention on "underperforming" schools in Massachusetts: Implications for policy and practice. *Education Policy Analysis Archives, 16*(18). Retrieved September 21, 2009, from http://epaa.asu.edu/epaa/v16n18/

Mediratta, K., & Fruchter, N. (2003). *From governance to accountability: Building relationships that make schools work.* New York: Drum Major Institute for Public Policy.

Miles, K. H., & Darling-Hammond, L. (1997). Rethinking the allocation of teaching resources: Some lessons from high-performing schools. *Educational Evaluation and Policy Analysis, 20*(1), 9–29.

Mintrop, H., & Sunderman, G. L. (2009). Predictable failure of federal-sanctions-driven accountability for school improvement—and why we may retain it anyway. *Educational Researcher, 38*(5), 353–364.

Mintrop, H., & Trujillo, T. (2005). Corrective action in low performing schools: Lessons for NCLB implementation from first-generation accountability systems. *Education Policy Analysis*

*Archives, 13*(48), 1–26.

Mishel, L., & Roy, J. (2006). *Rethinking high school graduation rates and trends.* Washington, DC: Economic Policy Institute.

National Association for Sport and Physical Education (NASPE). (2004). *Moving into the future: National standards for physical education.* Reston, VA: Author.

National Center for Education Statistics. (2009). *NAEP 2008 trends in academic progress.* Washington, DC: Author.

National Commission on Excellence in Education (NCEE). (1983). *A nation at risk: The imperative for educational reform.* Washington, DC: U.S. Government Printing Office.

National Commission on Teaching and America's Future. (1996). *What matters most: Teaching for America's Future.* New York: Author.

National Education Association. (1893). *Report of the Committee on Secondary School Studies (Committee of Ten).* Washington, DC: Government Printing Office.

National Education Association, Commission on the Reorganization of Secondary Education. (1918). *Cardinal Principles of Secondary Education.* In Bureau of Education, U.S. Department of the Interior, Bulletin No. 35.

National Institutes of Health (NIH). (1992). *NIH strategic plan.* Washington, DC: Author.

National Research Council (NRC). (1989). *Everybody counts: A report to the nation on the future of mathematics education.* Washington, DC: National Academies Press.

National Research Council (NRC). (1990a). *On the shoulders of giants: New approaches to numeracy.* Washington, DC: National Academies Press.

National Research Council (NRC). (1990b). *Reshaping school mathematics: A philosophy and a framework for a curriculum.* Washington, DC: National Academies Press.

National Research Council (NRC). (1999). *Improving student learning: A strategic plan for education research and its utilization.* Washington, DC: National Academies Press.

National Research Council (NRC). (2004). *Engaging schools: Fostering high school students' motivation to learn.* Washington, DC: National Academies Press.

National Research Council (NRC). (2008). *Common standards for K–12 education? Considering the evidence.* Washington, DC: National Academies Press.

National Study of School Evaluation (NSSE). (2004). *Technical guide to school and district factors impacting student learning.* Schaumberg, IL: Author.

National Study of School Evaluation (NSSE). (2005). *Breakthrough school improvement: An action guide for greater and faster results.* Schaumberg, IL: Author.

Newell, R. J., & Van Ryzin, M. J. (2007). Growing hope as a determinant of school effectiveness. *Phi Delta Kappan, 88*(6), 465–472.

Newmann, F. M., King, M. B., & Rigdon, M. (1997). Accountability and school performance: Implications from restructuring schools. *Harvard Educational Review, 67*(1), 41–74.

Newmann, F. M., Smith, B., Allensworth, E., & Bryk, A. S. (2001). Instructional program coherence: What it is and why it should guide school improvement policy. *Educational Evaluation and Policy Analysis, 23*(4), 297–321.

Newmann, F. M., & Wehlage, G. C. (1995). *Successful school restructuring.* Madison, WI: Center on Organization and Restructuring of Schools.

Niguidula, D. (1998). A richer picture of student work: The digital portfolio. In D. Allen (Ed.), *Assessing student learning: From grading to understanding* (pp. 183–198). New York: Teachers College Press.

Nord, W. A. (2001). Moral education, moral disagreement, and common ground. In D. Ravitch & J. P. Viteritti (Eds.), *Making good citizens: Education and civil society* (pp. 142–167). New Haven, CT: Yale University Press.

Obama, B. (2009). *Remarks by the President at the National Academy of Sciences.* Retrieved May 20, 2009, from http://www.whitehouse.gov/the_press_office/Remarks-by-the-President-at-the-National-Academy-of-Sciences-Annual-Meeting/

O'Day, J. A. (2004). Complexity, accountability, and school improvement. In S. H. Fuhrman & R. F. Elmore (Eds.), *Redesigning accountability systems for education* (pp. 15–43). New York: Teachers College Press.

O'Day, J. A., & Smith, M. S. (1993). Systemic reform and educational opportunity. In S. H. Fuhrman (Ed.), *Designing coherent education policy: Improving the system* (pp. 250–312). San Francisco: Jossey-Bass.

Odden, A., & Clune, W. H. (1998). School finance systems: Aging structures in need of renovation. *Educational Evaluation and Policy Analysis, 20*(3), 157–177.

Odden, A., Kelley, C., Heneman, H., & Milanowski, A. (2001). *Enhancing teacher quality through knowledge- and skills-based pay* [CPRE Policy Briefs]. Philadelphia: Consortium for Policy Research in Education.

Odden, A., Picus, L. O., Archibald, S., Goetz, M., Mangan, M. T., & Aportela, A. (2007). *Moving from good to great in Wisconsin: Funding schools adequately and doubling student performance.* Madison, WI: Wisconsin Center for Education Research.

Office for Standards in Education (OFSTED). (2002). *Progress file: An evaluation of demonstration projects in schools.* London, UK: Author.

Ogden, E. A., & Germinario, V. (1995). *The nation's best schools: Blueprints for excellence* (Vol. 2). Lancaster, PA: Technomic.

Organization for Economic Co-Operation and Development (OECD). (2009). *Education at a glance.* Retrieved on November 18, 2009, from http://www.oei.es/pdf2/Panorama_educacion_OCDE_2009.pdf

Pallas, A. (2009). *Just how gullible is David Brooks?* Retrieved on February 28, 2010, from http://gothamschools.org/2009/05/08/just-how-gullible-is-david-brooks/

Pangle, L. S., & Pangle, T. S. (2000). What the American founders have to teach us about schooling for democratic citizenship. In L. M. McDonnell, P. M. Timpane, & R. Benjamin (Eds.), *Rediscovering the democratic purposes of education* (pp. 21–46). Lawrence: University Press of Kansas.

Parker, W. C. (2003). *Teaching democracy: Unity and diversity in public life.* New York: Teachers College Press.

Pearson, P. D. (2000). Reading in the 20th century. In T. Good (Ed.), *American education: Yesterday, today, and tomorrow* (pp. 152–208). Chicago: University of Chicago Press.

Pelligrino, J. W., Baxter, G. P., & Glaser, R. (1999). Addressing the "two disciplines" problem: Linking theories of cognition and learning with assessment and instructional practice. In A. Iran-Nejad & P. D. Pearson (Eds.), *Review of research in education* (pp. 307–353). Washington, DC: American Educational Research Association.

Pelligrino, J. W., Chudowsky, N., & Glaser, R. (2001). *Knowing what students know: The science and design of educational assessment.* Washington, DC: National Academies Press.

Pennsylvania State Education Association (PSEA). (2009). *Getting on the right track: Using Race to the Top funds to support research-based reforms.* Retrieved September 5, 2009, from http://www.psea.org/uploadedFiles/LegislationAndPolitics/RaceToTheTop_PSEAComments.pdf

Phelan, P., Davidson, A. L., & Cao, H. T. (1992). Speaking up: Students' perspectives on school. *Phi Delta Kappan, 73*(9), 695–704.

Phelan, P., Davidson, A. L., & Yu, H. C. (1998). *Adolescents' worlds: Negotiating family, peers, and school.* New York: Teachers College Press.

Porter, A. C., Youngs, P., & Odden A. (2001). Advances in teacher assessments and their uses. In V. Richardson (Ed.), *Handbook of research on teaching* (4th ed., pp. 259–297). Washington, DC: American Educational Research Association.

Race to the Top Fund; Final Rule. 34 CFR Subtitle B, Chapter II, 59689 (2009).

Ravitch, D. (2001). Education and democracy. In D. Ravitch & J. P. Viteritti (Eds.), *Making good citizens: Education and civil society* (pp. 15–29). New Haven, CT: Yale University Press.

Ravitch, D. (2010). *The death and life of the great American school system.* New York: Basic Books.

Rein, M., & Schön, D. A. (1977). Problem setting in policy research. In C. H. Weiss (Ed.), *Using social research in public policymaking* (pp. 235–251). Lexington, MA: D.C. Heath.

Resnick, L. B. (1987). *Education and learning to think.* Washington, DC: National Academies Press.

Resnick, L. B. (1995). From aptitude to effort: A new foundation for our schools. *Daedalus, 124*(4), 55–62.

Resnick, L. B., & Glennan, T. K. (2002). Leadership for learning: A theory of action for urban school districts. In A. T. Hightower, M. S. Knapp, J. A. Marsh, & M. W. McLaughlin (Eds.), *School districts and instructional renewal* (pp. 160–172). New York: Teachers College Press.

Resnick, L. B., & Hall, M. W. (1998). Learning organizations for sustainable education reform. *Daedalus, 127*(4), 89–118.

Resnick, L. B., & Harwell, M. (1998). *High performing learning communities: District 2 achievement.* Pittsburgh, PA: Learning Research and Development Center.

Resnick, L. B., Stein, M. K., & Coon, S. (2008). Standards-based reform: A powerful idea unmoored. In R. D. Kalenberg (Ed.), *Improving No Child Left Behind: Getting education reform back on track* (pp. 103–138). New York: Century Foundation Press.

Resnick, L. B., & Zurawsky, C. (2005). Getting back on course. *American Educator, 29*(1), 8–46.

Richardson, V. (2001). *Handbook of research on teaching* (4th ed.). Washington, DC: American Educational Research Association.

Roderick, M., Nagaoka, J., & Coca, V. (2009). College readiness for all: The challenge for urban high schools. *The Future of Children, 19*(1), 185–210.

Rogers, J. (2006). Forces of accountability? The power of poor parents in NCLB. *Harvard Educational Review, 76*(4), 611–641.

Rogoff, B. (1994). Developing understanding of the idea of communities of learners. *Mind, culture, and activity, 1*(4), 209–229.

Rogoff, B. (2003). *The cultural nature of human development.* New York: Oxford University Press.

Rose, L. C., & Gallup, A. M. (2000). The 32nd annual Phi Delta Kappa/Gallup poll of the public's attitudes toward the public schools. *Phi Delta Kappan, 82*(1), 41–57.

Rose, L. C., & Gallup, A. M. (2001). The 33rd annual Phi Delta Kappa/Gallup poll of the public's attitudes toward the public schools. *Phi Delta Kappan, 83*(1), 41–58.

Rose, L. C., & Gallup, A. M. (2006). The 38th annual Phi Delta Kappa/Gallup poll of the public's attitudes toward the public schools. *Phi Delta Kappan, 88*(1), 41–53.

Rothstein, R. (2000). Equalizing education resources on behalf of disadvantaged children. In R. D. Kahlenberg (Ed.), *A notion at risk: Preserving education as an engine for social mobility* (pp. 31–92). New York: Century Press.

Rothstein, R. (2004). *Class and schools: Using social, economic, and educational reform to close the black-white achievement gap.* New York: Teachers College Press.

Rothstein, R., & Jacobsen, R. (2006). The goals of education. *Phi Delta Kappan, 88*(4), 264–272.

Rothstein, R., Jacobsen, R., & Wilder, T. (2006). "Proficiency for all"—An oxymoron. Paper prepared for the symposium *Examining America's commitment to closing achievement gaps: NCLB and its alternatives*, sponsored by the Campaign for Educational Equity, Teachers College, Columbia University.

Rothstein, R., Jacobsen, R., & Wilder, T. (2008). *Grading education: Getting accountability right.* Washington, DC: Economic Policy Institute & New York: Teachers College Press.

Rowan, B., Correnti, R., Miller, R. J., & Camburn, E. M. (2009). *School improvement by design: Lessons from a study of comprehensive school reform programs.* Philadelphia: Consortium for Policy Research in Education.

Roza, M. (2008). What if we closed the Title I comparability loophole? In J. Podesta & C. Brown (Eds.), *Ensuring equal opportunity in public education* (pp. 59–77). Washington DC: Center for American Progress.

Rueda, R. (2004). *The concept of achievement in sociocultural research.* Unpublished paper prepared for the National Education Association.

Rutherford, F. J., & Ahlgren, A. (1989). *Science for all Americans.* New York: Oxford University Press.

Ryan, R. M., & Deci, E. L. (2002). Self determination theory and the facilitation of intrinsic motivation, social development, and well-being, *American Psychologist, 55*(1), 68–78.

Salomon, G. (1991). Transcending the qualitative-quantitative debate: The analytic and systemic approaches to educational research. *Educational Researcher, 20*(6), 10–18.

Schoenfeld, A. H. (2006). What doesn't work: The challenge and failure of the What Works Clearinghouse to conduct meaningful reviews of studies of mathematics curricula. *Educational Researcher, 35*(2), 13–21.

School Improvement Grants; American Recovery and Reinvestment Act of 2009 (AARA); Title I of the Elementary and Secondary Education Act of 1965 as Amended (ESEA). Final requirements. 34 CFR Subtitle B, Chapter II, 65618. (2009).

Senge, P. M. (1990). *The fifth discipline: The art and practice of the learning organization.* New York: Currency Doubleday.

Shavelson, R. J. (1988). Contributions of educational research to policy and practice: Constructing, challenging, and changing cognition. *Educational Researcher, 17*(7), 4–11.

Shavelson, R. J., & Towne, L. (Eds.). (2002). *Scientific research in education.* Washington, DC: National Academy Press.

Shepard, L. (2001). The role of classroom assessment in teaching and learning. In V. Richardson (Ed.), *Handbook of research on teaching* (4th ed., pp. 1066–1101). Washington, DC: American Educational Research Association.

Shepard, L. (2005). Assessment. In L. Darling-Hammond & J. Bransford (Eds.), *Preparing teachers for a changing world* (pp. 275–326). San Francisco: Jossey Bass.

Shepard, L. A., & Bliem, C. L. (1995). Parents' thinking about standardized tests and performance tests. *Educational Researcher, 24*(8), 25–32.

Shepard, L., Hannaway, J., & Baker, E. (2009). Standards, assessments, and accountability [National Academy of Education, White Paper Series]. Retrieved December 11, 2009, from http://www.naeducation.org/NAEd_White_Papers_Project.html

Shulman, L. S. (1986). Those who understand: Knowledge growth in teaching. *Educational Researcher, 15*(2), 4–14.

Smith, D. R., & Ruff, D. J. (1998). Building a culture of inquiry: The school quality review initiative. In D. Allen (Ed.), *Assessing student learning: From grading to understanding* (pp. 164–182). New York: Teachers College Press.

Smith, P. (1995). Outcome related performance indicators and organizational control in the public sector. In J. Holloway, J. Lewis, & G. Mallory (Eds.), *Performance measurement and evaluation* (pp. 192–216). Thousand Oaks, CA: Sage.

Smith, T. M., & Ingersoll, R. M. (2004). What are the effects of induction and mentoring on beginning teacher turnover? *American Educational Research Journal, 41*(3), 681–714.

Smylie, M. A., & Evans, A. E. (2006). Social capital and the problem of implementation. In M. I. Honig (Ed.), *New directions in education policy implementation* (pp. 187–208). New York: State University of New York Press.

Snipes, J., Doolittle, F., & Herlihy, C. (2002). *Foundations for success: Case studies of how urban school systems improve student achievement.* Washington, DC: Council of Great City Schools.

Spillane, J. P. (2000). *District leaders' perceptions of teacher learning.* Philadelphia: Consortium for Policy Research in Education.

Spillane, J. P. (2005). *Standards deviation: How schools misunderstand education policy* [CPRE Policy Briefs Series]. Philadelphia: Consortium for Policy Research in Education.

Spillane, J. P., Reisner, B. J., & Reimer, T. (2002). Policy implementation and cognition: Reframing and refocusing implementation research. *Review of Education Research, 72*(3), 387–431.

Spillane, J. P., & Thompson, C. L. (1997). Reconstructing conceptions of local capacity: The local education agency's capacity for ambitious instructional reform. *Education Evaluation and Policy Analysis, 19*(2), 185–203.

Stein, M. K., & D'Amico, L. (1998). *Content-driven instructional reform in Community School District #2.* Pittsburgh, PA: Learning Research and Development Center.

Stein, M. K., & D'Amico, L. (1999). *Leading school and district-wide reform: Multiple subjects matter.* Pittsburgh, PA: Learning Research and Development Center.

Stein, M. K., Harwell, M., & D'Amico, L. (1999). *Toward closing the gap in literacy achievement.* Pittsburgh, PA: Learning Research and Development Center.

Sternberg, R. J. (1990). *Metaphors of mind: Conceptions of the nature of intelligence.* New York: Cambridge University Press.

Sternberg, R. J. (2003). *Wisdom, intelligence, and creativity synthesized.* New York: Cambridge University Press.

Stigler, J. W., & Hiebert, J. (1999). *The teaching gap.* New York: Free Press.

Stipek, D. (2002). *Motivation to learn: Integrating theory and practice* (4th ed.). Boston: Allyn and Bacon.

Stipek, D. (2004). *The concept of achievement in child development research.* Unpublished paper prepared for the National Education Association.

Strike, K. A. (1991). The moral role of schooling in a liberal democratic society. In G. Grant (Ed.), *Review of research in education* (pp. 413–483). Washington, DC: American Educational Research Association.

Sunderman, G. L., Kim, J. S., & Orfield, G. (2005). *NCLB meets school realities: Lessons from the field.* Thousand Oaks, CA: Corwin Press.

Sunderman, G. L., & Orfield, G. (2006). Domesticating a revolution: No Child Left Behind reforms and state administrative response. *Harvard Educational Review, 76*(4), 526–556.

Supovitz, J. A., & Klein, V. (2003). *Mapping a course for improved student learning: How innovative schools systematically use student performance data to guide improvement.* Philadelphia: Consortium for Policy Research in Education.

Supovitz, J. A., & Weathers, J. (2004). *Dashboard lights: Monitoring implementation of district instructional improvement strategies.* Philadelphia: Consortium for Policy Research in Education.

Suri, H., & Clarke, D. (2009). Advancements in research synthesis method: From a methodologically inclusive perspective. *Review of Educational Research, 79*(1), 395–430.

Talbert, J. E. (2002). Professionalism and politics in education reform. *Journal of Educational Change, 3*, 339–363.

Talbert, J., Eaton, M., Ennis, M., Fletcher, S., & Shuer, C. (1990). *Brief report on goal divergence among U.S. high schools: Tradeoffs with academic excellence.* Stanford, CA: Center for Research on the Context of Teaching.

Tharp, R. G., & Gallimore, R. (1988). *Rousing minds to life: Teaching, learning, and schooling in social context.* New York: Cambridge University Press.

Toch, T. (2006). *Margins of error: The testing industry in the No Child Left Behind era.* Washington, DC: Education Sector.

Toch, T., & Rothman, R. (2008). *Rush to judgment: Teacher evaluation on public education.* Washington, DC: Education Sector.

Togneri, W. (2003). *Beyond islands of excellence.* Washington, DC: Learning First Alliance.

Tough, P. (2008). *Whatever it takes: Geoffrey Canada's quest to change Harlem and America.* Boston: Houghton Mifflin Harcourt.

Tucker, S. (1996). *Benchmarking: A guide for educators.* Thousand Oaks, CA: Corwin Press.

Turnbull, B. J. (1982). The federal role in educational improvement. *Harvard Educational Review, 52*(4), 514–528.

Turnbull, B. J. (1996). *Technical assistance and the creation of educational knowledge.* Washington, DC: Policy Studies Associates.

Turnbull, B. J. (2006). *Citizen mobilization and community institutions: The Public Education Network's policy initiatives.* Washington, DC: Policy Studies Associates.

Turnbull, B. J., & Laguarda, K. G. (2006). The surprising challenges of knowledge use. Retrieved November 20, 2009, from http://www.policystudies.com/studies/technical/Challenges%20of%20Knowledge%20Use.pdf

U.S. Department of Education (USDE). (1996). *Blue ribbon schools 1996–1997 elementary program nomination requirements.* Washington, DC: Author.

U.S. Department of Education (USDE). (2010a). *Fiscal year 2011 budget summary.* Retrieved February 2, 2010, from http://www2.ed.gov/about/overview/budget/budget11/summary/edlite-section1.html

U.S. Department of Education (USDE). (2010b). *A blueprint for reform: The reauthorization of the Elementary and Secondary Education Act.* Washington, DC: Author.

U.S. Government Accountability Office (USGAO). (2007). *Teacher quality: Approaches, implementation, and evaluation of key federal efforts.* Washington, DC: Author.

Viadero, D. (2009). "Race to the Top" said to lack key science. *Education Week, 29*(6), 1, 18–19.

Vogel, S. (2009, September 29). Equal raises for defense employees in 2010, no matter the pay system. *Washington Post.*

Von Zastrow, C. (2010). *Carrots and sticks are so last century: An interview with author Daniel Pink.* Retrieved June 11, 2010, from http://www.publicschoolinsights.org/carrots-and-sticks-are-so-last-century-conversation-author-dan-pink

Warren, J. R., & Halpern-Manners, A. (2007). Is the glass emptying or filling up? Reconciling divergent trends in high school completion and dropout. *Educational Researcher, 36*(6), 335–343.

Watson, G. H. (1992). *Strategic benchmarking: How to rate your company's performance against the world's best.* New York: Wiley.

Wechsler, H. S. (2001). Eastern standard time: High school-college collaboration and admissions to college, 1880–1930. In M. C. Johanek (Ed.), *A faithful mirror: Reflections on the College Board and education in America* (pp. 43–79). New York: The College Board.

Weiner, K. G. (2009). Obama's dalliance with truthiness. *Teachers College Record.* Retrieved August 4, 2009, from http://www.tcrecord.org/PrintContent.asp?ContentID=15731

Weisberg, D., Sexton, S., Mulhern, J., & Keeling, D. (2009). *The widget effect: Our national failure to acknowledge and act on differences in teacher effectiveness.* New York: New Teacher Project.

Wenger, E. (1998). *Communities of practice: Learning, meaning, and identity.* New York: Cambridge University Press.

Wenger, E., McDermott, R., & Snyder, W. M. (2002). *Cultivating communities of practice.* Boston: Harvard Business School Press.

What Works Clearing House (WWC). (2009). *Dropout prevention: Interventions with reports.* Retrieved November 18, 2009, from http://ies.ed.gov/ncee/wwc/

What Works Clearing House (WWC). (2010). *WWC quick review of the article "Are high-quality schools enough to close the achievement gap? Evidence from a social experiment in Harlem."* Retrieved April 14, 2010, from http://ies.ed.gov/ncee/wwc/

Wiley, D. E. (1992). Policy research. In M. C. Alkin (Ed.), *Encyclopedia of educational research* (Vol. 2, pp. 1013–1016). New York: Macmillan.

Wilkinson, R., & Pickett, K. (2009). *The spirit of level: Why greater equality makes societies stronger.* New York: Bloomsbury Press.

Wilson, S. M. (2003). *California dreaming: Reforming mathematics education.* New Haven: Yale University Press.

Wilson, S. M., Darling-Hammond, L., & Berry, B. (2001). *Connecticut's story: A model of teaching policy* [CTP Teaching Quality Policy Briefs, No. 4]. Seattle, WA: Center for the Study of Teaching Policy.

Wilson, S. M., & Peterson, P. L. (2006). *Theories of learning and teaching: What do they mean for educators?* Washington, DC: National Education Association.

Wilson, S. M., & Youngs, P. (2005). Research on accountability processes in teacher education. In M. Cochran-Smith & K. M. Zeichner (Eds.), *Studying teacher education: The report of the AERA Panel on Research and Teacher Education* (pp. 591–643). Mahwah, NJ: Erlbaum.

Wilson, T. A. (1996). *Reaching for a better standard: English school inspection and the dilemma of accountability for American public schools.* New York: Teachers College Press.

Wixson, K. K., Dutro, E., & Athan, R. G. (2003). The challenge of developing content standards. In R. E. Floden (Ed.), *Review of research in education* (pp. 69–107). Washington, DC: American Educational Research Association.

Zeichner, K. M., & Conklin, H. G. (2005). A research agenda for teacher education. In M. Cochran-Smith & K. M. Zeichner (Eds.), *Studying teacher education: The report of the AERA Panel on Research and Teacher Education* (pp. 645–725). Mahwah, NJ: Lawrence Erlbaum.

Zigler, E., & Muenchow, S. (1992). *Head Start: The inside story of America's most successful educational experiment.* New York: Basic Books.

# Index

167

# About the Author

**Elizabeth Demarest** (Betty) is an education consultant who lives in Alexandria, VA. She is retired from the U.S. Department of Education and the National Education Association. While with the government, she served in a variety of senior civil service positions in the areas of education research, policy, and program management. She was director of the Blue Ribbon Schools Program and director of planning and policy coordination for the Office of Educational Research and Improvement. At NEA she was a senior associate in the research department. She began her career as a middle school social studies teacher in New York City.